Ages 5-12

Parenting Your Child by the Spirit

Yes, you can be God's instrument to re-create your child's character

Sally Hohnberger

Pacific Press® Publishing Association
Nampa, Idaho
Oshawa, Ontario, Canada
www.pacificpress.com

Designed by Linda Griffith

Copyright © 2005 by
Pacific Press® Publishing Association
Printed in the United States of America
All Rights Reserved

Additional copies of this book are available by calling toll free 1-800-765-6955
or by visiting http://www.adventistbookcenter.com

Scripture references are taken from the King James Version
unless otherwise marked.

Library of Congress Cataloging-in-Publication Data:
Hohnberger, Sally, 1948-
Parenting by the Spirit : yes, you can be God's instrument to re-create your child's
character/Sally Hohnberger.
p. cm.
ISBN 0-8163-2070-5
1. Child rearing—Religious aspects—Christianity. 2. Parenting—religious
aspects—Christianity. 3. Christian education of children. I. Title

BV4529.H625 2005
248.8'45—dc22   2004060152

05 06 07 08 · 5 4 3 2 1

Dedication

This book is dedicated to all the people I love and care for—which is everyone . . . which is . . . *You!*

May God become *real* to you, *ever present,* and I hope you will discover by experimentation that *He is there to help you!* He will never turn you away. He longs and loves to help you manage your children and raise them for His kingdom. You cannot do it without Him, and He looks forward to your calling upon Him in every need you have.

My love to every one of you!

Acknowledgement

No one is an independent atom. God brings different individuals into our lives to round us out, spur us on, add to or enchance our gifts and talents. For me, that special someone was Jeanette Houghtelling. She'd comb through each chapter, make suggestions, improve, enhance, and upgrade the stories. I cannot thank my dear friend enough! Thank you for all your effort, time, talent, and your great big heart!

Contents

Preface

This book is the second in a projected series of four. *Parenting by the Spirit,* the first, focused on the preparatory work of the parent learning to walk and talk with God. Two more books will follow this second book: *Parenting Teens by the Spirit,* which will focus on the adolescent years—that sometimes slippery bridge between childhood and independent adulthood—and *Parenting Infants by the Spirit,* which will deal with the years when the child is fully dependent. It is during our child's infancy that we build the foundation of obedience, trust in God, and all the right responses to life. During this time of life, the parent needs to be mind, will, and judgment for the child.

This book you hold in your hand, *Parenting Your Child by the Spirit,* addresses **ages five through twelve** predominately. The years of childhood are an incredibly important time to build on the foundation of "trust and obey" that has been established in infancy—or to build that foundation if it was neglected, and to add to the child's character-building self-government, initiative, and industry. This volume represents practical principles for solving typical difficulties that arise during this time period, and each principle is thoroughly illustrated with true stories. You will see that the underlying foundation of each principle is that "God is a very present helper."

Each parent is unique in the baggage he or she carries into parenting. In my early years, I grew up to be timid and prone to despair; feelings of inadequacy and unworthiness made me their slave. God has freed me from this mindset and from the feelings and emotions that kept me a slave to serve them. When it came time to write this book, feelings of unworthiness were still there. But a longing to work with God to help set more captives free by sharing what God has done for me overrode my inherited tendencies and gave me courage.

This book was written with my hand in Jesus' hand; we wrote it together. Of myself, I could not do this, but with Him at my side, instructing me, I could. He led me chapter after chapter, giving me direction for each one. It required me to turn to Him often for ideas and ways to bring across the basic vital principles involved in child rearing. We all need to rear our children for, with, and in Christ Jesus *our* Savior.

This book is *not* restricted to parents with children aged five to twelve! This book can reveal to single parents, to parents whose children are out of the home—even gone astray—and to grandparents how they can still influence their children by gaining that more personal walk with Christ that I illustrate in these pages. The principles of child rearing are the same principles by which God longs *to raise us up* into His character. These principles teach us how to walk with Him as His child. Enoch, after having his son, walked more closely with God because now he could better understand the heart of the Father in heaven. His own longing and experiences in directing his son as a parent revealed to him God's heart toward himself.

We all long for successes in molding our children's character after that of Christ. Only by fellowship, communion, and beholding Jesus will you find the success you desire. Only by spending quality time and quantity time and by connecting with Jesus with an honest heart day by day will you discover how He can bring ideas to an idealess parent. He has a thousand ideas for us. One at a time, He will share them with us to direct our steps. As we follow Him, more ideas will come, and success in changing your character and that of your children will come in its train. This applies to children in the home as well as out of the home.

Time with God will comfort your sorrows in the moment. He will comfort the sorrows of a parent whose child is out of the home and away from God. He has a program for you to influence them, even now, if you will come to Him. God will give you His wisdom and His courage to trust in Him at every step of this learning process. That is what I have done to raise my boys successfully and to write these books for you.

For example, a seventy-two-year-old grandmother came up to me after a meeting. She was so delighted with the message of a personal Savior and yet so convicted of how bad a parent she had been. Her heartache was great. Her daughter was out of the church and had no interest in God. What could she do now? She wanted to know. She was sure there was no hope!

Inquiring into her life, we recommended she apply the principles she understood now, as a grandmother, to her granddaughter. She could offer to baby-sit the grandchild to help the daughter—a working, single parent.

She made a plan with God. She dedicated herself to be used by God and to study to understand these principles better. When she approached her daughter, offering to baby-sit the grandchild, she expected to be refused, but her daughter was willing.

After six months, the daughter said to her mother, "What are you doing with my daughter? She has changed so nicely. She is kind in her words; she prays nice prayers at meal times; she's helpful in the home duties and such a joy to be around."

"I'm raising her with Jesus, the way I should have raised you but didn't know how," the grandmother responded tenderly.

The grandmother and her daughter were reunited in a new and loving relationship. The grandmother shared the principles, tapes, and books she was learning from. Old wounds were addressed and healed as each drew closer to Jesus personally. Today they are raising this child together, united under God. Jesus wants to heal your sorrows, too, whatever they may be. He is a big God, and He is still here for you!

May God's presence be with you. May He open your blind eyes to see, your deaf ears to hear, and your fearful hearts to do.

Chapter 1
BACK TO THE BASICS

"But refuse profane and old wives' fables, and exercise thyself [rather] unto godliness" (1 Timothy 4:7).

Lord, what do You expect a parent to be and to do? This is such a basic question; yet the desire for the answer burns within my soul. I'm confused. Can You help me?"

A long silent pause followed. Then several texts popped into my head with corresponding thoughts and suggestions, but no clear solution appeared. I pursued the direction these thoughts indicated by studying and recording key Bible texts that gave me specific "how to's" for parenting. God was guiding me, but as yet, I had not grasped His answer in a practical way.

Later, when I was in the greenhouse pulling weeds, God put the picture together before my mind.

"Parenting is much like gardening! I want you to pull up the weeds of unrighteousness, of selfishness, and of independence from Me. Do this thoughtfully and prayerfully. I am the Master Gardener, and I will direct you in your work. True parental love restrains, hinders, and eliminates the wrong, unsightly traits of character that come up so naturally. Just as you plant good seeds in an orderly, timely fashion, so I want you to cultivate, water, and exercise the good traits of character in your children. A good gardener tends his garden daily and continues to give it careful attention."

As I pulled each type of weed from the soil, I labeled the common weeds in the hearts and characters of my sons. " 'Interruptive Ivan' should not be allowed to interrupt me," I thought. "That selfish 'I-want-it-now' weed needs to be hindered, restrained, and eventually pulled up. If the root, or even a portion of the root, remains, it is guaranteed to return, and I'll face it at another time. God wants me to persevere in pulling this weed until it is gone, while cultivating the opposite trait— showing my sons a better way to respond. We want to replace the old ways with new ways. Hmm, what would that be Lord?"

"What would you like to see in its place?"

"Well . . . to wait patiently."

"Then plant this goodly seed of patience in an orderly fashion. I'm with you."

The voice of God is a still, small voice. It's not an audible voice but rather thoughts that come into the mind in response to our crying out to God. His thoughts direct our reasoning. Every thought or impression is not from God, for Satan communicates through the mind as well. So we must judge our thoughts according to Isaiah 8:20 and Isaiah 30:21, according to the Spirit as well as the word. Experience and the final outcome of the situation best indicate where our thoughts originated.

I pondered this concept and called it the *replacement principle*— exchanging good for evil, right for wrong, God's character traits for Satan's. Leaving the heart-garden merely weeded by just denying the wrong is not enough; rather, we must preoccupy the character soil with those lovely traits that are the opposite of the weeds we've pulled up (see Matthew 12:43-45). Soon I had opportunity to experiment with this principle and learn more.

I was visiting at a friend's house when Matthew, age seven, interrupted our conversation with what he perceived as a crucial need. This lack of courtesy showed my ineffective teachings so far. To answer him would have taken only a moment and seemed to be the quickest solution. It was what I had done many times before.

"Allowing him to interrupt is how you water this weed and give it life, Sally," God said.

In a moment my thoughts brought all the former thinking into play. "I want to pull this weed and cultivate a lovely plant in its place," I decided. "Lord, what do I want him to do instead?"

"Mother?" Matthew asked impatiently.

"Son, you know you shouldn't interrupt me like this. I want to help you learn a better way," I said with a sweet spirit. "You need to go over to the garage and come again with your question. But instead of just blurting out what you want, tug on my skirt and then wait patiently and quietly for me to turn to you at a proper time."

He grimaced at this request to restrain himself; he wanted an answer immediately as he typically had gotten before. I saw the struggle as good and evil strove for the mastery. I prayed for God to speak to Matthew and call him to choose right over wrong. "Matthew," I whispered, "pray to Jesus to help you do the right. It's your choice."

This practical, experiential union and communion with God is the highest education we can gain ourselves and give to our children. To come to know a personal God is truly primitive godliness. We and our children can become like Enoch, walking and talking with God.

Now Matthew was well exercised in the art of prayer, which is communion with God. He knew this was the right thing to do, and he had experienced Jesus changing his inner disposition before. Yet at this moment, he still struggled with "I want," with opposing thoughts and emotions. (Restraining self is a great trial for our children, so be compassionate yet firm. Until they learn to see the wonderful benefits of the new way, it will appear to them foolishness. But as the good becomes stronger by doing, and the selfish ways fall away by neglect, they will see its wisdom and be happier for the change.)

Matthew surrendered and went over to the garage. I saw him bow his head there. My friend and I resumed our conversation. While talking, I was also praying for God to continue to work in Matthew's heart and for him to cooperate all the way. Pulling weeds from the heart-garden is delicate work, requiring the proper balance of tenderness and firmness. To be successful, I must be under the influence of the Holy Spirit and listening for His directions.

In a few minutes Matthew returned, tugged on my skirt, and waited quite patiently. We ladies continued talking.

"How long, Lord, do I make him wait? It's been fifteen seconds, and he's finding this waiting hard. Should I turn to him right now?"

"No, let patience have its perfect work. I will tell you when to turn to him."

I placed my hand on Matthew's shoulder encouragingly while I continued talking; he settled into waiting a little better. He tugged once again on my skirt, fearful that I had forgotten.

"Now, Lord?" I asked again.

"Not yet; wait a little longer."

"But he looks discouraged. What if he gives up? I surely don't want to discipline him for this now—here—but I will if necessary. Shouldn't I encourage him by responding quickly?"

God was silent, so I chose to continue talking to my friend.

At least ninety long seconds passed before God said, *"Now will be a good time."*

"Matthew, you did splendidly. Good boy! This is the proper way to ask your question. Now what did you want to ask?"

I answered him, and he was off. The beauty of this experience is that the weed of impatient outspokenness was drastically restrained and cut off.

Our next experience with "Interruptive Ivan" involved a longer period of waiting and cultivated greater patience. In Christ, we were encouraging the sprouting of that goodly plant of patience which grew day by day with repeated exercise, taking the place of interrupting. The Creator fashioned a good thing as Matthew did his work of cooperating and trusting in God to change him inside. And God did! Matthew's attitude, perspective, thoughts, feelings, disposition, and habits all changed. To God be the glory!

Just as plants need food and water on a regular basis, so do our children need encouraging, thankful words for their surrender, their cooperation, and their change in character traits.

"Matthew," I told him, "calling out to God in prayer as you did, surrendering your wrong thoughts and feelings to Him, and then cooperating in doing the right brings happiness and peace to your mind and life. It's the best way to go. It's God who changes your disposition and attitude inside when you do this. You want to do this again and again." And my Matthew smiled.

Working under God has good benefits. "Interruptive Ivan" was transformed into "Patient Paul" by God's grace and divine power working in the heart, mind, and life of my son. Yet it was *my* connection and surrender to let Christ first lead me that made me a link between Him and my son for this miracle to take place. Truly the transformation begins with me.

This experience needs to be repeated daily to form the right habits we desire in our home and to make sure that they excel in strength over the old ways. "Therefore if any man [be] in Christ, [he is] a new creature: old things are passed away; behold, all things are become new" (2 Corinthians 5:17).

I pondered, "Lord, pulling weeds and replacing them with goodly plants would be working with You in practical terms to transform my 'Sassy Susie' into 'Sweet Sue,' cultivating sweetness in her by repetition and the grace of Christ. It would be bringing my 'Disobedient Danny' to You so that by instruction and discipline we could weed out disobedient thoughts, feelings, and habits and sow seeds of obedience in his life until he becomes 'Obedient Ollie.' This must be what Revelation 2:17 is talking about when it promises us a 'new name.' I think I'm getting the idea clearly now. Every selfish, evil trait of character can be overcome by cultivating the opposite trait of character in and with Christ! Oh how exciting!

"What else is parenting supposed to be Lord? Surely there is more."

"Every good gardener takes the time to stand back and evaluate his garden. I have a blueprint for every heart garden. You will find it in My Word, which is like a gardening manual for every parent. You need to carefully evaluate all aspects of the heart-gardens that I have entrusted to your care." God responded to my reason.

"Evaluate what type of soil exists. Is it soft and fertile—or does it need to be softened with the gentle rain of family fun and loving attention? Does this garden have clear boundaries to define what belongs in it and what does not? Is it receiving all the nutrients it needs to flourish—and in the proper proportions? Does its soil need to be tilled up with painful consequences for ungodly behavior so that your sons will 'Come unto Me' for new life?

"What types of plants are growing in their heart-gardens? Are there weeds and thistles, or are there fruits and flowers? You know, many weeds appear harmless and even attractive when they are small. You need My wisdom to identify those young weeds and to learn how to pull them up before they put down tenacious roots. Under My teaching, you will learn to recognize them quickly.

"Being an instrument in My hands to re-create the character of your child into My image is a very important work. Few parents have begun to touch this work with the tips of their fingers. This work of training your children underlies every other work."

I thought, "If we parents would cultivate early in our children such Christlike traits as kindness, helpfulness, patience, and sweetness, these characteristics would be a part of them for life. That's awesome!"

Whatever we allow to grow in their heart-garden during those first seven years—good or evil—shapes them for life. Few parents understand the importance of these early years, and Satan gains an astronomically far-reaching advantage by sowing his weeds in the heart-garden!

Our God-given work as parents is to shape the characters of our children. We are cultivating in them dispositions to follow either Christ or Satan. Our children can grow up with a lovely, orderly heart-garden—or with characters that resemble overgrown weed and thistle patches. We must come to see that our children's character traits are *largely* the result of our diligence or slackness in tending to their heart-garden.

I reasoned, "If I expect my child to flourish, I can't pick up this work with enthusiasm one day and neglect it the next. I must be willing to consistently encourage and implement consequences at the right time and in the right spirit. I must remain in Christ and have no variableness in training."

As I considered the magnitude of the task, I responded, "Oh Lord, the big picture is scary because there are so many traits in my sons that need changing. I made out a list for each, and there were over a dozen per child. How can I do this? I try, but my failures loom up to discourage me. My history reminds me how I lose self-control trying to bring my children under control. Must I address all these needed changes at the same time? It's so easy to become frustrated, angry, or impatient. I long to say with Mary, 'Be it unto me according to thy word,' but I fear failure in my own strength. What do I do?"

"Without Me you can do nothing, but with Me you can do all things! Keep your hand in Mine; don't try to do it alone. I am beside you always even if you can't see Me.

"The biggest difficulty you face is that you're warring against powers and principalities of darkness [see Ephesians 6:12]. In your efforts to do right, you will be opposed by the devil. His efforts are directed toward you even more than toward your child. When you strive to correct your child, if you allow thistles of a wrong spirit to bloom in your own heart, you will be planting more weeds than you pull out! You need to be continually reaching out to Me for guidance and seeking My strength to empower and sustain you in doing right. You are to sustain your relationship with Me by faith, not by sight or feeling. I will instruct you and teach you in the way that you should go. I will guide you with My eyes [see Psalm 32:8]. You can't war against 'self' in you or in your child without a vital connection with Me [see John 15:4, 5]. You must first face your own weaknesses and gain hold of Me before you are prepared to contend with your child and the pull of his flesh."

"Silly Sally" and "Disobedient Danny" soon dropped by and wanted to pull my boys off to some silly, mischievous activity. My boys were inclined to these traits of character, and I sent up a prayer to my helper, Jesus. "Lord what shall I do?" (see Acts 9:6).

"Keep a close watch over them. Don't even let them out of your hearing, but keep them close to you and show them a better way."

"How do I do that?" I wondered. "Well, I could direct and participate in their play. That way it will remain proper and appropriate—and crowd out the wrong ways. Oh Lord, help me love them!"

Then a wonderful idea popped in my mind. It must have come from my helper, Jesus. I would play jump rope together with the children. "Okay, that's what I'll do! These children are young; it will be fun and challenging for them to learn how to jump rope together." I suggested the game to them, showing and teaching each one how to have fun. It was a hit! They had no time to be tempted to mischief.

"Be not overcome of evil, but overcome evil with good" (Romans 12:21). My boys did not get involved in mischievous activity and didn't need to be corrected. And "Silly Sally" and "Disobedient Danny" want to come back again because they enjoyed our time together doing wholesome, fun things! They even happily helped me move rocks for a project and prepare our meal. They wanted to be beside me and do whatever I was doing because they knew that not only were they corrected and restrained from wrong, but they were also loved and appreciated. (You know, most children get into mischief because they have never been shown how to play and enjoy wholesome, fun activities. Parents need to be playmates with their children, showing them how to play, how to interact nicely with siblings or others, and exchanging poor activities for good ones.)

Afterward, God impressed upon my heart an evaluation of my playtime with the children. *"What atmosphere surrounded your 'garden' today? Was it pure and healthful—a cheerful place with a dependable routine? Or was it a toxic place with negative attitudes, evil influences, and irregularity?"*

"Lord, I tried to cultivate the good plants of uprightness in the heart-gardens of our little visitors, rather than let them and my boys be growing weeds. Looking back, I can say that no noxious weeds were planted today to require rooting out. Only under You can the atmosphere be right."

When we have children, we assume the responsibility to raise them under God's guidance. This must become our priority above all others—to raise our child to know Jesus in his or her heart, transforming the natural naughty disposition to a sweet one. The goal is to teach our child to learn to recognize God's voice from the voice of his flesh and how to connect with Jesus' power in order to live above his flesh. That means we must detach ourselves from our overcommitted lives so that we have time to let God show us what we should do—and then do it. Once we have children, our time is no longer ours for fun, for socializing going here or there, for this and that. We must understand what the basic values of life are and see to it that we take the time to meet those basics, leaving the cracks and crevices of the time that remains for less essential things.

When we have children, life needs to be focused on praying for them in our personal worship time, making logical plans with God for teaching and training our children in His ways, evaluating their dispositions and habits, making plans to correct imbalances and character weaknesses under Christ's guardianship. To do this, we must have a vital connection and experience with God ourselves, for we can share only what we possess. Our relationship with God must become more consistent and intimate. We must learn to instruct, correct, and apply consequences *in Christ*, rather than "in self."

God has provided us with the Comforter, "the Spirit of truth . . . [to] guide [us] into all truth" (John 16:13). As we become sensitive to the Holy Spirit's influence, we can have wisdom and strength sufficient to our task of parenting our children in the way of God and not in the way of self. As we take every noxious weed to Jesus, it will be uprooted by divine power cooperating with human effort.

A friend told me about her experience with planting peas. She had planted peas in her garden. About a week later she was weeding and happened to discover a pea on the ground that had not yet sprouted. As she tried to pick it up, to her surprise she unearthed a six-inch root that was hidden underground! God spoke to her just then and told her that her life must be like that pea. She must take the time to learn how to put down her roots in Him and have the strong experience of a life hidden with Him. And then, she must learn how to grow one little shoot above ground, and then one leaf at a time—always maintaining her connection with Him—until she became a mature plant with many leaves above ground, after His likeness.

Parent and child alike must be rooted and grounded in Christ—this is letting our abiding tap roots grow first, which is the unseen foundation work of every healthy plant that brings life. Getting our children in touch with, and coming to know, God personally is the most important work; it lies at the foundation of all the work of character development that follows. Rooted in Him, our children can sprout one stem and one leaf, which represent exercising patience instead of interrupting, sweetness instead of sassiness, or playing jump rope instead of doing mischief. As the plant's root system grows, it can support more stems and leaves. And in due time my list of twelve character traits can all change and find new life in Him because the pattern for life in each trait is being rooted in Jesus. We can all become beautiful, fruitful vines for Jesus when we are connected and grow in this way.

Many mistakenly think that parenting is providing their children food, water, clothing, shelter, and opportunity for an education. True Christian parenting is far more than this. It's bringing our child to Christ in the morning to learn. It's bringing our child to Christ when his will is crossed, when he needs instruction on how to respond, when he is doing his work, when he is in school, and especially when he is in need of experiencing the consequences of wrong behavior. It's communing with God before communing with our child. It's showing a Christlike spirit in correction or instruction. It's meeting the emotional needs of our child. It's providing a practical spiritual connection with Christ to enable him to do the right thing instead of the wrong. It's supervising his character and weeding out all bad traits while cultivating the good traits under the direction of Jesus Himself. It's training him to surrender his will to God rather than letting evil weeds come up in his heart-garden. It's reasoning, educating, disciplining, and praising him. It's overcoming myself so that I can practically instruct my child how to come to Jesus to overcome self and all that self encompasses. It's a very large work—too large for any human being alone. But it's not too large for Jesus. He must become our constant Companion and Friend, guiding us in the way we should go.

We teach most effectively by our example. Our children watch our principles, demeanor, and character under provocation, and they imitate us—good or bad. In this way we teach very loudly what a Christian is or isn't. So we must change, improve, or learn what we need to so that we can instruct them properly in the way to go.

We do this teaching when we rise up, when we sit down, when we eat, and when we sleep. Parenting is truly giving ourselves to our children, as completely as the wheat plant gives its life for the next generation. Parenting must consume our best time and energies.

In summary, every parent is a gardener. Every parent is sowing seed—either good seed or noxious weeds. God is the master Gardener who knows the fruit of every kind of seed and who understands the requirements of every type of heart-soil. He has the wisdom to uproot harmful character traits and to replace them with lovely ones. He is willing to take parents into His training school and teach them how to govern and cultivate their own little garden plots so that they may present them to Him, and to the world, fruitful in every good work, lovely and attractive as He has designed they should be.

THE LONE EMBRACE
A SPECIAL WORD OF ENCOURAGEMENT FOR SINGLE PARENTS

Being alone is scary and unsettling for single parents. All parents must come to know God as a personal Savior, but, single parents, you have a special promise that He will be your faithful spouse in your special need. You need never be alone again. Christ will be ever at your side when you seek Him and call upon Him with all your heart. He will be your invisible God and faithful Companion, directing your steps, giving you wisdom, strength, and comfort according to your need. You will know He is by your side—not by sight or by feeling, but by His Word and by His promises. Try God, and you will find Him to be faithful. Others in your life may have proved not to be faithful, but He will be. He will help you as you daily attempt to manage your children and build up their characters after His image.

Chapter 2

FINDING THE TREASURE

"To him that overcometh will I . . . give him a white stone, and in the stone a new name written, which no man knoweth saving he that receiveth [it]"
(Revelation 2:17).

We were already in the elevator when "Sassy Sam," age five, and his parents were approaching. Sam halted at the entrance, staring at the three-inch gap in the floor revealing the elevator shaft and the cables that operated the mechanism. His parents got in the elevator, but Sam refused to step over the gap. His parents told him to get in. "No!" Sam insisted emphatically. "I'm not going in that thing!"

His parents were obviously embarrassed. They coaxed; they reasoned. Finally, they tried to force Sam into the elevator, to no avail. He fought valiantly and won. Then Sam put his hands on his hips in an authoritative manner to which he seemed very accustomed, and demanded, "Get off this elevator right now. We'll take the stairs!"

Mortified, his parents retreated; in submission to "Sassy Sam" they took the stairway. As the elevator closed, we could hear "Sassy Sam" scolding his parents for not obeying more quickly as they ascended that stairway!

It is amazing how well parents obey their children! It's a shame, and it's totally the opposite of God's plan for parenting. For parents to be under the control of Satan through their children is a seriously flawed approach to parenting. The spirit of compulsion, force, and anger reflects Satan's character, not God's. No parent should surrender to such a spirit nor allow it in the home. This is not love! This is letting Satan marshal our children under his banner. This upside-down family government is against God and right. It robs our children of their birthright in Christ Jesus.

Poor Sam needs to be brought out of his bondage of fear of the elevator shaft. Through a personal understanding of, and surrender to, God he needs to find out that his fears are lying thoughts that he need not obey. He needs to be brought out of the bondage of an un-Christlike spirit and connected to the power source found in Jesus. He can serve his parents with love and respect and find the happiness he desires. To let him obey his fears and be a servant of Satan is the worst cruelty his parents can perform—all in the name of *misguided* love.

"There is no fear in love; but perfect love casteth out fear" (1 John 4:18). God says, "I [am] the LORD, the God of all flesh: is there anything too hard for Me?" (Jeremiah 32:27). God is able to change each of us, but we must come to Him and learn by our own experience of His power, enabling grace, and empowering love.

Jesus wants us parents to bring our "Sassy Sams" to Him in prayer, to show them how to give Him their fears, sassy thoughts, dispositions, and habits and ask Him what to do in place of these wrong ways. He will never leave us nor forsake us; He has promised to be with us always. He is our Friend, Savior, and Redeemer. He is invested with divine grace that can empower anyone to serve Him. Then our children can learn to love and obey their parents *in the Lord.* Jesus in the heart is the key and the hidden treasure.

"Sassy Susie," age six, was visiting in my home. She had fears and a very low sense of self-worth. Her parents were frustrated, not knowing how to help her, and were asking for our help and advice.

God put it in my heart to draw near to Susie. I understand the crippling effect of fear and a poor sense of self-worth; I longed to connect her to the source of her strength—a personal Jesus. I wanted her to know that He could free her from her prison of lying thoughts and misconceptions. I determined to treat Susie as one of my own children, showing love to her.

Our two families played freeze tag, and I chased her often with joy and glee. This drew her closer. She fit in with our work routine, and I taught her a few jobs she would be responsible for during her family's stay. She responded well for a time.

Then it happened! She didn't sweep the floor properly and needed correction. I prayed to God that I would know how to approach her in the right spirit, knowing this could become a trial for her. And sure enough it was. She pursed her lips, her eyes grew distant, and then in disgust she threw the broom on the floor and said, "You can sweep your own floor! I'm out of here!" And she walked away in a huff.

Experience has taught me that hurt people tend to hurt others, so I wasn't personally offended at her behavior. Also, I felt her reaction was likely a self-preserving, problem-solving technique. She likely felt rejection, and this was how she was protecting herself—by blaming me for the problem so that she didn't have to face the fact that she had done something wrong.

"Lord what would You have me to do?" I prayed. I have experience and understanding about children's hearts, and I knew Susie needed to come to Jesus and connect with Him in order to be empowered to change. But only Jesus knew what would reach her heart that day. He can read hearts, and He knows just how to bring them to Him that they might experience change. So I would seek Him and follow His directions for this situation.

"Appeal to her heart to do right. I am with you."

"Lord I don't know what to say. Be with my mind and direct me," I responded.

I went to Susie and looked deep into her eyes with a sympathizing heart. "Why did you speak so sharply to me? Why did that hurt you so much?"

Her eyes showed surprise at my care for her. They softened momentarily then flashed with anger again. "I can't do anything right for anyone! I won't work at home because I'm always being corrected. I'm worthless. No one loves me!"

"Susie those are lying thoughts that you are thinking."

"No they are not!" she said with determination and a heavy heart.

"Lord attend my words; convince her in some way," I prayed.

"Susie they *are* lying thoughts, and Satan puts them in your mind to hurt you. I love you. Remember yesterday, playing freeze tag? And what about the good job you did for me here—and here? I love you." Correction, rightly done, is love!

Her eyes softened; her disposition changed. The Holy Spirit was coming into her heart, and she was cooperating with these new thoughts. I continued, "Your mother and father love you truly, and Jesus loves you the most. Do you know Jesus personally?"

"My mother reads me Bible stories."

"That's good, but do you know Jesus personally?" She shrugged her shoulders. "Jesus wants to be your best Friend. He doesn't want Satan to hurt you in this way anymore. If you will talk with Him and ask for help, He will show you the way out of these awful feelings and lying thoughts about yourself. Why don't you try Him right now?"

"I don't know how."

"I'll show you how. You know, I sometimes have the same feelings about myself that you are feeling right now. And Jesus brings me out of it every time I ask Him to and do what He tells me to do. Let's begin by kneeling down and praying to Him to do this for you."

I watched her struggle between the two masters vying for her heart—Satan pushing her old emotional buttons that were very sensitive, very responsive, and God through His Holy Spirit affirming that my words were true and awakening hope in her heart for a happier life. She said nothing, but knelt down by the couch with me to pray.

"Lord, poor little Susie is so sad, thinking many lying thoughts about herself. Help her reach out to you and see that You and her parents and I all love her. Help her see that she can be a good floor sweeper when she puts her hand in Yours. Help her see that my corrections and instructions are signs of love. Help her have the courage to go back and sweep the floor well; help her to know that with You she can do good work."

By this time, Susie had softened and looked hopeful. I had her repeat a little surrender prayer after me, so that she was expressing it with her own lips. This is a helpful step in making a full surrender. She gave God her lying thoughts. We returned to the kitchen, and she picked up the broom hesitantly. Then I saw by the look on her face that evil angels must be pressing the old ways of thinking on her again.

"Don't believe their lies, Susie! You don't have to obey them; Jesus is here. Take His hand and trust Him—not your feelings right now. You can sweep the floor well."

The struggle was severe. She faltered and said, "You just want me to do your work. You don't love me. Nobody loves me. Not even Jesus can love awful me!" And she threw the broom down again.

"Lord what would you have me to do now?"

"She will need to experience a consequence as a motivation to choose."

"I'm sorry you did this, Susie. Because you didn't choose to believe me, you have chosen to accept the consequences of that decision. Afterwards, we will come back to the kitchen to sweep this floor well. You *can* do a good job of sweeping. Whenever you believe Satan's lying thoughts and cooperate with him, life will be hard and unhappy. When you choose to believe Jesus' thoughts and cooperate with Him, life will be happy and pleasant. You must choose. No one can choose for you."

Susie cried, grumbled, and said more nasty things.

"Come with me. You will need to clean and organize this drawer. Take everything out, wipe it out, and put everything back in it neat and orderly. Talk with Jesus while you do this, and He can clean out those naughty thoughts from your mind and give you nice thoughts to think. Then you can be happy."

Two such tasks were necessary before she swept the floor well. Little by little, Susie trusted Jesus. She needed "consequences" as a motivation to change her negative, destructive ways. She didn't need harsh, angry words spoken to her—she already had enough of those in her own little heart for Jesus to get rid of. More such words would only wound her afresh and cause her to erect further bars to seal her heart against hurt in an attempt at self-protection.

By the time Susie had finished sweeping the floor properly, she was convinced that Jesus, her parents, and I loved her. She was beaming with a light, free heart. She had grasped the treasure of Jesus in her life. She could sweep the floor well, and she wasn't what she thought she was. Hope reigned. She went through the rest of the day with a happy spirit. She could sweep the floor well and please a parent.

The next time she was corrected, she cooperated more quickly, wanting the freedom she had already tasted. "Sassy Susie" was transformed into "Sweet Sue" through a loving person connecting her to God, the One who performed the *real* miracle regarding her inner thoughts and feelings.

James says, "Submit yourselves therefore to God. Resist the devil, and he will flee from you" (James 4:7). When we are in Christ—or when our child is in Christ—and submitted to Him, then we resist the devil in Jesus' strength, which is sufficient for every temptation. Then the devil will flee from us because Jesus has told him with authority to leave.

Parents, we need to trust in a big God who will work in our behalf, helping us to move our children away from wrong techniques of problem solving, fears, wrong habits, lying thoughts, or whatever weakness they are dealing with. In Christ Jesus, all this is possible. Why do we pray and talk with God so little when He is our source of wisdom, strength, and love? In any corrective process, we need to commune with Him before communing with our children, for He will direct our course wisely as He did for Solomon.

When we correct our child, we should demonstrate the right disposition, the right spirit, so that he or she has a proper example to imitate.

A child responds to love, understanding, and sympathy, and at the same time, these attributes call them to move higher still. This is much more effective than a pitiless hail of harshness and anger or belittling, demeaning statements that destroy the child's courage and desire to cooperate. Fretfulness and faultfinding by the parent will create a war, a wall, and a defensive, noncooperative posture in the child. When our children trust us, then we can turn them toward God for power to change their lives. This process awakens gratitude and cooperation and a better outlook on future correction.

Parents, we are responsible for the atmosphere in the home. We make it pleasant or miserable according to which spirit leads us. We are the adults who should understand that all correction is a battle between good and evil. The child is still learning and doesn't understand what is happening when the flesh drives him in selfishness—unless we explain it to him, teaching and training him. When a child experiences a change in heart and mind, it encourages him to continue following God and facing those things in his life that need correcting.

The goal we all are seeking is "Christ in me, the hope of glory, the hope of change, the hope of redemption." When we, as parents, make Jesus our constant Companion and familiar Friend, we can expect to raise our children in the ways of Jesus. We'll find the courage to face our wrong parenting practices. We can look realistically at the shortcomings, weaknesses, and character defects in our children and plan with God how to correct them. We battle under the leadership of our general, Jesus, who has never lost a battle. Of course, some battles require many skirmishes before the victory is won, but we can put forth the effort courageously, knowing that God wins in the end.

Larry, age six, had a hard life. His parents allowed him to tell untruths and laughed when he did so, encouraging him in the art of lying. It seemed so "cute" to them when Larry was two or three or four. The early years began something like this. At age three, Larry was out in the blueberry patch eating blueberries at a forbidden time between meals. A few moments later his mother saw him coming toward the house, his face well stained with blueberries. "Larry have you been eating blueberries off the bushes again?"

"No, Mom," he said with a grin.

"Oh, aren't you the darling!" Mother giggled and gave him a big hug. "You're always so mischievous. Let's go for a wagon ride!"

By the time Larry reached five years old, his lying was becoming a nuisance, and by age six, he had developed such a bent to telling lies that nothing his parents did to correct the habit seemed to release "Lying Larry" from his prison. He was a compulsive liar. Even the pastor couldn't convince Larry of his wrong course. Reasoning, scolding, reproof, censure, punishment—all was in vain. Larry was still the center of attention—admittedly, negative attention—and he seemed to thrive on it.

When their children are very young, many parents believe Satan's falsehood that telling lies is normal behavior and that they should just leave the child to grow out of it as they become older. The truth, of course, is that letting this behavior continue instills Satan's lying traits of character most tenaciously in those important first seven years when character is formed and solidified. We serve only one of two masters—God or Satan. Whose side do your parenting practices support?

Our children will become what we continue to tell them they are. The Bible says as a man "thinketh in his heart, so [is] he" (Proverbs 23:7). If we continue to tell our son that he is mischievous, what will he become? Mischievous. If we continue to tell our daughter that she is naughty, what will she become? Naughty. True or not, whatever we tell our children, their minds will process that information and internalize it. Every sin or weakness begins in the thoughts. Habits for good or evil that we sow in these formative first seven years will grow as the child grows and become stronger as he gains in strength. If we discover our course is wrong, we need to come to Jesus and plan with Him to change our course. He will empower us, give us wisdom, and direct us.

Larry's mother wanted her child to change; she knew that for her son to change, *she* must change. The process had to begin with her; she must change her wrong concepts. Prayer, study, and planning a new course with God commenced. Determined to live in Christ and no longer in the flesh, she decided to filter all she said and did through Christ. She gained experience as she made these changes in her own life.

She read Romans 12:21, "Be not overcome of evil but overcome evil with good." First, God led her to identify and name Larry's sin. Then He led her to understand that under the guidance of Jesus, she needed to cultivate in her son the opposite trait of character. So using her dictionary, she made a list of synonyms and antonyms to help her understand what weeds should be pulled up, restrained, and denied. She made another list of the opposite traits that needed to be cultivated and exercised in "Lying Larry" to bring him out of his wrong ways of thinking and responding.

She knew that her son's lying should be denied and restrained through Jesus, while cultivating truthfulness in its place. Instead of being deceitful, Larry needed to be transparent. Instead of being dishonest, he needed to be honest. He needed to exchange falseheartedness for God's attitude of truth, his insincerity for God's sincerity, his falseness and untruthfulness for God's truthfulness. She spent time each day talking with God about how to cultivate the needed character traits in her son.

One day she was inspired of God to ask Larry some questions designed specifically to test, train, and exercise honesty. When he responded in the old way of deceit, evasiveness, and lying, she applied the consequences in love—consistently and matter-of-factly. She explained what the right response should be, and discussed it with him briefly, but sufficiently. Then she brought him back to the same scenario and reenacted it until he responded in truth, with the right spirit and the right words. Often she took her son to God in prayer to connect him to Jesus for the power to obey.

Another day she'd be impressed to read all her children a story about honesty and extol its benefits throughout the story and discuss it with them, getting them all involved in the discussion.

Still another day she knew the Holy Spirit inspired her to have her son collect Bible texts about lying for his personal worship time. Yet another day he'd collect texts about how God was able to keep him from falling. Each activity served its purpose to correct the thoughts while exercising the opposite trait in his responses during the day. She could see the good fruit that resulted.

Then one day a major victory changed "Lying Larry's" life forever. Mother gave him money to go to the corner store and buy a few items. She had been teaching Larry how to recognize Jesus' voice and to always obey Him, and Larry understood. Before he left, his mother said, "God wants to give you a new name, son."

"He does? What is it?"

" 'Honest Henry.' This is a very desirable name and comes with a cost. It's a small cost although Satan likes to lie to you and tell you that it's a big cost so that you will continue to serve him. Satan is a liar and wants to hurt you. Jesus is your friend and wants to redeem you from lying. He wants to remake you into 'Honest Henry.' But He can't do that unless you cooperate as He leads you. You will be very happy, truly happy, following Jesus. Remember that today."

"Yes, Mother," Larry replied.

Now Mother had made an arrangement with the clerk at the grocery store to give Larry more money in change than he deserved in order to give him an opportunity to exercise honesty. She knew that if Larry exercised the Christlike trait of honesty, he could one day see it replace Satan's trait of lying in his life.

"Lying Larry" gave the man at the grocery store $10.00 for the items his mother had asked him to buy. The clerk gave him back $13.25 plus his purchases. As Larry walked out of the store on his way home, the Holy Spirit brought the thought, *"Did you get the correct change?"* Larry counted the money, recalling clearly that he had had only $10 to begin with. "He gave me too much money back," he said to himself.

Satan then suggested, "He gave you ten dollars too much. Why don't you just keep it to buy yourself something you'd like? No one will ever know."

"That wouldn't be right," Larry reasoned. "But ten dollars *is* enough to buy that toy I wanted. Hmmm."

"Larry you want to be honest now. Do you remember your decision?" the Lord spoke to his heart.

"Yes I do! Mother said You want to give me a new name—'Honest Henry.' I like that. She said it would cost me something. Is this what she was talking about?"

"Yes, Henry. This is the cost. Won't you taste and see that it is good?"

Larry struggled through the desires pulling him both directions—the easy path of lying and the hard road of giving away the money he could have. Then he put his will on the side of right and good. He'd try. He resolutely turned around to return the grocery clerk the money due him.

The clerk could hardly believe his eyes. Larry said, "I think you gave me too much money." And he placed all the money on the counter, holding nothing back. He was being transparent. The clerk gave him the correct change and sent "Honest Henry" home.

After this victory, Larry and Mother made major inroads against lying and dishonesty day by day. "Honest Henry" set his feet on a new path each day as Mother, led by God's wisdom, pointed out the way for Henry's feet. "Lying Larry" became paralytic by lack of exercise, and he died. Meanwhile, "Honest Henry" continued to receive exercise and was rewarded with a new life of happiness. Jesus performed this great miracle and brought a compulsive liar to freedom through a mother who was willing to look at her own ways and let God lead her.

Who gave Mother all these ideas about how to move "Lying Larry" toward honesty? Our loving heavenly Father has a thousand ideas, and He will give you one idea at a time for working out your dilemmas as you deal with your child's weaknesses. Like Larry's mother, you and I will find that is the time we spend with God at the beginning of the day, laying plans with Him, and the time we spend in the evening evaluating how Jesus has led us during the day, that will be our secret to successfully teaching our children how to overcome wrong habits learned in the school of the world.

True love is kind, yet firm, and has consistent boundaries. True love does not let our little ones disobey God's ways. We must love them too much to let them disobey. We do not want our children to have even one habit that needs to change. Rather, let's give them the treasure of proper parental government under the lordship of Jesus Christ. We need to teach our children in practical ways how to talk with God, how to recognize His voice to their minds, hearts, and souls, and how to connect with His power in order to carry out the right they choose. Divinity must unite with humanity to redeem us from self and re-create us into the image of God.

Let me introduce you to "Slothful Sam." Sam is eight years old, a strong young lad at getting out of work. Sam is tenaciously unavailable when he is needed; in fact, he is often out of sight. When he is doing the dishes, scrubbing the toilet, or sweeping the floor, at least a hundred things distract him or slow him down. Homework is tedious; it takes an hour to do ten minutes worth of work. His mind wanders; he dreams of this or that.

As a consequence, I gave him more schoolwork or more housework, but I was more tortured than he was. He accepted that he was slothful, and neither extra work, spanking, nor loss of privileges seemed to motivate him. As his mother, I came to the Lord for help. "Lord what am I to do?"

"What does Romans 12:21 tell you to do?"

"Cultivate the opposite trait." So I looked up the definition of various words and their synonyms in order to label his weak character trait accurately. I learned that instead of being slow and lazy, Sam needed to be lively. Instead of allowing him to be inactive or idle, I needed to get him moving. Instead of being laid back and indolent, he needed to be industrious. Instead of letting him be apathetic and indifferent, somehow—in Jesus—I must exercise him to become energetic.

That night I talked to the Lord again about the situation. "Lord, these definitions have only kindled despair in my heart. How do I motivate a sloth to move? I can't!"

"Why does 'Slothful Sam' respond the way he does?"

"I don't know. Let me think . . . He is much like me—prone to despair. He has the fear of failure looming beside him, discouraging him from believing he can do things well. He *can* do things very well, but he doesn't believe he can. Oh, Lord, I see it now! He needs to believe in what he can be in You rather than believing and obeying the lying thoughts that Satan insinuates in his mind. Lying thoughts are the enemy, holding him hostage to slothful, slow work habits. He is slow because he fears failure. If I worked simply on training him to be diligent, without working on the root problem, I'd be fighting the wrong battle, wouldn't I?"

Correcting our children is more than applying a particular discipline for a particular offense. True correction is correcting the defect that is driving the character weakness, while at the same time, in Jesus, we cultivate the opposite trait. The power of God works from the inside out. So the Lord and I need to start by correcting the wrong thoughts and feelings inside. God wants to purify his mind and heart. Then the outward habit of diligence will match the inward thoughts and feelings.

Correction is the opportunity to exercise our child in the two aspects of re-creation—surrender and cooperation. Just as a bird needs two wings to fly, so our children need to develop both the "wing" of surrender and the "wing" of cooperation. To exercise only a mental surrender to God does not change the character. We can hope and desire to be changed until Jesus comes—and still be lost—if we are exercising only the one "wing" of surrender. A bird with only one wing flops around in a circle, unable to fly. Many professed Christians are flopping around in their Christian experience, unable to obey, for the same reason. But when we add the second wing of cooperation, we give God our permission to come into our lives and re-create us into His image, after His likeness. This is how Jesus' re-creative power re-creates us. His character will become ours. His thoughts, His feelings will become ours. God will not force His way against our will. So we must give our consent and cooperate with His leading before He will come in and evict Satan's character traits from ruling over us. With two wings exercised, the bird flies above the pull of gravity—and we are able to rise above the pull of our flesh.

My son wasn't too excited when I took him aside and said, "Son, we can get you out of your prison of slothfulness. You can be a diligent worker. You can sweep the floor perfectly with Jesus on the throne of your heart. You can even scrub the tub, your most abhorrent job, with cheerfulness and find pleasure in a job well done. Slow work habits are history, and you will have a new name—'David the Diligent'—for with God you can slay the giant 'Lying Thoughts' and his brothers, the giants 'I Can't' and 'Fear of Failure.' Let Jesus be your General!"

I went on to tell him that all he had to do was filter his thoughts, feelings, and actions through Christ before he believed or acted upon them. If God's Word said, "Fear not," he should lay down his fear and trust God. Then Jesus would free him from fear, and courage would take its place. If Jesus said to him that the thought "I can't do this job well" was a lying thought, he could ignore that thought and refuse to act on it. He could take Jesus' hand and say, "I can, with Jesus."

"Jesus wants to deliver you from being a captive of Satan's thinking," I told him. "But without your cooperation, son, Jesus cannot deliver you."

I've found that spending time with God to come up with a plan for transforming my children's character weaknesses into strengths can be both fun and difficult. Why? Because at times God would give me a clear idea; I'd implement it; and it would work wonderfully. Then at other times God seemed far from me, so I'd begin searching His Word and will to gain a concept or idea. Eventually it would come.

Sometimes I'd implement other ideas, and they would seem to be a big flop. Slothfulness and slow work habits are first an attitude and second a habit. In this case, my "Slothful Sam" believed he couldn't do well. This third aspect complicated answering the question, "Why does he respond the way he does?" Was his response driven by attitude, habit, or lying thoughts and feelings? This was getting too hard for me. I became frustrated and turned to God.

"Lord what would You have me to do? We have come a distance, but we haven't overcome yet. To motivate him seems impossible. I've done this, this, and that—but still I see no real changes. What's next?"

"Sally, you are one step closer to the solution. Don't despair over what has not worked. It all has its part in putting the puzzle together. Each is an important piece. Have trust in Me and patience with yourself and your son. Have you considered trying My suggestion of working with the slothful?"

"What is that, Lord?"

"If any will not work, neither should he eat." (See 2 Thessalonians 3:10.)

"Oh my, that one is tough on me. Yes I have considered it, but it seems too severe a consequence. Is it loving?"

"Is it loving to let Satan keep your son in bondage to slothful habits? To grow up destined to be cursed by this trait? Is it loving to let him continue in a way that he doesn't recognize as detrimental and that has eternal consequences?"

"Well, when You put it that way, I must agree." I took time to think all this over very thoroughly, and the conclusion was consistently the same. "I can't leave him where he is. With God directing me, I'll trust His wisdom and do all I can to cooperate with Him to bring 'Slothful Sam' out of this snare."

"Have not I commanded thee? Be strong and of a good courage; be not afraid, neither be thou dismayed: for the LORD thy God [is] with thee whithersoever thou goest" (Joshua 1:9).

During personal worship time I had a nice chat with my "Slothful Sam" and explained what he could become in Jesus—a "Diligent David." "Your Father and I want you to be the best you can be in Jesus. You want to be 'David the Diligent,' and we're here to help you. You haven't responded to the discipline we have given thus far, so the consequences have to become more difficult in order to motivate you to reach out to God and find the freedom you desire. The next time you are slothful or slow in your duties, your decision not to work will grant you the right not to eat, as the Bible says. It's up to you. Your too-soft mother will follow through in the strength of Jesus because I love you too much to let you continue obeying this bad trait."

That very morning his bed was not made before breakfast. He had been reminded and shown mercy—and still it was slothfully left undone. "My poor 'Slothful Sam,' you have chosen to miss breakfast this morning by not choosing the right. I'm so sorry you did that! Not to decide is to decide!

"Father and I talked; we're in agreement to follow through. There is no other way. But to make this as easy on you as possible, we want you to weed your section in the greenhouse while we're eating so that you don't have to see or smell what you're missing. Remember, this is because we love you. Be sure to decide before lunchtime how you intend to handle your chores so that this doesn't happen again. You have your list. Be sure you do everything on it so that you don't miss the next meal. And while you are working diligently in the greenhouse, talk with Jesus, your best Friend. He will take away your sadness and give you His diligence as you choose to exercise it."

And "Slothful Sam" did just that. He was most diligent and dependable that day. He was putting forth his effort as never before. That day, he laid down a cornerstone upon which we were able to build new thoughts and feelings day by day, creating new and different responses. The motivation was sufficient for the task.

Occasionally, he fell back to the old ways, and we'd follow a similar procedure. Then I'd check him as he carried out whatever duty he was given and find him singing a cheerful song, fully accepting the consequences of his decision. In the evening we'd talk about what he thought and felt through this process. His disposition and attitudes were being transformed in such a lovely manner. God knows just what to do to bring them out.

Correction should be given to change a wrong course and put our children's feet upon the straight and narrow path, empowering them to obey through a connection with Jesus.

Redemption is God's plan to restore us completely so that we are once more His sons and daughters. God's redemption requires us to cooperate in the purifying process. We put off the old ways and put on the new ways. God knows that we cannot change our thoughts and feelings as we wish by ourselves, but He gave us our will to exercise. We can put our will on God's side and consent for Him to perform transformations in the inner mind and heart as we cooperate with Him in the moment of temptation. This is how we live "in Him." God's power, united with our surrender and cooperation, can re-create us into His image in our thoughts and feelings. Thus the character of Christ becomes ours. "Whosoever abideth in him sinneth not" (1 John 3:6).

Unless we have the mind of God, every effort to purify ourselves will be useless. Unless Jesus is planted in the mind and heart—our thoughts, feelings, emotions, inclinations, habits, etc.—we cannot control the life ourselves. We need Jesus, and He loves to answer our prayers for deliverance from temptation. The whole Bible is calling us back to a condition in which God is in charge and we are His subjects. Only in this relationship will we find the joy, peace, and love we desire. Otherwise, Satan will taunt, tempt, and press us on to resemble his character of selfishness. Parenting involves teaching all this to our children and showing them in practical terms how to connect themselves to God and how to abide in Him and be His child.

Susie need never be sassy again in Jesus. Larry never needs to lie again. My son can be a "Diligent David." We all can be redeemed from evil, selfish habits and grasp the treasure of Jesus within our hearts.

The Lone Embrace
A Special Word of Encouragement for Single Parents

"Jesus in you" is the treasure to be sought. Have you found it? Do you want to possess it? You can, and Jesus will personally teach you how as you communicate with Him and are willing to follow Him. Jesus called the paralytic to walk, the deaf to hear, and the blind to see. Fear Him not when He comes to bring deliverance to you.

"Leave thy fatherless children, I will preserve [them] alive; and let thy widows [or single parents] trust in me" (Jeremiah 49:11). Truly, you need never be alone! Satan is lying to you when he whispers that you are forsaken, alone, or at any disadvantage. God's presence and wisdom in your life are sufficient for whatever you may face today.

Chapter 3

THE VOICE OF THE PARENT

"But now ye also put off all these; anger, wrath, malice, blasphemy, filthy communication out of your mouth. . . . put on the new [man]"
(Colossians 3:8, 10).

Y ou stupid kid! What is the matter with you? Why did you do that? Haven't I told you a thousand times?"

Have you heard such a voice in your home? Have you found yourself blindly following the demands of your carnal nature, passionately venting upon the poor victim like pitiless hail? After the fact, you realize that your child didn't respond with repentance, love, or obedience. You feel guilty, but you don't know what to do to make it right. Children fear to trust such parents because they are so flammable and unpredictable. In order to survive, the child puts up all kinds of self-protective responses.

Or there is another voice.

"Son, what happened here?" The lamp lies broken in innumerable pieces on the floor. The parent listens quietly and inquires kindly, "What were you trying to do?"

This parent is looking for the child's motive, his intention, rather than jumping to conclusions and harassing him for a mistake in judgment or the inconvenience he has caused. He corrects the wrong and instructs the child in a calm spirit, and the child apologizes, cooperates in cleaning up the mess, and strives to please. They hug. This child is willing to honestly share his thoughts and feelings with his parents even if he feels they may not agree with his thinking. He trusts his parents to have his best interest in mind, thus engendering open communication.

Which parent are you?

All too often, the voice of the parent is like pitiless hail. This voice needs the redemption brought to view in the text for this chapter—"But now ye also put off all these; anger, wrath, malice, blasphemy, filthy communication out of your mouth. . . . put on the new [man]" (Colossians 3:8, 10).

The parent in the second example above started his correction by communing with God before communing with his child. He didn't respond to his flesh—like the first—but to the influence of the Holy

Spirit. His steps were directed by the Spirit, just as ours may be. As parents, we need to pattern ourselves after Christ's character as it is portrayed in Galatians 5:22-25, Philippians 4:8, and, above all, by the love described in 1 Corinthians 13. Self must die, and God must live through us if we are really serious about redeeming our children from the tyranny of these traits of the devil.

The voice of the parent needs to be under the control of God's voice—hearing and discerning His voice and saying His words. The authority of the parent needs to be under the authority of God. In God's plan for parental government, parents are not to oppress their children or provoke them to anger, and the children are to obey their parents *in the Lord*. The voice of the parent needs to portray the Holy Spirit—not an unholy spirit!

"If any man among you seem to be religious, and bridleth not his tongue, but deceiveth his own heart, this man's religion [is] vain" (James 1:26). The voice of the parent must never, never correct or punish in harshness or anger. This kind of voice drives more devils in than out. There is no respect for such a parent. God says, "Children, obey your parents *in the Lord*" (Ephesians 6:1, emphasis supplied). We parents need to be in the Lord if we want our children to obey us.

A five-year-old child was throwing a temper tantrum. His mother was trying to restrain him physically, but he threw himself on the floor and began to beat his head against it. Exasperated, his mother picked him up and shook him, yelling, "Stop that, you brat! Stop that right now!"

She turned to me. "What am I supposed to do with this naughty boy?" She continued in this railing, faultfinding manner, telling me how terrible her child was.

I breathed a prayer, "Lord, what should I say and what should I not say?"

"Tell her the truth in love."

"Sandy," I began, "change in your child begins with you. First, your spirit has to be right. You need to recognize God's voice to your heart, mind, and soul. You discipline in harsh passion, and you get back the same spirit you have shown. You can't expect your child to know how to respond rightly unless you demonstrate a right spirit to him. He is just copying you. The voice of the parent is to be the voice of God in truth and spirit."

"You're right," she replied. "I can't believe you said that to me or that I let you say it! You know, I am doing just what my mother did to me. When I had my first child, I vowed I would never be like her, and yet here I am. What can I do?"

"Stop excusing your past failings and be honest with yourself. You have inherited and cultivated fleshly thoughts and have exercised harsh, angry control over your child. Your solution is to come to Jesus. Filter all you think and do through Him before you do it, and God will bring you out of all these wrong habits." Then I explained, simply, how to surrender and cooperate in order to live in Christ Jesus.

"What about my son? Will he ever forgive me? Do you think I can really change?"

"Yes, children are like a rubber band—very forgiving and flexible—but only to a point. So don't continue as you are. Yes, you can change as soon as you face your history and commit to do nothing until you know what Jesus wants you to do. Before you administer correction, you'll need some time apart with Jesus to let Him gain your heart and pronounce His "peace be still" on your emotions, passions, thoughts, and feelings. Only in that way will you be prepared to be God's messenger to your child instead of simply passing on your own history.

" 'Lord, what wilt thou have me to do?' (Acts 9:6). This is one of your weapons in the warfare against the mountain of self that you face both in you and in your child. God is big enough for this!" Then we talked about the distinction between the voice of God and the voice of her flesh. She saw it clearly.

She turned to her son and apologized genuinely. But I could see the distrust, the hate, the insecurity still in her son. She had wounded him so many times before—physically, verbally, and emotionally—that he was fearful to trust her again. He needed to be corrected, but first she had to become trustworthy in restraining her passions through Jesus.

I took the child aside and talked with him. He was an intelligent, tender child. We spent some time together, and I found he had a very strong desire to please, to do a task well, but he frequently gave up on himself. His mother's derogatory comments had sunk so deep he believed them. Later, he threw down his hammer and nails on a building project, throwing his head back, and voicing derogatory thoughts about himself. I went over to restrain him, and he threw himself on the floor just as he had done before.

"Lord, save this child from himself! Tell me what to do."

"Be firm, be loving, bring Him to Me."

"Stuart, you may not do this; I want you to stop right now." I spoke kindly, but firmly. It was as though my words fell on deaf ears.

"Stuart, Jesus is here. Cry out to Him for help! He loves you, and He can free you from these bad feelings and lying thoughts. You don't have to obey them; they are a lie. Trust me, Stuart. You must do what I say no matter how hard it is. You did a fine job of building, for a beginner. You must give God these hurtful thoughts and feelings. Jesus will take them from you. Now stop struggling." God had been speaking to this child. Now Stuart cooperated with my voice and stopped his tantrum.

I prayed with him and told him how Jesus would come into his heart and change those ugly feelings and thoughts, how he had to cooperate so that Jesus could come in. And he did. His countenance became free from stress, strain, and anxiety. He had hope in Jesus. God freed this poor child from the viselike grip of Satan and his demons. After some time, Stuart considered me his best friend and said to his mother, "Mrs. Hohnberger loves me too much to let me disobey. Jesus is strong and pushed out all the darkness and ugliness. I love Jesus."

His mother and I talked about how she was wounding his spirit and about how to stop doing that and how to open his little heart to her again. We talked about how important it is to speak to her children the words that God wants her to speak and in the spirit He wants her to have—rather than letting her past history come through in her words and attitude. We discussed how all children who feel loved, long to please and will strive for the approval of their parents and how our approach can either nurture or stifle that good trait. She needed to know that God would be there for her, too. He is a strong God, able to save her as well as Stuart.

After a while, the mother called me to tell me how well things were going. The voice of God was guiding her steps, but she was surprised that the voice of her flesh was still so much louder, stronger, and easier to follow. Even so, the Holy Spirit was teaching her the distinction between the two, and her history was losing ground. She was so pleased. Her son was doing much better and had not thrown a temper tantrum since we were together. She was learning! And so can any of us. Jesus has the solution for every difficulty and the power sufficient for any history we may be carrying into our home life.

Our children thrive well in a loving, growing environment when the voice of the parent is the voice of God. "Let the word of Christ dwell in you" (Colossians 3:16).

Parents, it is your duty to have your children in perfect subjection, having all their passions and evil tempers subdued in this way. Women may have a transforming influence if they will only consent to yield their ways and their wills to God and let Him control their minds and affections. God has assigned the woman her mission—to make a heaven of her home and to brighten all around her by a virtuous life. This is the voice of God to all parents. There is a work for all of us mothers. It is to be kind and patient, and to educate our children to become acquainted with Christ from their birth up.

Few parents realize that their children are what their example and discipline, or lack thereof, has made them and that they are responsible for the characters their children develop. Character is made up of our thoughts, feelings, and responses. If you find yourself in need of change, Jesus has said, "Come unto Me, all [ye] that labour and are heavy laden, and I will give you rest" (Matthew 11:28).

"Fathers, provoke not your children [to anger], lest they be discouraged" (Colossians 3:21). Provoking our children is not the voice of God, but the voice of the devil and of our flesh. Many parents provoke their children in harshness and anger, but the Bible says, "The wrath of man worketh not the righteousness of God" (James 1:20). Harshness and anger is not the voice of God and should never be the parent's voice.

The voice of the parent in cooperation with Christ must require prompt and perfect obedience. When parents fail to require this obedience in their children, they fail to lay the right foundation of character in their little ones. They prepare their children to dishonor them and bring sorrow into their lives. The parent's requirements should always be reasonable and expressed with kindness. We are to teach our children pleasantly, without scolding or faultfinding, seeking to bind their hearts to us by cords of love.

In the training of my own children, and in the training of the children of others, I have proved that they never love parents less for restraining them from doing evil. So take courage in Jesus.

"Overbearing Orville," age ten, came up to "Quiet Carol," age nine, took her dolly away rudely, and ran off. "Quiet Carol" cried quietly, for that was her favorite doll. What would happen to her dolly? Would he hurt her? "Lord," she prayed, "that's my favorite dolly. Please keep her safe and return her to me."

About that time Mother came out of the house to hang up some clothes. She saw Carol crying and asked what had happened. Carol told her, and Mother prayed as well. She was impressed to go talk with her neighbor about "Overbearing Orville." God asked her to give away her feelings of unfairness and retaliation regarding this boy and to be willing to follow His leading. And she did. As she walked to the neighbor's house, she was thinking how she could help Orville to come to know Jesus so that he didn't have to be so nasty. This was far from the first time something like this had happened, but she didn't get angry this time.

Knock, knock! Knock, knock! No one answered the door. She walked behind the house, and there was "Overbearing Orville." Two doll arms lay on the ground. He quickly hid the rest of the doll behind his back and stepped in front of the doll's arms on the ground to hide them as well.

"What are you doing, Orville?"

"Nothing."

"Where is your mother?"

"Gone shopping."

"Lord," she prayed, "I was planning to talk with his mother. What should I do?"

"Approach Orville tenderly as you were thinking about doing on the way over here."

"Carol lost her doll; she is very sad. Would you happen to know anything about it?"

"No!" he said nervously.

"You know, I feel real sorry for the fellow that took it. God will not give him rest until he returns the doll because we prayed to God for him. God loves that fellow and wants to show him how to be kind instead of overbearing. We want him to find that happiness, too. He will never be happy doing what he is doing. I'm concerned for whoever it is because he doesn't know Jesus, and he won't be able to shake this sadness and guilt until he lets Jesus into his life. I'd be glad to show him how. Well, if you see or hear of anything, do let me know, won't you?"

"Oh, I . . . I will . . . I . . . I sure will." He stuttered as the red color rose in his face.

Mother went home and prayed again with her daughter. "You know, honey, sad things like this happen in life. How do you think Jesus would respond if something like this happened to Him?"

"Well," she cried, "I lost my dolly, didn't I?"

Mother felt God asking her not to answer, and she didn't. "What would Jesus do in your situation?"

"I know He'd forgive the boy like He did the soldiers when they nailed Him to the cross. He said, 'Father, forgive them for they know not what they do.' "

They talked further along this line until "Quiet Carol" was at peace about losing her doll to this bully and she had forgiven him. She was sad, but accepting. Time would heal her hurt the rest of the way, and Mother would keep an eye on her thoughts and feelings, should negative ones return later, in order to help her get rid of them and regain her peace.

A week went by. Mother had to deal with Carol a few times to help her give away "I'm-going-to-get-even" thoughts and attitudes. As Carol let go of these, Jesus faithfully took them away, and happiness again filled her heart in spite of her loss. She and Mother continued to pray for "Overbearing Orville." They were surprised they never saw him.

One evening a knock came at the door. It was Orville. He held a bag in one hand and a box wrapped nicely in the other.

"What's up?" Mother asked.

"I . . . I came to give you back your doll, Carol. I'm sorry for taking it. Your mother came over last week, and I haven't been able to sleep at night until I decided to make my wrong right. She said I couldn't be happy doing wrong, and she was right."

"Where is my doll? I missed her so much."

"Well, your old doll is in this bag. I had pulled her arms off. I . . . I'm real sorry now! That was nasty. I tried to sew them back on, but I don't think I did a very good job. So I bought you a new doll." And he presented her with the box and the bag.

"Oh, this is so wonderful! Carol pulled out her old doll and looked closely at the stitches. "These are beautiful stitches of love. I'll never get rid of this doll. You're wonderful!" She opened the box and found a lovely doll, far finer than anything she had ever had. "Now I have my old dolly back—and she has a new sister! God multiplies for good everything we give to Him. Thank You, Jesus, and thank you, 'Kind Karl.' "

"Kind Karl" blushed and smiled a half grin that grew into the most brilliant smile. "Quiet Carol" shook his hand vigorously with gratitude.

"Will your mother teach me how to get to know your Jesus? How do I let Him in so I can get rid of my overbearingness and find that peace you talked about?"

Together they did just that.

The voice of God through the parent's voice can help our children no matter on which side of a difficulty they may find themselves. But we must die to self, letting God lead and do His will, not ours. God is a big God and has a peace for you and me that passes understanding.

The voice of the parent must communicate to the child early in life that the parent is in charge. If you haven't done this before your child reaches five years of age, the work is much tougher but not impossible with Christ at your right hand. It will take much prayer and death to your way in order to follow God's way and bring happiness back into your home under the lordship of Jesus Christ.

It is not love to allow a child to "run the show." Such mismanagement results in chaos and bondage—bondage of the parent to the child and of the child to himself. We are to give our children choices within the parameters of right, but never choices to do evil or harmful things to themselves or others. Giving unwise control to the selfish heart of your child raises a "little Hitler" that grows into a bigger and bigger Hitler. Selfishness grows and cannot be satisfied. A young child doesn't have the wisdom or experience to handle this kind of control. God's Word teaches every one of us how to submit to Him and how wives are to submit to husbands and children to parents *as unto the Lord.* There is a purpose in this. When we don't expect our children to submit, we do them a great disservice. How will they ever submit to God whom they do not see if they are never trained to submit to the parents they see?

The voice of the parent under God is to be mind and will for younger children—not in a dictatorial manner, not in the spirit of "because I said so," but for their best good and to instill character traits of Christ in those young, formative years. We choose whom they will play with, for how long, and how often. We choose their associates. We train up our children to know the voice of God and to surrender to do His will above their own will and teach them that to do so is true happiness. We protect them from evil, even shield them from knowing about it at times. Our schedule makes time not only for play but also for developing good work ethics that are habituated in and with Jesus. We give them choices of what foods they will eat or how they will respond within the boundaries of what we have chosen for our families. God will guide the parent's steps to tell their children in a pleasant manner how to be a Daniel, an Esther, a Simeon, or an Anna and develop in them the traits of character that will produce such fruit. In this way we are mind and will for our children, making good and upright traits of character attractive and rewarding. We will not let Satan take our children captive. Instead, we will introduce them to Jesus, the Friend of sinners that can save them from sin and self.

As our children grow older and have proved themselves to be upright and under God's control, we will give them more freedom to make choices of where to go and what they do. This is not a license or a free reign to sin, but a schoolroom in which to learn how to live upright lives in a sin-sick world. With our boys, we began, little by little, when they were about twelve years old and encouraged them forward to ever increasing dependence on God. We must decrease, and He must increase.

Of course, you will still keep watch, praying and letting your children exercise their wings, pulling them in if necessary to reposition them in Christ so that they will have better judgment and more knowledge as they make their next choices. Children need to learn to base their standards and values in the Word of God, studying to know His will as the foundation of their problem-solving techniques. At first, we give them space for this process in simple situations and allow them to face more complicated circumstances as they grow. As they develop and connect more fully to Jesus, we take a lesser guiding role so that they become comfortable in seeking, knowing, and following God's will before they leave the home. Eventually God must become the supreme Ruler over them. And if we do our job right, we will always be their coach, respected and honored, but not necessarily always followed as they reach young adulthood, for they must follow God.

Christian parents cannot use Satan's tactics. That means we cannot use anger, hostility, physical or verbal intimidation, threats, dictatorial commands, dominant gestures, or compel or force our children into obedience. There is no place for deceit, hypocrisy, pretense, two-facedness, insincerity, the silent treatment, or misconstruing what happened for our own benefit. This is the voice of the devil and has nothing of the character of God in it. The voice of the parent should have none of these traits.

God cannot use these tactics, and neither can we parents! Our flesh will tell us that we are at a disadvantage without these weapons, but we really are not. Compulsion and force are the mark of Cain. Stay away from it, for the Bible shows the negative path down which this spirit leads. You see, a Christian parent—one who follows Christ—cannot use the spirit or the character of Satan to bring about obedience, nor will he want to.

God wants free-will obedience. Why? Because it is of much greater value than any forced, coerced obedience. Think about it. When I command in a dominant tone, "Sit here!" my child sits out of fear, and his mind resents being forced. In his mind, he may well be standing up; he just isn't big enough to defy you yet. When he is big enough, he will likely perpetuate your treatment in a more severe way in dealing with his own children. Do you really want this kind of obedience?

Free-will obedience calls for the heart to grapple with right and wrong and for the mind to freely choose to go in opposition to the flesh. If your child takes these steps, he will discover *in Jesus* that his choices are empowered by divine power, which evicts the wrong and nurtures the right. God allows free-will choices, and so must we!

When the child disobeys and chooses the way of evil or selfishness, there are natural consequences. The Bible says, "The way of transgressors is hard" (Proverbs 13:15). Parents who are living under God, in His Spirit, wisdom, and power, will consistently see to it that these consequences are administered in love, not harshness and anger. Consequences are to show that the selfish way is not a good way. Consequences are motivators. They quickly show the child where his behavior is taking him, rather than leaving him to reap the result years later. This is love!

Parents need to come under God's direction because human reason is faulty. They will use these occasions to teach the child the error of his ways, using reason, intellect, and conscience accompanied with motivations as necessary. Parents will call the child to a decision, showing him the choices before him. They will point him to Christ for the power to obey, and then give him the opportunity to make a free-will choice. Praying with our children is a wonderful approach to awaken love in both parent and child. If the child chooses wrongly, the parent will, by God's grace, give consequences in a matter-of-fact manner and not in fretfulness and faultfinding. Then the parent brings the child to a choice again.

Turn often to God for wisdom and courage. You will continue to lead your child through this circle of decision, choice, and consequences until he chooses right.

Once the right choice is made, God indwells the child, and inner miracles occur. The negative attitude or disposition, hostility, or anger dissipates and leaves. The child relaxes, is reasonable again, and now, led by God, you can do a deeper work. These experiences of being changed inside help the child make right choices more quickly the next time because he sees that it is possible to change and that it's pleasant to the soul. We want our children to gain an experience with God redeeming them from sin and selfishness through a free-will choice. God is working in this triangle. There is the parent, the child, and God. God is directing both child and parent. When parents cooperate with God, He is also working in the mind and heart of your child to cooperate with you. God wants you to learn to use His tactics in place of Satan's. The choice is yours, and so are the consequences.

True obedience goes after the heart, not just the outward obedience. Inward obedience is what we want, and this requires Christ in your child, the hope of glory, the hope of change (see Colossians 1:26, 27).

The voice of the parent needs to be God's voice speaking through you at all times and under all circumstances. Even under provocation, God's grace is sufficient.

The Lone Embrace
A Special Word of Encouragement for Single Parents

As a single parent, you have a hard life alone. You may feel that it's easy to become upset and vent at home. No, it isn't easy. It makes life harder on you. God wants the voice of the parent—that's you—to reflect His voice. If you consent to let Him put His voice in you and if you choose to cooperate with Him, your home can be a little heaven on earth. Now that is what you really want, isn't it?

The reality is that venting in anger hurts yourself and your child, and causes you to lose the atmosphere of heaven in your home. Won't you commit yourself to God, letting Him keep you and your mouth, that your home can be all that He intends it to be? Home and a loving parent is an oasis for your children, a place where they are nurtured, loved, and grow up knowing God—a place where their love, in turn, comes back on you to fill your heart to the fullest. There are no greater riches on this earth than to be a vessel for God, to be His voice to your children, to be the messenger of His love and power. Try God and see!

Chapter 4

THE VOICE OF GOD

"I will instruct thee and teach thee in the way which thou shalt go: I will guide thee with mine eye" (Psalm 32:8).

I was kneading my bread in the kitchen after breakfast and talking with God. "Lord, I keep a close watch over my boys, looking out the window occasionally as they play. But what if I'm not looking and Lonesome [our wild 'pet' bear] comes for her visit? Is this safe?"

No answer or inspiration came.

I took my lump of bread to the kitchen table to knead it, so that I could watch the boys, and continued, "What if Lonesome came while the boys were playing in the sandbox? Should I be out there with them at all times?"

"Can I take care of bears?" He asked.

Now that was a loaded question for me. You see, God delivered me from the fear of the bears in a most remarkable way (see my earlier book, *Parenting by the Spirit*, pages 99-102). "Why, of course You have control of all the wild beasts. Ezekiel 34:25 says You, 'will cause the evil beasts to cease out of the land: and they [Your people] shall dwell safely in the wilderness, and sleep in the woods.' In Genesis 9:2, You tell us that You put the 'fear of us' upon the beasts. But Lord, the question remains: Is it enough to put my boys under Your care at the beginning of the day, or must I put them into Your hands often throughout the day for them to be safe?"

Just then I saw Lonesome, our two-year-old black bear, turn the corner of the garage heading toward the tree under which Andrew was playing in the sandbox with his toy trucks.

"Lord, surely You want me to go out there right now. What if the boys don't respond rightly? What might Lonesome do?"

"No, Sally, I want you to stay right here and see."

I was strongly inclined to go outside, say our usual prayer, and greet our dear little bear friend. "Well, if you say so, Lord, I'll stay here. I sense this to be You."

Lonesome meandered between the tree and Andrew. The sandbox is about ten feet square, with the tree in the middle. This means that both Lonesome and Andrew were side-by-side, almost touching each other in that space. Andrew was on the outside of the sandbox moving his toy truck along his newly constructed roadway. Andrew, on all fours, turned to greet Lonesome beside him. "Good morning, Lonesome," he said and resumed playing with his truck as if this was normal business. He was treating Lonesome more like a house pet than a wild bear.

"Lord, do I need to go out there and give him some cautions on nose-to-nose conversations with wild bears? He may not recall that we always put Lonesome in Your hands when she comes for a visit."

"Leave him in My hands, Sally. I can talk to Andrew."

"Oh dear, this is a trial! I'm not comfortable about this. But I know You are faithful. I can trust You! Okay, Lord, I'll watch what You will do."

Just then I saw Lonesome step in front of Andrew to sniff the toy truck curiously. Then Andrew protectively gave Lonesome a push, saying, "No, Lonesome, no! You are ruining my roads!"

I gasped, and God immediately said, *"He's alright; keep trusting Me."*

Lonesome gave way and moved back. As Andrew proceeded to round a curve with his truck, Lonesome again slowly moved to get a closer look at this curious object and stepped on Andrew's road a second time. Again Andrew pushed the bear back, harder this time. Lonesome was too curious and didn't budge even with Andrew's pushing. Now Andrew jumped up, stomped his foot, and said as authoritatively as a five-year-old child can, "No, Lonesome! You can't step on my roads!"

Instantly, *out of fear,* Lonesome jumped for the tree beside them and pulled herself up ten feet before she stopped to look back on the scene. Andrew, now feeling sorry for Lonesome, coaxed her down, gave her some attention, and came into the house for something special to give her to eat.

I joined Matthew and Andrew, and we all enjoyed Lonesome. She loves apples, homemade bread—or any grain, for that matter—and, of course, honey. After her little snack, we all walked to the front porch, and Lonesome snuggled up at my feet and just lay there while the boys and I talked. "You know," I told them, "we are the only family she has left. Her mother was shot illegally last fall, and her two siblings died in the den. She is the only survivor. Poor Lonesome. Truly, we are her family."

I added, "Thank You, God, for keeping my boys safe."

God's voice directed me that there was nothing to fear as long as He was there. How does God inspire such questions in my mind? How does He cause the bear to come to answer my question so practically and so timely? I surely can't explain it all, but I can declare that He does it. Nothing happens by chance with God; this experience was not a coincidence. The outcome confirmed that it was truly God guiding and directing not only *my* steps and thoughts but Andrew's as well. The voice of God spoke to my son, and Jesus gave authority to my son's words and put fear in the bear toward that little boy. The lesson learned is that if we are under God's care and control, He will tell us when we are to flee, when we are to go outside to be with our children, and when we don't need to go. He is a wise Father, watching out for us at all times. I want nothing between my soul and my Savior so that He can keep my children and me safe even in the wilderness.

Job 5:22 says, "Neither shalt thou be afraid of the beasts of the earth." The "beasts" you deal with may not be bears like ours, but you may have fear when you face sharks, snakes, spiders, mice, man, or whatever. God is able to care for you in the same way He cares for us. We need not fear because we know God to be greater than any supposed threat. We have come to know His voice. He can direct our steps and put fear in these beasts so that we are kept safe in Him.

"And they shall be all taught of God" (John 6:45). How important is it for parents to teach their children to distinguish between the voice of the flesh and the voice of the Spirit, as well as between the spirit of Satan and the Spirit of God? It is extremely important!

Matthew was very sad. He was attempting to build a birdhouse in the garage. Now, Jim and I were city kids and hadn't learned practical things such as hands-on carpentry. When our boys were about six and eight years old, I felt impressed to let them gain this experience even though we weren't qualified to teach this skill. I had a book with pictures of different birdhouses and had put the boys outside, each with a hammer, saw, and nails. I told each to build a birdhouse. After a short while, Matthew became very frustrated with himself because his first cut wasn't straight. When I checked on him, he was grumbling at himself. Then he told me that the saw was his problem; it wasn't a good saw. "And the nails," he complained, "they don't pound in straight." His house was not perfect like the one in the picture, and his faulty equipment was all to blame. To a perfectionist like Matthew, this was a terrible trial.

"Lord, attend my words. Help me give Matthew better, more realistic problem-solving techniques."

I continued, "Matthew, the saw isn't the real problem, nor is it the nails. The problem is your attitude toward your task. The voice of your flesh is telling you to be 'Sad Sam,' and God's voice wants you to become 'Pleasant Pete' right now."

He argued with me, trying to convince me it was the saw and nails that were giving him this grief.

"Lord what shall I do now? Shall I continue reasoning or do something else?"

"Take him to prayer to let My Holy Spirit soften and subdue his disposition."

So I did, and Matthew gave his stiff, sad disposition to God to take away.

"So, do you feel any different after prayer, Matthew?"

"No, Mother, not one bit."

"That is okay. Your wrong feelings will hang around a while until Jesus can put happy thoughts and feelings in the place of those sad thoughts and feelings. You need to cooperate with whatever God wants you to think right now. Listen for His voice to you."

We stayed on our knees and gave Matthew opportunity to listen for God's voice to his soul and mind. In a little bit he said, "I think God wants me to ask Him to help me make the birdhouse while I'm making it. He said it will be better if I take instructions from Him rather than doing it on my own. He said He'd be with me and teach me."

That was excellent advice for my son. God knew his character well. And Jesus was a carpenter, so surely He could teach him well. "Now Matthew you need to forgive yourself for not making it perfectly the first time. You can't put that kind of expectation upon yourself. That's Satan's voice! When you have had the experience of making a hundred birdhouses, you will have that skill. Right now that is not realistic. Is that right?"

"I guess so." And he picked up his hammer and saw and began again. This time he gained instructions from Jesus as he tried. God taught him carpentry skills with hands-on experience that Jim and I could not. And God also directed his thoughts toward right and good. Thankfully, Matthew cooperated. In a short time a smile was on his face as he was learning new skills and performing them nicely. Matthew tasted grace, changing his disposition from sad to happy in Jesus. Knowing the distinctions between the two voices is paramount; otherwise, we find ourselves fighting against God.

Matthew was a very strong-willed child under the molding and shaping process of God to bring balance to his personality and character. Parents, we can be instruments in God's hands to do His will by being sensitive to the Holy Spirit's influence "in the moment" of a situation. He will instruct us how to direct our child's thoughts. In Him is our success. But we don't have to wait for a particular set of circumstances. We can be His instrument by making plans how to overcome a particular weakness in our child even before a situation arises. God will guide us ahead of time as well as in the moment. Matthew grew patience to a new height by making birdhouses under God.

Jesus needs to be our children's constant Companion and familiar Friend. They need to be taught, exercised, and trained in knowing Him, for only by acquaintance and association with Christ will they become like Him. Who are your children conversing with and imitating—God or Satan?

Andrew was ten years old and becoming a good bicycle rider. I asked him to take something to a neighbor for me. Now, neighbors aren't located very close together where we live, so this meant he would ride his bicycle. Usually Andrew would be happy to do so because he liked riding his bike. But this particular time he was Mr. Grumpy. It was obvious all over his face that he was going to do what I asked grudgingly.

"Lord, what should I do with this attitude?"

"You need to faithfully correct it."

"Andrew, you can't go with that attitude. It isn't good for you or anyone around you, myself included."

"Lord, He wasn't communicative with me nor cooperative. What will work for him today?"

It has always been a trial and frustration for me to decide what consequences would be best in a given situation. But I had been learning how to come to God and listen for an idea. I had learned that if I followed Him, I would successfully get to the heart of the matter and that lasting heart changes would take place. I liked that!

God gave me an idea in this situation. I followed through, and it improved Andrew's disposition nicely, but didn't entirely transform it.

"Lord I've been wanting to help Andrew learn to take You with him so that You can become that constant Companion and familiar Friend You need to be. I want to help him develop more confident conversations with You that will draw him even closer to You. I want to use this opportunity to do so, but his disposition isn't very good. Is now a good time?"

God spoke to my heart, *"Yes, this would be a good lesson for him today."*

"Okay, Lord, give me words to use and divine love and firmness in my approach."

Now God had given me an idea previously during one of my "baptismal" tub baths, which is a time I use to talk with Him, where self dies and God gives me solutions to my problems. I had thought about it and decided to do it. So God knew what I was asking.

"Andrew, I'd like you to take Jesus with you on your trip. Whenever we go on a trip in the car, what do we do first?"

"We pray first for God's protection and blessing during our trip." He rolled his eyes backward to show that my question was annoying to him. "I'm just going for a bike ride."

"Well, son, your bicycle is your 'car.' You need to practice becoming a father and husband by doing the same as Father does."

"Aw, Mother!" Andrew stood there, not making the decision I had hoped he would.

"Lord, now what?"

"Just wait a bit." And I did.

"Andrew, you must decide. Your spirit needs to change. Give the wrong thoughts and feelings to God so that you can have peace and enjoy this day. You know where this attitude takes you. It isn't worth it. It's the devil bringing these thoughts to you."

After a few more minutes, he dragged his feet to the porch where we both knelt to pray. He didn't pray on his own, so I nudged him.

"Lord, does this mean I have to give him a 'consequence' to motivate him to obey?"

"Be patient for now."

Andrew prayed. He began in a disinterested attitude. I prayed silently for God to touch his heart. Quickly his prayer took on a different tone; it was evident that he had responded to God in his heart, that Jesus was coming onto the throne of his heart, making changes in his disposition. "Praise God!" I prayed silently.

Andrew went off on his bike with a smile and a hearty wave goodbye.

I went into the house and prayed for him. "Lord, please keep him safe and give him a good experience with You so that He will see You are his best Friend and Companion." A few minutes passed; again I was impressed by the Holy Spirit to pray for Andrew, and I did.

Suddenly I heard the sound of gravel churning under bicycle tires and a screeching halt at the back door. How could Andrew be back so soon?

"Mother, Mother!" Andrew shouted excitedly. "There are two grizzly bears on the driveway—great big ones! I want you and Matthew to come see them! Come quickly."

"Oh my! Two grizzly bears? How can that be? They're too ill tempered to travel together when they're that big. Grizzlies are loners. Are you sure there were two?"

"Yes, Mother, there are two."

"Are you sure they're grizzlies?"

"Yes I'm sure! They have that big hump and a silver stripe across their shoulder."

"Let's all get into the truck and go see."

The boys tumbled in quickly. Less than a quarter mile down the road was the hill where Andrew said he had encountered the two bears. There were no bears at this time.

"So, Andrew, tell us what happened."

"Well, I came to the hill here, and there were two grizzlies standing still in the road, right in my way. I told those bears to get off the road, but they didn't! I thought I could get past them on the right before they could react because I can ride fast on my bike. They can't see well, you know. Then I thought, 'No, I shouldn't do that.' Then I thought I'd go into the woods a little ways and get around them. Then I thought, 'No, I need to ride home real fast and tell Mother and Matthew so that they can come see these bears before I go to the neighbor.' "

"Whew!" God had been with Andrew! God had helped his young mind to reason correctly; He had revealed to Andrew which options were not good. It was Jesus that thrilled his heart with the idea to share this experience with those he loved. What would have happened if I had allowed Andrew to go to the neighbor with his disgruntled attitude uncorrected? Would he have been as inclined to listen to God or to be moved by love to return home? And if not, what might have happened? "And thine ears shall hear a word behind thee, saying, This [is] the way, walk ye in it, when ye turn to the right hand, and when ye turn to the left" (Isaiah 30:21).

Everything good comes from God, and this experience had been a good thing. Andrew found that Jesus was there for him, instructing him in the way to go. He had experienced hearing God's voice to his reason and conscience. He had learned the need for prayer before going anywhere on his bicycle. He had learned that God would keep him safe.

That evening, we talked further with Father about prayer—and about the proper response when one encounters a bear! Neither charging a bear nor running away from him is a good response, and we discussed why that is true. We told Andrew, "Jesus is your best defense and protection; call upon Him. Jesus will tell you what you need to do and will handle the bear in your behalf as long as you are not presumptuous and are listening to God's directions. You need to be under God's direction, not telling Him what you want Him to do for you. It is so important that your heart is right with God whether you're taking a short trip on a bicycle or a longer trip in the car, because safety comes from God."

Two weeks later the family was in the car and saw this unusual grizzly pair still running together just as Andrew had seen them. God is so good!

Our children need a personal acquaintance with God's voice through the impressions of the Holy Spirit, His Word, nature, and providence. Are we teaching them in the school of life that walking with God means to give our wrong thoughts, feelings, and dispositions to Him to cleanse, purify, and return to us to be used for righteousness? Are we teaching them how to cooperate with God? Are we making our children aware of God's presence directing them in their lives? Are we showing them their need of praying to God in every time of need or emergency? Can they distinguish between God's voice and that of Satan? Are they gaining the experience of having God with them, speaking to them like He did Samuel, Paul, Enoch and all the disciples of the Bible?

Likewise, God's voice will direct us, their parents, into this same pathway. Are you aware of His presence, and do you know His voice? If not, God will personally teach you.

We moved to the mountains of Montana when the boys were four and six. After two years, the Lord laid on my heart the need for them to have their own personal worship time to get to know God personally. This was not something I desired. After all, it would reduce the time I had to spend with God myself—praying and reading. After I worked through that and surrendered to reason, we began a new road in our life.

"Boys! Time to get up." I'd shake them lovingly. Both were sleepyheads, and I knew this would be trial number one for them. I was determined to be as positive and cheerful as God would enable me to be. So cheerfully I'd tease them out of bed with their little moans, groans, and playful falling back into bed. "Now, boys, as we have read about Samuel, we've seen that God wants to talk personally with each of us. Today we will begin experimenting. Matthew, I want you to go downstairs and take your shower, drink your water, and get out your Bible for study. You need to be first because you are the bigger sleepyhead of the two. Meanwhile, Andrew, I want you to get on your knees here and have your prayers while Matthew uses the bathroom. When Matthew finishes, it's your turn to do those things, and Matthew will have his prayer time alone.

Matthew went right away. "Now Andrew," I continued, "you need to learn how to pray. You begin by telling God how you want to walk and talk with Him today and asking Him to teach you how. Recite the Lord's Prayer and stop to think of each thought as you pray it. Then bring all your special needs to Him—remember? We discussed what those might be. Then spend some time listening for God to impress you through His Holy Spirit what your solutions might be."

"Sally, have Andrew recite back to you the list of things in their proper order."

"Okay, Andrew, tell me exactly what you will do in prayer and in what order you will do them."

"Umm . . . , first pray for Him to teach me how to walk and talk with Him. Then recite the Lord's Prayer, and umm . . . ?"

"What else will you do while reciting the Lord's Prayer?"

"I will think about it. Then I should listen quietly for God to speak to me if He so chooses."

"Very good! If you get sleepy in the dark with a blanket around you, call me to turn on your gas light for you."

"Okay."

Developing a routine is important, and understanding *why* you do what you do is also important. Some days the boys have wonderful experiences in which God draws close and leaves them with some great or helpful thought. Other days, God seems distant and noncommunicative. They need to experience both. They need to understand that the Holy

Spirit is to control us, not we the Holy Spirit. We cannot dictate when He talks with us; we must learn submissiveness and be content when He speaks to our heart and when He doesn't. We must take God at His word that He is with us. Our feelings are not always to be trusted, especially if they do not agree with God's Word. But we can trust His Word.

These experiences afford us the opportunity to point out the voice of the flesh in contrast to the voice of the Holy Spirit. It is best, we've found, to talk about the theory during the morning quiet time and then very specifically to help our children identify these principles throughout the day as the voices of God or Satan are actively pushing them toward good or evil.

You can know the voice of the flesh because it is characterized by selfishness, anger, pouting, feeling sorry for oneself, hatred, an unwilling disposition, impatience, feeling "I can't," being a bully, insisting on "me first," etc. (See Galatians 5:19-21.)

You can know the voice of the Holy Spirit because it agrees with God's Word (see Isaiah 8:20). It's characterized by unselfishness, happiness, freedom, kindness, love, helpfulness, honesty, truthfulness, a cheery disposition, and caring for others just like Jesus did when He walked this earth. (See Galatians 5:22, 23.)

There is also the *spirit* of Satan, which is made up of compulsion, force, threats, dishonesty, domination, and hurtfulness. You do not need to obey this spirit. This spirit wants to hurt you and lead you to do wrong. Then it makes you feel guilty for giving in, and thus brings you to the point of hopelessness and despair.

In contrast, the *Spirit* of God is kind, patient, and inviting. The Comforter calls to your heart in a still small voice, leaving you free to choose His way or not. He never forces or compels. He's loving, not critical. He encourages you to do right; He offers His helping hand to empower you to do it. He pursues you always.

God's voice and the voice of Satan are not audible voices. Rather, they are thoughts in your mind; you must decide whether they are good or evil. Often, you will need to cry out to God to help you distinguish whether a particular thought is good or evil. Sometimes God will not give you a distinct impression, and then you will need to search to know His will from His Word. As you learn through the school of life how to distinguish between these two very different voices to your soul, you will be able to instruct and teach your children.

So I taught my boys how to study their Bible to know God's will.

We first became familiar with the Bible stories in family worship. This is gaining general knowledge. When they could read for themselves, I took them to certain books of the Bible to familiarize them with God's character and words in contrast to the character and words common to the usurper—Satan. Then I encouraged them to summarize what they read and also to think how it applied to them today.

It's important for parents to teach children how to do topical studies in the Bible so that they can research God's will on specific points. These studies are very valuable in gaining an experience with God. Then there are also doctrinal studies. As much as possible, we need to let the Bible interpret itself. If we rely on human interpretations, these can take us down many a dead end. Pray to God as you read His word that the Holy Spirit will interpret His word to you (see John 16:7, 13). Isaiah said we gain knowledge by adding "precept upon precept; line upon line, . . . here a little, [and] there a little" (Isaiah 28:10).

I wanted our sons to become good Bible students. In order for Bible study to be interesting, it has to meet real needs and give answers that work when we try them under God's guidance. We want our children to discover a living, powerful God—not the powerless God commonly served in "professed" Christendom today.

As our boys gained this foundation, we built upon it by adding a deeper understanding of how to walk and talk with God as men such as Enoch, Moses, David, Daniel, Joseph, and others had done. Often, the lessons learned in the morning would relate to something in their day and allow them see how God is with them right now as they follow by faith, not according to feelings. The Bible became very practical and made more sense to them. Their personal walk with God was the most important lesson, and it grew stronger day by day and year by year. Understanding God's word is much like mining for gold. Effort and persistency will be well repaid.

The boys read their Bibles through from Genesis to Revelation and we, their parents, helped them understand the concepts and solid truths as best we were able. Are you giving your offspring your concepts and views of Jesus, or are you leaving that work to another? Leaving it to others is allowing Satan to have opportunities to confuse, bewilder, and discourage them by wrong concepts. But if we are willing to learn of Christ, as did Saul, we can make a difference. When he was blinded on the road to Damascus, Saul finally listened to heaven. He spent three years in the wilderness of Arabia to develop an ear tuned to heaven and recognize God's voice. He had been duped into believing the voice of Satan, the usurper, and was persecuting God's people in error. He didn't want to be duped again, so he laid the right foundation as he studied in Arabia. So must we. And how much more important it is for our children to learn to hear God's voice in the generation in which they are living today, amidst Sodom and Gomorrah. There are many false teachers out there. We must introduce our children to the true Teacher, Jesus Christ.

As we, ourselves, learn how to distinguish between the Spirit's voice and the voice of the flesh or of Satan, we can teach our children to do the same at their level. When we learn the distinction between the spirit of Satan and the Spirit of God by the working of the Holy Spirit, we can teach our children to do the same—simply and practically—and give them an advantage so that they need not fall into Satan's snares. Then they do not have to come out of a horrible life of evil in order to find God; instead, they can escape this corruption. They need not sow their oats in a life of sin and selfishness and waste their health, life, and energy until they are old. Why would we want pain and heartache like this for our children? How much do you want to save your children from that kind of life?

When Matthew was twelve and Andrew was ten, Jim and I found it was better to leave the boys home when we went on trips to town. At home, they could do school work or their chores, feed and play with the deer, and cook. It was a lot harder for them to concentrate on their school work in the busy, noisy real estate office. And there were some things in town we preferred that they didn't see or hear at their tender ages. They were responsible boys, and leaving them at home was working wonderfully.

I would leave them a list of plenty of things to do—as well as some activities for their own amusement—so that they wouldn't have lots of idle time that Satan could make use of. I also have a standing list on the side of my refrigerator to keep track of things needing to be done. For instance, if I'm in the garage and see something that needs to be done—yard work, greenhouse projects, and the like—I put it on my list for use as a "consequence" or an occupation when needed. I even include things on that list that I'd like to have done, things that are unlikely to happen but nice to hope for.

On one occasion, we returned home from town to a heartwarming surprise. The boys had faithfully accomplished all the things on the list I had left them. But they wanted to do something special as well. So they consulted my list of extras. They had strung up a trellis for my pea vines, made cages for the cantaloupes and tomatoes, had the garden all weeded and freshly watered. And they still had time to make Jim's favorite carob fudge cake with thick carob frosting.

"My sheep hear my voice, and I know them, and they follow me" (John 10:27).

The boys were so thrilled when we came home and showed our excitement about all that they had done. My squeals of joy gave them joy. Listening to God's voice is a heavenly thing.

Everything good comes from God. Oh, how God must rejoice when He can inspire the hearts of our youth with good, Christlike things to do to bring pleasure into our homes, lives, and hearts! Won't you give God access to your children by teaching them how to recognize the voice of God and follow it?

THE LONE EMBRACE
A SPECIAL WORD OF ENCOURAGEMENT FOR SINGLE PARENTS

When you're in despair or discouragement, which voice do you usually listen to and obey? Satan's voice or God's voice? Is God your Pilot? Do you let Him guide your thoughts, feelings, words, deeds, and responses? Colossians 4:6 says, "Let your speech [be] alway with grace, seasoned with salt [Christ], that ye may know how ye ought to answer every man." Christ in you is the hope of glory in your home today, right now, even under difficult circumstances. Coming to know the voice of God to your soul will free your home to be heavenlike although it does not necessarily change any of your irritations or daunting circumstances. Christ can give you an oasis even in the storm, if you abide in Him.

Once you gain confidence that God is with you, prepare a "fire escape" plan for those situations where you are weakest. Remember when you practiced fire drills in school? You knew just what to do and where to go when the alarm rang. So, too, with spiritual alarms. With God you can make a plan about how not to get angry, upset, or irritated. You'll know what to do *instead,* and you can have the assurance that God will help you carry out the choices you have made before hand. He will give you power to live above the pull of the flesh. He is always there with you, ready to help you. Remember, practice makes perfect! You can have a real heaven here on earth under His wings.

Chapter 5

TEACHING AND TRAINING

"Train up a child in the way he should go: and when he is old, he will not depart from it (Proverbs 22:6).

But, Lord, I taught Andrew his math facts. What is the matter with him? He knows what is right, but he doesn't do it. For example, he went upstairs to review his math cards the other day, and I heard him bouncing his ball up there instead of practicing his math. I can't take all the responsibility for making sure he learns his math facts; he has to take responsibility as well. So what is wrong?"

"Teaching and training are very different learning processes. Teaching deals only with the mind—telling your child what is right. But training deals with the will and seeing to it your child does what he knows is right. This is your responsibility."

"So teaching is telling, transmitting information into the mind," I mused. I reviewed Andrew's attitude toward math. I had drilled him daily with the flash cards so that he could become proficient with the facts. He started to master them, then something happened, and he lost interest and self-motivation. He developed a very negative attitude. It began with dislike and then progressed to a hatred of math class and a fear of timed tests. It grew into a real problem. He came to feel that he could never be a good mathematician.

"Where did we go wrong, Lord?"

"What was your part in this?" God asked.

"Well, I drilled him with those flash cards daily for a while, and he was coming along well." Then I remembered. "Lord, as You know, I would get on the phone helping other mothers to bring their children to surrender, and I'd send Andrew up to our bedroom to drill himself on his math facts alone. Soon I'd hear him bouncing a ball up there. I knew he was playing, not practicing. You called for my heart to go take care of *my* child and correct him, but I didn't heed Your call because . . . it was too awkward and uncomfortable. I was at fault for helping other children while leaving my own child without help. Satan had an inroad and planted the seeds of lying thoughts in Andrew's mind. Those seeds have sprouted and grown with time and repetition. Months of that pattern is what has brought us to where we are right now. Yes, I did have a big part in this, didn't I? I'm so sorry. I need to change and be consistent.

"But, Lord, Andrew's attitude is so set that he believes the lie that he can't do math. He believes this heartily. It will be very difficult to overcome, but I'm willing to do whatever You tell me to do right now. I want Andrew to be the best mathematician he can be in Jesus. Help me, Lord!"

God chose not to reason with me at this time. So I committed to make time for Him by arranging for another "baptismal" tub bath that evening. Jim agreed to watch the boys. Here God inspired me with a solution and courage.

"Lord I don't have one idea about how to help Andrew. This case is very complicated to my mind, but I know You have a thousand ideas. Please give me one or two. I'm so sorry for not heeding Your voice to me earlier regarding Andrew; I'm sure it would have been a lot easier then. But I'm ready and needy now, so I trust You will answer." I put my head under the water thinking I must die to self's way and instead, follow God's way.

"Sally, you need to approach Andrew in a new and different way. It would be best to drill him outdoors—daily, faithfully, with Me guiding you. Don't try to drill those facts the old way, fighting against all the lying thoughts that have been developed upstairs in your bedroom or with you at the table. Let's bypass all the prejudices we can."

"Sounds good to me! Should I just drill him while we're walking?"

"You can vary how you drill him. Remember how you took Matthew down the driveway, bouncing a basketball?"

"I sure do. I discovered that, for him, it worked well to have his hands busy while his mind worked math mentally. Maybe this can work for Andrew as well to hinder those lying thoughts and get him over the hump. Say, I'm excited about this. There is hope when You are with me. You can help me out of this trouble just as You have so many other times. I love Your ideas and especially Your empowering presence!"

Excitedly I came away from that talk time with God with renewed energy and courage. That next morning as we began school I said, "Okay, Andrew, I have a surprise for you. We'll do math first today. God gave me a wonderful idea about how we can get you over your fear and lying thoughts about not being able to do math. First, I commit to you that I will be with you to do your math drills until you have them down well. The phone will not distract me as before.

"You will soon discover how well you can do these facts trusting in Jesus. You'll do much better than you've been doing upstairs the last few months, trusting in self. I want you to be the best you can be in Jesus. After you learn these facts well, you'll never need to fear those timed math tests again, either. It will become fun!"

Andrew looked drawn, fearful, and without courage. "It looks like you need to connect with Jesus," I told him, "so that you can have courage and faith. So let's pray right now."

We both prayed, but Andrew still looked worried and unsure.

"Is he surrendering well enough, Lord?"

"For right now he is. Let's get him into his new program."

"Andrew, we'll go outside to do your drills today. It'll be fun! This is a new, different way, and you will learn the math facts very well. You can do it, Andrew!"

"It's not fair for you to expect me to be like Matthew. I'll never be a good math student like him. Never, never! You don't understand!"

"Those are lying thoughts, Andrew, and you'll discover it in time. First, you can't allow yourself to think discouraging thoughts like that. They are lies, believe me. Whenever they come up, you must give them to Jesus. Throw them away. If they don't go away, tell me, and we will both go to Jesus and get rid of them. I can show you how.

"You must put forth your effort and let God put new thoughts in place of the wrong thoughts. This you must do willingly. God will take away all the negative thinking that you will allow Him to; He'll perform that wonderful miracle inside you. You can be happy and do well. He can change your disposition, your feelings, and even your thoughts. You've given God these things; now believe that He is working for you against what your feelings say. Exercise your will on God's side, and He will return your wrong thoughts, feelings, and habits to you purified. Trust God now and let go of all the 'I can't.' "

He dragged his feet, and we began.

"Now, Andrew, you *can* learn these math facts. Think of the little engine that could and choose to think, 'I think I can; I think I can; I can!' " He recited these phrases after me.

I began the flash cards, and he said slowly and rhythmically, "Two and two are . . . ," and he put up two fingers, then two more fingers, then counted them slowly, and said timidly, "Four." I showed him another flash card, and in similar fashion he said, "Three and two are . . . five"—counting his fingers.

"No, Andrew, you can't count your fingers and toes to get the answer. When you get beyond twenty, you will be lost," I said lovingly, but firmly. "This habit must go. You can't do math this way. Instead, I want you to say quickly out loud, automatically—"two and two are four"—without adding up your fingers. If you don't know the answer, tell me so. Then I will show you the answer side of the card, and you will recite the facts and answer automatically. Math facts must become automatic; then they become fun! You can do it! Let's try again."

And he did try. It was painful for me to watch; he was so timid and insecure. As we went through more math cards, I asked God if I needed to address Andrew's disposition now.

"Yes, address it, and I will be with you."

"Andrew, you're doing better. Do you see that?"

"No, I'm not doing better, Mother! You don't understand who I am."

"Well, maybe I don't understand you, but God does. He told me you can do it, and I trust God. You must too. He knows you better than you know yourself. Right? You have to choose to turn away from all these oppressive lies you are thinking. When you cooperate with them, do you see how they hurt you and make you sad? Lying thoughts are the enemy, the giant that needs to be slain—not God or I."

Andrew broke down into tears. My tender heart was drawn out mightily to his emotional condition. I wanted to relieve him of this pain and difficulty. I consulted with God, and He convinced me that it would not be love to relieve Andrew. Rather, it would be love to help him out of all this heartache by having him face his fears and lying thoughts, label them rightly, and overcome them with God's help. So I found the firmness and wisdom from above to follow God's leading. (See James 1:5.)

"Andrew," I said, "you cannot think these thoughts. They are lies. We need to stop right here on the road and give them again to Jesus to throw into the sea. You can't bear such a heavy load. Give it all to Jesus, son."

He couldn't face it, and he wouldn't pray with me. So God led me to send him on a half-mile run up the road and back. When he returned, he was motivated to pray and put his will on God's side and try God again.

We returned to drilling. I was walking backward, facing Andrew, and he was reciting the facts as we had discussed. He was still very slow. "Lord, can I push him to go faster?"

"Yes, that would be fine. You're doing well, Sally. Keep up your courage."

"Andrew, you're doing better, but you must do the math problems faster." So I pushed him faster and faster in his responses by flipping the flash cards faster. I was cooperating with God to exchange new habits for old.

We did a long session the first day—an hour and a half. And Andrew's disposition was really much better at the end. He was gaining success, and he was learning his facts. He even smiled and enjoyed it a little bit. The hard work was keeping him positive, knowing when to push, when to give a hug to encourage him, and when to give consequences to motivate him to come out of his comfort zone and to try a new way. I wanted him to taste grace working in his heart, mind, and soul to free him from his present bondage to fear and believing "I can't."

The next day we repeated this process, varying how we practiced the flash cards by using the basketball approach. First I drilled him in mental math from the textbook—five minus two plus three minus one plus four equals. . . . While Andrew bounced the ball he did addition and subtraction. Hopefully, he wouldn't be able to think those debilitating negative thoughts about himself and would just work on learning the math facts automatically. He did pretty well the first time, and each day we practiced, he did better. Then we drilled, using the cards as before.

I was still dealing with the exercise of his will as often as necessary, in order to free him up to learn those facts in Jesus. This is the important art of training. As we progressed, the corrections and consequences were needed less; he was learning well. God led me to challenge his slow responses each day so that he wouldn't revert to counting his fingers and toes. After a few days, the slow responses were no more. Each change helped him to learn better. And God did change his sadness, took away the oppression, and changed his disposition as he cooperated—bringing hope into his hopeless heart. Some days the negative thoughts disappeared for the whole day; at other times they would return for a short season.

When Andrew would fall back into the old thinking and disposition of fear, God—through me—would faithfully address these things. After a month, Andrew was noticeably improved. God had to deal with me when those phone calls came. I got stronger, more confident, and decisive about deferring those calls to a more convenient season so that I could be there for Andrew faithfully.

Titus 2:12 says, "Teaching us that, denying ungodliness and worldly lusts, we should live soberly, righteously, and godly, in this present world."

"Sally, do you see now the difference between teaching and training Andrew?"

"Oh yes, Lord! What a contrast. Teaching truly deals with the mind. The boys have the knowledge of what is right, but fears, habits, feelings, or emotions compel them into the old way of serving sin and self against Your will and way." Knowing what is right is not enough to be an overcomer. We must know by experience how to get rid of the lying thoughts and compelling feelings that push us against the knowledge and the will of God.

Training deals with the will and sees to it our child does what he knows is right, empowered under God. It's training that gets us in touch with God, and then His divine power brings the wrong thoughts and feelings into line. Apart from Him we do not have the power to do that! Andrew must surrender his will to God and cooperate with Him, not his feelings. Only Andrew can make this step. Christ wants free-will obedience, not just an outward obedience without the heart cooperating. And the heart cannot cooperate unless God is in the equation to evict wrong thoughts and feelings—and re-create the right ones in their place. Under God, training transforms the child, freeing him to obey what he knows is right.

"You are learning well." God's still small voice encouraged.

"Lord, I've been thinking that it's time to bring Andrew to face his fear of those timed tests."

"Let's do it."

And so that day, after our addition flash card drills outside; I brought Andrew in to do a timed test. Immediately, his face showed fear.

"Andrew, you need not fear these tests anymore. Trust Mother! You cannot think these hurtful, debilitating thoughts. God has freed you from them outside on the road, and He will do so inside the house, too. You must give them to Jesus until they are all gone from you. Let's pray."

Andrew knew the right words to say and said them willingly, but timidly. His face, however, showed that fear still reigned in his thoughts and emotions.

"Are you going to trust what you feel or what God's Word says?"

"Mother, this is so hard! You don't understand!" His little body shook nervously with fear.

"Son, I *do* understand," I said compassionately. "Because I love you, I want you to face your fears and think trusting thoughts of what Jesus can do for you right now."

He struggled, he grimaced, and I saw him decide. His shoulders relaxed, and he went to his knees on his own and prayed the same words again, but added, "Lord, in You I can do my timed test without fear. Take this fear from me and help me believe more."

I sensed God's presence. We did the timed test, and he was more calm and free to concentrate than I'd yet seen him. This time there were no shaking limbs, tense shoulders, or fearful countenance. Excitedly, I told Andrew how well he had done and showed him his last timed test as a contrast to the present one. He had concrete evidence that he was doing much better than he ever thought he could, and he thanked Jesus for it.

"But look how much better Matthew's times are than mine." Andrew noticed, because I marked the timing for each drill in my book for reference. "I can never be like Matthew in math. You are expecting too much from me."

"Andrew, I just want you to be the best you can be in Jesus. You are doing very well and have improved greatly," I encouraged. "God is making you into a good mathematician. Whether you match Matthew or not is not an issue. The question is: Are you doing the best *you* can?"

Matthew 28:20 says, "Teaching them to observe all things whatsoever I have commanded you: and, lo, I am with you alway, even unto the end of the world."

We went through a similar scenario several more times. Occasionally he needed to be motivated by consequences, which I gave in love. But he put forth increasing effort to do his best with God's help. At times, I watched him swing the sword of the Spirit by applying Bible texts in his own words, reinforcing thoughts of courage. I saw him exercise his will, submitting temptations to God and cooperating with Him to overcome them.

The big day of deliverance finally came. Andrew had developed a pattern of facing his fear, so when I announced the timed test, he was becoming skilled in his new pattern. This particular day he was very quick and was actually enjoying the challenge of the timed test. He was on the edge of his seat doing his best with all his effort.

"Oh, Lord, look at this score! He beat Matthew's score which I have written in the book. Oh, may I tell Andrew?" I sensed *"yes"* in my soul.

"Andrew! Andrew! Look here. You beat Matthew's score on this timed test! I knew you could do it in Jesus! You are better than you thought you could ever be."

"Mother, that isn't true! It can't be!"

"Yes it is. Come see for yourself, Andrew. All this effort to bring you out of those lying thoughts has been worth it. Are you convinced now? You are an excellent mathematician! God can help you do many impossible things!"

He was speechless, but his face said it all. He was an overcomer by taking Jesus at His word and not believing those lying thoughts that had held him hostage for so long. God had set another captive free. Andrew's smile was not due to pride, but to a mind set free to serve God, to trust and believe Him over the pull of his flesh.

Isaiah 54:13, 14 says, "And all thy children [shall be] taught of the LORD; and great [shall be] the peace of thy children. In righteousness shalt thou be established: thou shalt be far from oppression; for thou shalt not fear: and from terror; for it shall not come near thee."

The text that appears at the beginning of this chapter—Proverbs 22:6—does not say, *"Tell* a child the way he should go." Rather, it says significantly, *"Train up* a child in the way he should go: and when he is old, he will not depart from it." The promise comes with training, not merely teaching.

Many parents that think because in their home they have *told* their child what is right, that the young person will come back to God after sowing his wild oats. What a mistake! Knowing what is right and not doing it keeps us out of the kingdom of God, for it shows we are not God's children. We are obeying ourselves—our feelings, our habits—not Him. Training ourselves and our children to submit to the will of God, to say "No" to the flesh—while saying "Yes" to God, is the training process that allows God to adopt us as one of His own. Many parents see their children grow away from God and right. They cling vainly to this promise in Proverbs 22:6, hoping for their children to come back to God, but they never see it happen. The reason? Because simply knowing the right is not enough to save our children. Parents must train their children how to come to God and obey Him in His strength. When they possess this experiential knowledge of Christ, the promise applies.

Teaching deals with the mind.

Teaching your child is telling him or her what is right. It is drilling him to know what is right and to be able to repeat it back to you. It is transferring information from your mind to his. But does *knowing* he should not interrupt you necessarily keep "Interruptive Ivan" from interrupting? Does *knowing* that lying is wrong change "Lying Larry"? Does *knowing* she should not be sassy change "Sassy Susie"? No!

Teaching deals with the mind, but a mind that doesn't want to cooperate in heart, action, or life will not progress from knowing to doing. The real issue in parenting is learning how to capture our child's heart for God and bring about the transformation of his or her character.

Training deals with the will and sees to it that the child
does what he knows to be right.

In the case of "Interruptive Ivan," "Lying Larry," and "Sassy Susie," I had to go into deeper parenting. Dealing with the will motivates the child to engage his effort to connect with Jesus for power to go against the pull of their flesh. This is where most parents fail because the parent tires of the protracted effort. It's a daily struggle to deal with the will and establish those good habits of surrendering the mind and cooperating with the heart in our actions. (For more detailed information on the exercise of the will see the chapter "My Will—How to Exercise It" in my book *Parenting by the Spirit*.)

For two years, my "Interruptive Ivan" knew he shouldn't interrupt me. I taught him well; he could recite this fact to me. But when he was tempted to interrupt, all that knowledge flew out the window. Without *training* his will, without taking him to Jesus to change, what was the result? Interruptions! When training with the will and positive directions given in Jesus, what was the result? Character transformation—he learned to interrupt in a proper fashion.

"Lying Larry" knew he should tell the truth; he could give all the right answers in church. But he easily lied to his mother when she asked him about eating blueberries he was not supposed to eat. Knowing isn't enough, while exercising our will brings the desired change.

Likewise, "Sassy Susie" knew not to be sassy, but had her will been trained to be sweet in Jesus? Had she been trained to let Divine power work a change in her disposition through surrender and cooperation? This is what Susie—and all our children—need their parents to do for them.

Training is motivating our children to exercise their will and to come to God. Many times, this training will involve discipline and consequences for wrong actions. Led of God, I had to prescribe many hard things with my Andrew before he was fully free from his old ways of responding. Was this love? Absolutely! It freed him to be the mathematician he could be!

"O God, thou hast taught me from my youth: and hitherto have I declared thy wondrous works" (Psalm 71:17). How many character traits are holding back our children from being all they can be in Jesus? God is there to direct our steps out of Despairing Castle. In Him, we need no longer obey "Giant Fear"!

We need to train up our children to be free to serve God entirely (see Proverbs 22:6).

THE LONE EMBRACE
A SPECIAL WORD OF ENCOURAGEMENT FOR SINGLE PARENTS

Do you have fears, apprehensions, or oppression? Like Andrew, you can learn of God's perfect love that "casteth out fear" (1 John 4:18). As God was with Moses, so He will be with you in your household, in your dire straights, in your conflicting emotions. He longs to set you free! Give all these negative things to Jesus. As the song says, give Him all your wrong emotions, all your wrong character traits, and He will direct your path and show you a way of escape from every besetment. Whatever giants you face, they can all be slain with Jesus at your side. If you will hear His voice and be taught by Him, you will learn the truth as it is in Jesus, and this truth shall set you free so that you are free indeed. Your mighty Counselor can become your Prince of Peace! God can be more real than a husband living with you in your home. Try Him.

Chapter 6

WHAT IS CHARACTER?

"And you, that were sometime alienated and enemies in [your] mind by wicked works, yet now hath He reconciled" (Colossians 1:21).

*O*ur thoughts and feelings make up our character and drive our responses. Thoughts and feelings, prompted by God, yield good responses. Selfish, evil, unkind responses reveal thoughts and feelings instilled by Satan.

Likewise, our child's responses—good or evil—tell us to whom he or she is listening. It's our thoughts and feelings that drive us to react the way we do—parent and child alike. If we want to change the way our children react to us in any given situation, we must deal with their thoughts and feelings. We must let God lead us as we do this, for He knows how to redeem wrong thoughts and feelings and make them right. Through Christ we can effectively change our child's behavior, responses, and habits by giving him better thoughts and feelings that originate with God.

"Were you eating blueberries again, son?" Mother asked in a derogatory, accusing spirit! (See Colossians 3:21.)

"No, I didn't!" the child retorted defensively.

The blueberry stains on the six-year-old's face betrayed his lie. "Whatever am I going to do with you? You're a compulsive liar!" Mother scowled at the boy with her hands angrily on her hips.

I came in on this scenario, and the frustrated mother asked me to help her with her lying child. The child felt her spirit and demeanor. In fact, it seemed to me that he was reacting more to her harsh spirit than to her words.

"Why are you lying, Billy?" I asked tenderly.

"I'm not lying; I'm telling you the truth!" he persisted with coldness and fear.

"I'm your friend, and I want to help you. I'm not like your mother; I'm different. I want to help you out of your trouble, not make trouble for you. But first I need you to tell me the truth."

I saw in his eyes a struggle. He was looking down at the ground, and the strain of the situation was evident. Not knowing how to gain his heart, I sent a silent prayer heavenward for wisdom and help from Jesus! Then I gave him another chance, "I know you ate blueberries. You can tell me the truth."

Fear and confusion were evident in his eyes and countenance. He was displaying to me his history—his fear of his mother. I suspected that he was afraid to tell the truth for fear that his mother would retaliate and wouldn't accept him. I got a mirror. In an encouraging and loving fashion I showed him his face saying, "You need to tell me the truth."

He began to talk very fast, full of fear. He defended himself by saying that his mother also ate between meals. His anxiety level was obviously very high.

"Slow down," I said. "It's okay. Let's talk about all of this—but one step at a time. I'm here to listen and to help you. I love you. Jesus loves you and wants to get you out of all your trouble" (see Psalm 50:15).

I felt impressed to sit down and talk calmly with "Blueberry Billy" to lessen his anxiety and, hopefully, to gain honesty. "So tell me, *Why* did you eat those blueberries?"

"I was hungry. They looked so good. I knew they'd taste good, too." He was letting down now and being honest.

"Did you have any thoughts that you shouldn't have eaten the blueberries?"

"No!" He returned to his protective, defensive posture.

"Lord, do I challenge him on this? I sense this is not true."

"Yes, go ahead. I am speaking to Billy as well."

"Billy, when you say 'No,' that isn't true, is it? You need to be honest with me."

He dug at the ground with his foot, deciding what he'd say. "I did think that I shouldn't, but I wanted to eat them so much!"

"Thank you for being honest, Billy. You know that both the devil and God speak to your mind. Satan wants to get you into trouble, while God wants to keep you out of trouble. God wants to personally teach you how to know the difference between the good thoughts that come into your mind and the bad ones. And He wants you to find out that doing His will brings more happiness than does doing wrong. You need to learn to recognize God's voice to your mind so that you can do His will.

"The blueberries would taste better with your meal rather than eaten in secret. The devil is very good at making us believe that doing wrong is fun. But that is not true is it?"

"I'm not so sure." Again he was honest.

"Well, why don't we try it. You and I can go pick some blueberries for lunch, ask God's blessing, and let's see."

"Okay," he said, not fully convinced.

We picked the blueberries while having a pleasant conversation, and some trust began to grow from Billy toward me. He was finding me different from his fretful, faultfinding mother. He often looked deep into my eyes to judge my love for him. His little heart began to open up, and by the time we made a sweet cream to put on top of the blueberries, he was laughing and enjoying the work with me. We talked openly about why he'd eaten the blueberries in secret and then lied about it. I didn't scold him or belittle him for what he had done. Instead, we discussed the advantages of eating blueberries at an appropriate time. Making God's ways attractive and beneficial (as they truly are) appealed to Billy's mind. He dropped his defensive posture, and in his heart he decided to cooperate. His thoughts and feelings were now pleasant (see Philippians 4:7).

"When you choose to obey Jesus' way," I told him, "you'll find your thoughts and feelings don't always agree with your choice. You may still want to eat the forbidden blueberries. But all you have to do is to give those wrong thoughts and feelings to Jesus and ask Him to take them away. He will return them to you purified. God will put a suggestion in your mind of what to do or think in place of the wrong way. When you cooperate with God's thoughts, He will create right thoughts and feelings within you, but you must do His will, not yours. It will take a little while for the wrong thoughts to leave, but they will leave. Keep talking to Jesus. This is how you get to live 'in Jesus' and how you get the power to do right."

Romans 12:2 says, "Be not conformed to this world: but be ye transformed by the renewing of your mind." And Ephesians 3:16, 17, reads, "That He would grant you, according to the riches of his glory, to be strengthened with might by his Spirit in the inner man."

Lunch was lovely for all three of us. Billy's mother loved the blueberries topped with sweet cream and complimented him. She saw that her scolding made Billy feel unloved and was driving him to sneak the blueberries. She apologized with honest tears. God was drawing her heart out to her precious son, awakening a realization of her need to change in order to help him. She committed to show Billy a better way. She had seen the results of my approach, and she liked what she saw. Next she expressed her desire to replace her scolding, condemning approach with a more loving one. (See Colossians 3:8.) We discussed the fact that she needed to be under Christ so that He could empower her to exercise self-control. This awakened in her heart a desire to love her son in a new and different way—in Jesus.

Billy was beaming at this change of heart and spirit in his mother. He had hope. It was precious and heartwarming to see a loving hug between mother and son!

"So, Billy," I asked, "how good were the blueberries you ate the honest way?"

"Oh, very good, very delicious. I want to follow Jesus like you are teaching me. I think my mommy loves me again!" He looked so free and so happy!

"So the next time you are tempted by that nasty old devil to eat blueberries in secret, what will you do?"

"I will cry out to Jesus for help and run to Mommy to pray. I like Jesus. He cares for Mommy and me." "Blueberry Billy" smiled a great big smile.

Often our children are led into wrong paths of behavior, habits, or responses by the thoughts they think and the feelings they feel at the time. Sadly, we parents too often fuel the negative side of these thoughts and feelings—aiding Satan not God. By repetition, we set up an automatic response mechanism in our child for self-protection—undesirable behavior such as lying, coldness, "you can't hurt me," angry words, or disrespect. Instead, if we would lovingly educate our children how to evaluate whether it is the voice of Satan or the voice of God that is speaking to their mind, if we would teach them how to grow in Christ in order to have sufficient power to obey, they would follow God's lead and trust Him again.

If we show Jesus' spirit, we will gain cooperation in heart and mind from our children. If we use the devil's tactics of harshness, anger, scolding, or a demeaning spirit, we will get the spirit of resistance from our children. They feel hurt and unloved, and become self-protective. Then the devil takes advantage and suggests lying thoughts to the child—such as "Mother doesn't love me." This further separates our children in heart (feelings), mind (thoughts), and spirit from us. Resistance is their self-protecting response. Jesus can break down these barriers as we filter through God what we will think, say, and do in our dealings with them.

Home-schooling was becoming a frustration again. After several talks with the Lord, I labeled the major problem as a lack of thoroughness in my boys. I wanted my boys, then ages eight and ten, to become dependable, faithful men—good workers. I knew they could become such men in Jesus. But I knew that I would need to train them in thoroughness and help this character trait to become a part of them. Intellectually, my boys understood the importance of thoroughness. But that wasn't enough; they must *be* thorough.

We began school as usual, except that this day I added to our goals of neatness and orderliness the trait of thoroughness. God had inspired this thought during my prayer time that morning. We discussed that this meant they must read the English lesson before we did class discussion together. This was their responsibility. If they didn't understand the lesson the first time through, they should read it again—and again, and again—until it made sense to them. Our goal was thoroughness—in place of a half-hearted work. We talked about how they needed to thoroughly understand the lesson so that we could practice applying it in class and to deepen their learning.

Thoroughness also meant that their penmanship was to be their best. There must be no disorder in their written work or questions left unanswered in any class assignment. The math drills would be done with heart and mind improving every day. Attitudes such as grumpiness, unwillingness, "I can't," or "I don't want to" would be dealt with until a free heart was obtained in Jesus so that they could work thoroughly with heart and mind.

Then we sang a scripture song, prayed for God's presence and wisdom to attend us, and began English class. They went upstairs to read their lesson. During discussion time, it became quickly evident that neither boy grasped what an adverb was.

"Matthew, did you read your lesson before class?" I asked in a good spirit.

No answer. I repeated the question. No answer.

"Matthew, did you read the lesson at all?"

"No. I read *Paula the Waldensian* instead."

"Why?"

"I thought I could learn the English lesson while we read it in class," he admitted honestly.

"And Andrew, how about you?"

"I didn't read it either."

Often the younger child follows in the pathway of an older sibling. How important it is for parents to teach and train the firstborn properly, so that a good example will be passed down to the rest of the children. It's the most efficient and pleasant way.

"Well, boys, today we will learn what thoroughness really is. First, you will both return to your rooms to read the lesson through three times—more if you need it. You must become self-governing in your schoolwork. God will help you if you call upon Him. Let's pray together." And we did. "Now the time we will lose because of your wrong choice you will have to give up out of *your* free time this evening."

Andrew hung his head and went upstairs, but Matthew grumbled and complained. "This isn't fair, Mother," and he proceeded to explain why he thought this was unfair.

"The Israelites in the wilderness grumbled and felt just like you do," I told him. "Because they were unwilling to come under God's way and submit, they had a hard forty years in the desert, and so will you unless you learn your lesson more easily than they did. You can go for a grizzly run, son—no questions asked." A "grizzly run" was a half-mile course down our long driveway.

I was pleased he did as I said. He returned red in the face and hot, so I knew he had done an honest grizzly run.

"Matthew, you need to go upstairs now and prepare for your English class. You need Jesus because you can't change your thoughts and feelings without Him." We knelt together, and I asked him to pray.

His spirit and countenance still indicated obvious resistance. "Lord, I still don't have his heart. Do I let it go or discipline him further?"

"Do a thorough work. The heart work underlies every other work. You do not want an outward compliance without his heart—we want the whole heart."

"Matthew, you need to do God's will from your heart, not begrudgingly (see Ephesians 6:6). You need to let God have all the ugliness in your mind and feelings, and He will adopt you and re-create you to be like Jesus would be were He in this situation. To give you time to cry out to God I want you to go weed a ten-foot section in the greenhouse," I said affectionately.

"Oh, Mother! I'll never get my lesson done! I'll do my reading now; honestly, I will."

"No. This time it has to be this way. Next time, you can plan to give way to the right. But now you must accept your consequence and do it willingly. While you are in the garden pulling weeds, I want you to label your weed seed that is causing all the trouble this morning. Jesus can pull up that weed by the root today if you ask Him to and cooperate. That would be lovely. If you do this work willingly and heartily, it shouldn't take longer than fifteen minutes. If you hang on to your self-ish spirit, you'll lose even more of your free time this evening. It's your choice, dear," I said encouragingly.

He went out to the garden, yielded his will to God, talked to God while he pulled the weeds, and applied this lesson to his heart. This is bringing a child up "in the nurture and admonition of the Lord" (Ephesians 6:4). The Lord was leading me, keeping my spirit sweet and sympathetic, but lovingly firm. The Lord was leading my son, offering him power to change and making the right attractive to him, while leaving him the freedom to choose. True-hearted, free-will obedience is a pearl of great price.

"Mother, I've finished the weeding, and I'm ready to read my English lesson the right way," Matthew said with a free spirit.

"Well, what happened to you out there?"

"Jesus taught me a good lesson. While I was weeding, a hummingbird flew quickly into the greenhouse and took nectar from the flowers and then flew out. In and out he flew. Then I thought how I needed to fly quickly to Jesus. I had a good spirit during my worship this morning, but when my will was crossed about having to read my lesson, I left Jesus—flying away. This hummingbird knew where to go to get food for life. I knew that if I, too, would fly to Jesus, I could get the bread and water of life so that I could be happy and do right. So I gave God my heart, and He changed it right there. The weeding went quickly after that."

"Oh, that is lovely, son! God's ways are always the best even when they cross us. I'm so happy for you. Now what did you label your weed?"

"My weed was 'selfishness.' I wanted it *my* way. I gave it to Jesus, and He gave me a willing, happy heart. Next time, I'll give God permission to pull up my selfish weed more quickly."

In this fashion we incorporated thoroughness into our schoolwork, practical house duties, and yard work. Thoroughness in the things of this life begins with thoroughness in giving the heart into Jesus' hand and learning how to cooperate so that God can remove the wrong and implant the right.

That morning we had a lovely English class with good understanding and learning. How sweet is schoolwork—or any work—with a cooperative heart. The boys learned about adverbs and enjoyed diagramming many sentences on the chalkboard with diligence. We were able to make up some time, and the boys lost only twenty minutes of their free time that day. They had an enthusiastic attitude as they worked on a cleaning project in the garage. Here, Matthew shared with Andrew his wrong thoughts and feelings about English class and told him how much better it is to yield to God right away and let Him cleanse those wrong thoughts and to think God's right thoughts instead.

Character is how we react to any given situation. It is in a crisis that true character is revealed. It reveals whether good or evil is ruling in our hearts and minds. Christ came to redeem you and me at the level of our thoughts and feelings (see 2 Corinthians 10:5). If and when we give our wrong thoughts to Him and cooperate, He can then lead us out of the land of self and into the land of Christlike thoughts and feelings. Christ has come to take the captives out of the enemy's hand.

Thoroughness is gained by persevering efforts under the control of God. Everything good takes effort to obtain. With God we can teach and train our children in the way of the Lord lovingly and consistently.

"Lazy Lionel" and "Chaotic Casey" were *not* accustomed to helping mother in their home, and they were visiting at our house. Their mother and I were talking about her frustrations in getting on a schedule. We discussed the work habits of her boys. She shared their character defects of unruliness, unwilling hearts, sneaking away from assignments, and slothfulness. It took them hours to do the dishes, school assignments, or any small task. Arguing and bad temper disturbed the entire household. Then she asked, "How can I bring about the needed changes?"

"You don't know God's power, my dear friend," I replied. "This is all fixable, but we must begin with you." We discussed her need to spend time with God at the beginning of her day to connect with Him so that she could have Solomon's wisdom. "God is just as willing to share His wisdom with you as with Solomon," I assured her. "Connection with God is also a commitment to seek, listen, and do what God puts on your heart in answer to your present dilemma with your children. It's learning to let His Holy Spirit lead you, not you leading the Holy Spirit. It's studying for the purpose of application and experimentation in your home today.

"When you are connected to Jesus, attentive to His direction in your mind, your reason, and your spirit, you are prepared to direct your boys to Him to be changed in mind [thoughts] and heart [feelings, inclinations, disposition]." So we discussed a plan.

" 'Lazy Lionel,' after breakfast I want you to help Matthew do the dishes by rinsing and stacking them. 'Chaotic Casey,' you can dry the dishes and put them away. When you finish, Andrew will direct you to anything else that needs to be done," I directed.

In less than three minutes 'Lazy Lionel,' age seven, who knew no perseverance, wearied in well doing and began grumbling quietly to his mother about how unfair this was and wanting to be relieved of his hard work. He complained that it was too much work and that he didn't want to do it. Their discussion ended with him declaring loudly, "I will not do this!" He threw down the towel and walked off.

His mother was distraught and embarrassed. We discussed what course she could take. She chose to spank him. She went into another room for privacy, and the conflict was loud. He fought verbally against her. I offered to help, and she was glad to accept. We prayed and called 'Lazy Lionel' to a decision. He fussed; he argued and pushed away. Mother gave him another very mild spanking.

"Your consequences are insufficient motivation for him to change his course," I said. "You need to be much firmer." She couldn't bring herself to give him more than a mild spanking. So we tried reason, instruction, and more prayer—but without success. After forty minutes, she tried a firmer spanking, which almost motivated him to obey.

But like King Agrippa, he fell short of fully yielding his way to God.

The mother told me that this lawyerlike arguing was commonplace in their home. They'd go on for hours this way. His reasoning was very strong, and she'd often give in, thinking herself too severe or just to end the controversy.

We talked, reasoned, and implemented every idea—soft entreaties, stories, mild spankings—all trying to get Lionel to surrender and pray. We prayed out loud for God to intervene and open his heart. But in the end Lionel always refused to pray and remained uncooperative. This course of action wasn't working. I tried to help his mother see that love included firmness, but she was unable to be firmer. Thus, this correction took a very long time.

Lionel interrupted us, demanding, "I need to go to the bathroom!"

His mother quickly released him from her restraining lap.

"Did you ask God if you should let him go?" I asked.

"Well, no, I never thought of that." So he had to sit back down in her lap while she prayed to God for wisdom and direction.

"Filtering what we will say, how we will say it, what we will do, what we will not do, and to what extent we will persevere—all this must be done through Christ in every corrective situation with our child," I told her. "For God knows what will gain the child's mind and heart today. And connection with God is what we strive for. This connection will empower Lionel to obey no matter what his history has been. He needs this experience, and so do you."

She found this reasoning very hard on her soft personality, but God affirmed to her in her prayer that this was His will for her. So although not fully comfortable, she decided to try God and see. She knew she needed to change something in her parenting principles.

" 'Lazy Lionel,' you may go to the bathroom as soon as you pray and are willing to do the dishes as you were asked. This is a little thing. God will help you when you surrender to do His will. You must choose. I will stay here all day if necessary; you may as well give in now rather than making it harder on yourself," Mother said.

Lionel became inflamed and furious at this restriction of his liberty. He was accustomed to his mother being neither decisive nor consistent. What was happening here? She wasn't obeying him like she usually did. Hadn't he tried his best to convince his mother with reason, with tears, then with embarrassing bad language? The usual tactics were not working today. Now his passion inflamed, he threatened, "Well, then, I'll just go to the bathroom on you, if you won't let me go!"

Shocked she turned to me, "What do I do, Sally?"

"He may not go to the bathroom until he prays and does as you have asked him. This is a very reasonable request. It will take only a few minutes if he'll surrender to do right. Then he can go. God is speaking to him, but your son is rejecting His thoughts. Should he do this naughty thing, the consequences will have to be worse."

Now 'Lazy Lionel' fought for his independence in anger and tried to wrestle away from his mother. His countenance took on a notable look of fear. His mother spanked him again and called him to a decision to obey her simple request to pray to God, to apologize for his misbehavior, and to do the dishes.

He began screaming uncontrollably, "You're hurting me! You're hurting me!"

"No, son," his mother said calmly. "You're pulling so hard that you're hurting yourself. All you have to do is to relax and stop fighting me."

I felt sorry for the children downstairs who were hearing this awful wrestling and crying. I went downstairs to tell them to pray for "Lazy Lionel" that Jesus could gain his heart and that he could find God's peace. I assured them we were not hurting him. The three boys had all the dishes done, the laundry dried and folded, the floors swept, and Matthew was reading a story.

"I need to make bread today," I told them. "Matthew, would you please have the boys help you make bread while we continue to work with Lionel? 'Chaotic Casey,' don't be afraid for your brother. He's in the process of learning how to obey in Jesus, and Satan is speaking loudly, trying to convince him that we are being mean to him. We aren't! So won't you boys each pray for him before you make the bread?"

As I returned upstairs, I saw the boys in a prayer circle.

"Lazy Lionel" was still fighting against submitting to his mother. Self was striving for the mastery. Everyone looked exhausted. The battle lasted a long time, largely because of his mother's unwillingness to discipline him sufficiently to motivate surrender. Lionel returned to screaming again and again.

We had been in constant prayer, listening for any idea, any direction, and trying many different methods. He needed a grizzly run, but his mother wasn't willing to impose this on him.

Suddenly he screamed, "I'm thirsty. I'm thirsty. I want water!"

"That's it," I said. "I'll get a glass of water. Maybe this will work."

I returned with the water, and "Lazy Lionel" looked afraid. "What are you going to do with that water?"

I saw that this was the strongest motivator yet. "Well, you can drink it after you pray and surrender to Jesus. Or else I have a different use for it. It is all up to you."

To our surprise and joy, "Lazy Lionel" finally gave up his will and agreed to pray and ask Jesus what He'd have him to do. His prayer began in fear and anxiety, but soon calmed and became a sweet, submissive prayer. It was evident that God was speaking to his mind (thoughts) and heart (feelings) and that "Lazy Lionel" was cooperating at last.

He arose and said, "Mother, I'm sorry for being such a naughty boy to you."

They hugged and expressed a few sweet things together. The surrender was full and free.

"So 'Lazy Lionel' are you willing to do another chore instead of the dishes since they are all done now?" I asked.

"Yes, I am."

I had him sweep the porches and vacuum the living room, which he did cheerfully and thoroughly. Jesus was truly in his heart to make such a change in attitude and disposition. In Jesus he has become "Lively Lionel," persevering to do a good work willingly.

After this incident, we read a story about how Satan and his host of evil angels surround the tempted one with darkness and exert a stupefying influence to evil. God and the good angels are waiting to push away the evil angels, but He will not do so until the tempted soul cries out to Him for help. For God will not go against their will. But as soon as the soul cries out to God, the stronger, good angels drive back the evil angels, and they must give up their captive.

Now "Lazy Lionel" testified that the darkness he experienced upstairs was just like that. He told us how afraid he was and that when he finally prayed and surrendered to God, all the darkness, fear, and oppression left him.

"Lazy Lionel" was transformed by grace; through reaching out to Christ he became "Lively Lionel" instead. God wants to give us all a new name—an upright, holy name after His likeness. As long as we stay abiding in Him, we can have this life. "Lively Lionel" lived out the character trait of perseverance instead of laziness in his work duties during the rest of his stay at our house and even after he returned home. God still performs miracles today; whenever we yield to cooperate with His thoughts, feelings, and directions. This is Christ, re-creating His character in us.

What thoughts and feelings will you let God redeem in you and in your child today? God's next miracle can be yours.

THE LONE EMBRACE
A SPECIAL WORD OF ENCOURAGEMENT FOR SINGLE PARENTS

One important question to ask is: Why do I react the way I do? Why does my child react the way he or she does? Studying our children's disposition helps us evaluate their thoughts and feelings that are driving the way they are reacting right now. Often the trauma and trial of a death or a divorce drives bad behavior or bad problem-solving techniques that need to be given up. Under God's guidance, you can help your children understand why they respond as they do—and how to make plans for a new and better way. Take them to Jesus so that He can re-create them and set their feet on the right path, freeing them from the character damage of hate or fear, abandonment or rejection resulting from your divorce or your spouse's death. Don't allow them to retain hate, animosity, or rage toward the other parent, for these will destroy their spiritual life.

Their thoughts, feelings, and responses—rightly diagnosed with Jesus' help—will enable you to know how to properly instruct and discipline them. You will be able to bring them to Jesus for the power to live above the negative pull of their flesh. There need not be any lasting scars from going through a divorce or death, if we have Jesus building our characters aright.

May God bless you!

Chapter 7

DISCIPLINE IS DISCIPLING

*"And whosoever doth not bear his cross, and come after me, cannot be
my disciple" (Luke 14:27).*

*M*atthew, you have the privilege to be Christ's disciple. I know
that in your heart you want to be His faithful disciple. And yet, you
have been very foolish today, and neither our talking nor disciplining
has helped you change. Instead, you are defending your actions. Becoming hurtful to others through teasing is against God. This type of
foolishness must be admitted to, denied expression, and replaced with
something better. Will you crucify this foolishness?

"Remember when you changed from being 'Interruptive Ivan' into
'Patient Paul' by seeking to do Jesus' will? That was being Jesus' disciple,
following in His way. That was good! He often helped you to change
from being 'Sassy Sam' to 'Sweet Sam.' Remember? It took a decision
and an action on your part then, too. God loves to transform your
wrong ways into better ways. He is here for you right now. I'm going to
let you sit in your room to talk to God about what you should do. I'll
return a little later."

Matthew's foolishness at age nine was a recurrent weed in his character similar in character to a dandelion. We would think it was plucked
up by the roots, and then it would return to bloom again. It would start
with innocent fun, but then teasing would be overdone or fun play
would get too rough, and in the end someone would get hurt. He just
didn't know when to quit. I knew the solution was time and connection
with God. True discipline is discipling my child to Christ.

I prayed, "Lord, bind and rebuke Satan from getting into Matthew's
mind and feelings to stir up excuses. Make him mild and gentle by Your
Holy Spirit and change his disposition of stubbornness—please!"

When I felt God said it was time, I returned and said, "Well, Matthew, what have you learned?"

"Mother, I'm sorry for being foolish again. I really want to do right.
What can I do?"

"Let's get out our Bibles and concordance and see what God's Word can teach us about foolishness. And we began searching text after text, looking for a practical direction of what God would want us to do. "God's Word needs to be our guideline and standard, rather than what we or others think or feel."

After searching for some time, Matthew said, "Mother, I found a good one. Ephesians 5:4 says, 'Neither filthiness, nor foolish talking, nor jesting, which are not convenient: but rather giving of thanks.' I need to give thanks instead of being foolish." Matthew wrote down that text.

"That's really good," I agreed. "Let's keep looking for more. Oh, I found a good one, too. Proverbs 22:15 says, 'Foolishness [is] bound in the heart of a child; [but] the rod of correction shall drive it far from him.' I think we are doing that already." And Matthew agreed with me.

These were the best practical directions we found in the Bible. And Matthew was determined to be Christ's disciple, heeding His instructions and following His guidance. Matthew sought with a full heart to implement giving thanks when he was inclined to foolishness and found good success in Jesus. He also made efforts to respond positively when I would make him aware that he was going too far again. He'd have to choose in the moment of temptation to affirm his former commitment to follow Jesus his Savior. He prayed to God in the morning and responded often when God called for his heart through the day. Discipline is discipling my child to Christ. And Matthew was maturing through these choices.

Many parents show by their actions that their concept of discipline is that it affords an opportunity for them to vent their fleshly frustration upon their child. But this is not so. God wants us to filter our impulses, our thoughts, and our worries through Him. He knows what is best.

True discipline is calling self into restraint—first in myself and then in my child. Its purpose is to instruct, to correct, and to give reproof, in a Christlike way, while bringing the child in touch with God to change his heart and mind. It's also having a plan of what to substitute in place of the wrong. In this instance, Matthew put effort into giving thanks, rather than taking fun to the level of foolishness. Through a vital connection with Christ, your children can be healed of their disease of foolishness just like the woman with the issue of blood was healed when she touched the hem of Christ's garment in true faith! (See Matthew 9:20.)

A long time of victory passed, but one day foolishness cropped up again in ugly blooms. It occurred in an incident between the two brothers, likely started by Matthew.

"Lord!" I cried. "What do I do this time? Should I send him on a grizzly run? He could clean the work benches in the garage or go to his room." A long wait followed.

"This time, let's send him out under a tree with his lamp [the Bible], like Tip Lewis."

"Oh, that is a lovely idea! I would never have thought of that for this situation. Thank you Lord."

I was excited because we had recently read the book, *Tip Lewis and His Lamp,* and I understood the concept of putting Matthew in touch with God in order to change him on the inside through the influence of the Holy Spirit to his reason.

"Matthew, that weed of foolishness has bloomed again. I talked with God about how best to help you, and He suggested that you needed some time out under a tree with your 'lamp.' That is what I want you to do right now."

A flash of disagreement crossed his face, but he chose to check this spirit and said nothing. God was working even now, and Matthew was cooperating! Wow! He went to get his Bible without an argumentative word and then went out to find a favorite tree in order to talk over this problem with God.

After he left, I knelt down and sent up a prayer for God to be with him and direct his reasoning—to bind and rebuke Satan from his input into his mind, feelings, and prejudices. Periodically I wondered if he were truly under a tree with God or if he were off playing instead. So I'd send up another prayer. I sensed God assuring me that he was all right, so I didn't go looking to see. How can we know what is right to do unless we check with God?

About forty-five minutes passed, and Matthew returned excited and in an attractively sweet spirit.

"Mother, you won't believe what God told me out there." And he proceeded to tell me every detail. He expressed honestly what his spirit had been to begin with and how God subdued all his selfish thoughts and feelings. One thing about Matthew—he was always honest.

Then he said, "God impressed me to look into my Bible at this text and that text." And showed me each text and its significance. They were not texts on foolishness but on the attitude of the heart toward God and what God would do for him if he would follow those texts right now. Matthew chose to be obedient to His voice. Matthew's conscience was very moldable to God's reasoning out under that tree.

Our children want to do right. Our approach, our spirit, and our conduct under provocation is giving them lessons that either draw them to Jesus or repel them from Him. We parents, too, need to be a disciple of Christ's, under His direction, under His authority, and under His wisdom in order to direct our children aright.

The discipline that God led me to, in this situation, was discipling my child to Christ so that He could withdraw the evil and instill the good by His divine power working with Matthew's human effort and cooperation. God is good!

He will do this for you as well. "Seek ye first the kingdom of God, and His righteousness; and all these things shall be added unto you" (Matthew 6:33). Learn how to depend on Jesus to direct your steps in child rearing and placing your child's heart into His hands. He will become your General, and you will find success in this way.

Discipline, properly done, can teach the child how to surrender and cooperate in heart with Jesus and thus to his parents. Our goal is the transformation of heart (thoughts, feelings, and habits) from serving sin to serving God.

Enlisting our child's cooperation in heart makes parenting much more pleasant. To gain this we must connect our children to Christ using restraint or discipline as a lower motivator to come to Him. For in this connection God molds, shapes, and fashions the child's thoughts, feelings, and concepts after His divine character. The child's cooperation is a must in order for God to have permission to do this inner work on the heart. Our dependency upon God to lead us is essential in order to accomplish this character transformation. It requires our ears being tuned to heaven, asking and discerning the voice of God to our soul and then following His direction no matter how crucifying this may be to our flesh. And it will be, but this is good!

Don't expect success overnight. The above illustration is the result of several years of learning and practicing these principles. We each must deal with our own personalities, imbalances, and poor problem-solving techniques. Poor consistency and lack of follow-through delay or defeat this goodly experience. Yet a good outcome can be yours as well and sooner than you think, if you are willing to make hard changes, to experiment with new concepts, to unlearn and relearn to work under God's direction.

We had returned from a visit to a close friend. Matthew, twelve years old now, was much quieter than his usual interactive self. The next morning, during our personal worship time, it was the same. So I opened up an opportunity to talk. "Matthew, what's the matter? Are you all right?"

"Mother, you and Father keep too close a watch over us kids. We are good kids, and we don't need the supervision you gave yesterday. I felt insulted because you obviously didn't trust us—but we were trustworthy! We wouldn't do anything bad!" Then he explained in detail his view of how we had directed their work and play. The children wanted to play "Surprise Package Company" and had a hard time surprising us with good things because various parents checked on them too often. "I felt treated like a *child!*" Matthew concluded. "This was unfair!"

I was dumbfounded. Matthew had some legitimate objections, but I didn't know how to handle the situation. I looked into his eyes and saw that he felt strongly that he was right. Strong feelings of fairness appeared to be driving these strong words.

Parents, we want to know what our children are *really* thinking so that we can direct them the best we know how. Matthew has a leader personality, and I want this strength to be directed toward good, not evil. His judgment and fairness are strong traits among his faculties. I concluded that no reasoning by me would change his position, so I silently cried out to God.

"Lord, this one is too big for me, but not for You. What do I do? How do I respond? What does he need to bring balance into his thinking? Surely reasoning won't work now? It's not good to reason when there is passion."

A thought came into my mind as clear as day. As I began presenting it to Matthew, the next thought came in logical fashion. This continued until the idea was complete. This was God's still small voice, but I wasn't sure of that until the end of the story.

"Matthew, it doesn't really matter what you think or what I think." He was surprised at my comment and was listening. "I know what you think, and obviously you already know what your Father and I think. All that really matters is what does God think? You are twelve years old now, a young man preparing for adulthood, and that means you need to take responsibility to know God's will for your life. You need to study this topic out for yourself until you know the will of God in parental supervision for you. Then you can order your life to God's will. Let's change your personal study time for you to study out this topic until you have your answer."

He listened very attentively to my explanation. His disposition softened, and he responded, "Okay."

He immediately took out his Bible and our reference books. He began his course of seeking the will of God by reading here and there. During our personal worship time, the boys and I sat at our kitchen table. It appeared that I was having my own study at the end of the table, but in reality Matthew was heavy on my mind. I was praying, wanting God to direct his mind to the right texts. I desired the Holy Spirit to interpret the texts rightly to his reasoning mind. I knew Matthew wanted to do what was right. But I wanted to help him come to the right conclusion—mine of course—and the quicker the better!

A bright idea dawned. I recalled a little booklet that deals with texts on this topic and reaches a conclusion that was in harmony with my view. So I shared it with Matthew to help him. I had not filtered this through Jesus. Matthew read it and handed it back to me without a word or comment.

"Well, did it answer your question?" I asked.

"No. It didn't address the issue at all," he responded.

"Doesn't address the issue at all? But of course it does!" I thought. "You didn't want to hear the right conclusion."

"Lord, he isn't reading it right. I spoon-fed him his answer. This concerns me! What do I do? Where is he going?"

"Leave him in My hands, Sally. You don't want to spoon-feed a young man. You want to let him dig as for hidden treasure in order to become a man, in order to exercise concepts and decision based on My word. He needs to learn to be led of Me. Isn't this what you are raising him for—to follow Me and not you?"

"Yes, Lord, that is what I want! But I'm concerned because topical studies like this can be tedious and repetitive. I don't want him to give up before he gets the right answer. Shouldn't I be helping him?"

"Not now. If you want to raise a real man, he must learn persever-ance and tenacity, and it is best learned in situations like this. You do not want to save him from the repetition or the hardness of the quest for hidden treasure, but rather encourage him in it. This is how he grows good muscles for right—through exercise. Pray for him and trust Me to direct him."

I didn't want to work against God. He knows what my son needs. So I was thankful and prayed, not only during personal worship time but also throughout the day when it would come to my mind. I put Matthew into God's hands and asked Him to direct his thoughts. God says, "Let this mind be in you" (Philippians 2:5), and I wanted to coop-erate.

Several times during the next seven days Matthew would come to me with a text that interested him enough to want to share. At times I'd cry out to God before I'd comment because it seemed like the text was correcting me. God encouraged me to respond with openness and to hear what he had to say. My example would help him see how he should take correction as well.

"Well that is an interesting text," I'd say. "Are you trying to tell me that I am not following this as your mother?"

"Well, no. I shared it with you because I felt you and Father are doing that, and I wanted you to read it to be encouraged."

"Thank you, son. That is lovely."

Another time I responded, "I like this text; it's a favorite of mine. What do you see in it, Matthew?"

And Matthew said, "I think you could follow this text better than you do. You are too soft on Andrew and me here."

"Well, I'll take that to heart, dear. Thank you for sharing."

Then after seven long days like this, Matthew came to my chair at the table, excited and confident of his conclusion. "Mother, Mother! You have to have a closer watch care over me now than ever before!" he exclaimed.

"I do? Why do you say so?"

"I've read a lot now. I see how often children ages ten to eighteen think that there is no harm in coming and going as they please. Yet they need parental supervision more than they realize. We can have high goals and morals, but we still need God-fearing parents giving guide-lines and input as we grow in Him."

What a beautiful summary of one week's worth of research in the Bible and other quality reading! "How beautiful!" I responded. "So, is it all resolved now? Was it worth all your effort? Do you have peace?"

"Yes, I have a peace that this is the way God wants for me right now. My heart issue is resolved. Yes, it was worth the effort. God showed me that my real issue was not the supervision, but fairness, and you know how strong I am there. I had thought that the supervision wasn't fair, and so I got upset following my feelings that you didn't trust me. That's what disturbed me. I know now that you trust *me*. It just seemed unfair that day. I'm convinced God wants you to have a close watch care over me even now."

God knew all along that Matthew's issue was not submission to supervision, as I had thought, but rather it was all over trust and fairness. God used His Word to lead my son to resolve the real issue. No wonder my booklet was not the answer!

The Scriptures say, "If ye continue in my word, [then] are ye my disciples indeed; And ye shall know the truth, and the truth shall make you free" (John 8:31, 32). Christ's disciples heard His messages and followed Him, forsaking that which was not according to His word and His direction for their life, and were thus set free from false thinking. So it can be with our children when they are guided by God!

Our children need to make God's Word—interpreted by His Holy Spirit—their standard rather than the way they think or the way we think. God's standard is consistent and never changing. Human standards are variable and unreliable. Children need to be trained to be morally independent from their peers in this way. Most peers soften down or eliminate God's higher standard of conduct, deportment, and love. Are you training your children in how to know God's standard? This standard will not fail them. Are you training them how to be guided by Christ and His Word? Do they know His voice to their heart and soul by experience? Christ will be there for you and your child.

Let mothers come to Jesus with their perplexities. They will find sufficient grace to aid them in the management of their children. The door is open for every mother to lay her burdens at Jesus' feet. If we live in communion with God, we, too, may expect the divine Spirit to mold our little ones in the path of right. Jesus can give us each the blessing we come for when we bring our little ones and our youth to Him.

It is so important to realize that *we all* come to disciplining—correcting wrong behavior, thoughts, desires, or feelings—from an unbalanced perspective. We may be, to a greater or lesser degree, severe, cold, harsh, and dictatorial without compassion, or we may come from the equally harmful perspective, which is being so kind and gentle that we lack decision and firmness, and as a result, lack authority. Children suffer from either imbalance.

The too-kind mothers, as I have a tendency to be, have an unbalanced love called *sentimentalism.* This imbalance excuses a child's selfish, disobedient way. It coaxes and reasons at great length with the child, hoping vainly that he or she will choose to obey. This kind of mother sees she has little or no authority and that she cannot change her child's heart or will through reasoning and talking—so she gives up. And since she has no real control, this mother fears to cross the child's will because of the upheaval that results. So she lets the child express selfish words, play with things he should not play with, be unkind, or behave loudly and distractively without correction. Often she excuses this behavior to avoid conflict and another failure.

This false love creates a weak, boisterous, undesirable, and selfish child. Such a child is not pleasing to parents, friends, or society and, most important, is not pleasing or acceptable to God. When parents accustom their children to indulging their own selfish ways, they are unfitting them for heaven. This is a terrible evil. Parents must come to see that this indulgence of self is harmful and unloving. The indulgent method of parental government is without Christ's blessing and seriously misrepresents God's love.

On the other hand, the parent who is too severe and dictatorial suffers from the imbalance of *brutality.* This kind of love dictates what the child is to do according to the parent's mood, often in a cold, unbending, and militant spirit. The unspoken message is that the parent's perspective is the only perspective! Such a parent can be silently manipulative or explosive and unpredictable. The least inconvenience can set him or her on a rampage of anger and merciless punishment with no hope of compassion, discussion, or drawing instruction in right doing. This parent strives to maintain order and obedience with a rod of iron from a forceful, "my way" perspective. Verbal and spiritual abuse is common to this parent. Excessive government and dominance also misrepresent the love of God. Like the devil, their imbalance dictates their interpretation of right.

A stronger child will retaliate to the dictatorial or condemnatory parent by manifesting a rebellious or bitter spirit in response. The child mirrors the parent's angry outbursts. This attitude is acted out by physically dominating siblings or playmates. It says verbally or nonverbally, "You can't hurt me." The child hasn't been shown how to have love, patience, or self-control in difficulties or trials through surrendering to Jesus. Scripture says, "And, ye fathers, provoke not your children to wrath: but bring them up in the nurture and admonition of the Lord" (Ephesians 6:4).

The softer child responds more like an animal broken into submission. He has no will or personality of his own. This child doesn't dare to think for himself, for if he disagrees with the parent, he will be reduced to ashes critically or dominantly. The pleaser child will ask lots of questions so that he or she does it their way. But they cannot please and, as a result, have a poor image of themselves. Making decisions is stressful because a decision that disagrees with the parent—even in a minor matter—means another rejection. For one mind to have dominant rule over another mind is destroying individuality and is taking the place of God. This is not the government of God.

This child does not know how to show godly love or even have hope to change his or her weaknesses. These children will also grow up unfit for heaven, for this type of submission is not pleasing to God. This child is under the autocratic rule of the parent, instead of God.

We must understand that every home must have reasonable rules of conduct and behavior in order to function properly. There must be consequences, given consistently but lovingly, when these rules are broken. The parent is to be the authority to establish the rules and to oversee and give proper motivations or consequences when the rules are violated. The child is not to rule the home; the parents are to be the authority. There is to be no disobedience on the part of the child, and on the part of the parent there is to be no oppression or indulgence. The parents are to rule in love, balancing both softness and fairness—led of God. They are to be under God and not ruled by their flesh. "For the wrath of man worketh not the righteousness of God" (James 1:20).

Friends, the *only solution* for our children and us is for each of us to learn how to unite vitally with Christ as our Savior. We all need deliverance from our former ways of thinking and disciplining. God wants to bring us each from our unbalanced disciplines to the right mix of firmness and justice with love and mercy. This can be done *only* as we become Christ's disciple, surrendering to be led and instructed by Him.

We can take comfort, for God says, "I will never leave thee, nor forsake thee" (Hebrews 13:5). We are not alone in those corrections, conflicts, or trials with our children. God promises us, "I will guide thee continually" (see Psalm 32:8; Isaiah 58:11). We must seek His counsel situation by situation (see Acts 9:6). The Holy Spirit will call us to a life of self-denial and self-control. God wants parents to surrender their overdominant or overindulgent ways. Jesus will subdue these cultivated tendencies and feelings as we give them to Him. Jesus encourages us in Jeremiah 32:27, "I [am] the LORD, the God of all flesh, is there any thing too hard for me?" There is true freedom in following Christ.

Our children need very close watch care when they are young. In the early character-forming years, we hover over them very closely, being mind and will to train them in God's way of thinking, feeling, and reasoning. If we are doing our work of discipling our children to Christ properly, they will know and follow God's voice and their character will reflect His. Our watch care when they are eleven or twelve years of age takes a new and different approach. We reduce our management and put them increasingly under Christ's management as they learn. Of course, we interpose when it's needed. Teaching our children how to make good decisions *under God* is our work!

If your young teens were not trained in Christ, it would be dangerous to give them this degree of freedom, for Satan would grasp them tighter in the habits of sin. For the youth bound in habits of selfishness, return to your first work; pick up the dropped stitches in character development. Yes, it will be more difficult now than it would have been at ages one through seven, but it is not impossible to build this foundation now. Once they are connected with Jesus, show them how to mature in Him.

Discipline is discipling my child to Christ. It is truly the work of redemption, and in this work there is no compulsion. No external force is employed. Under the influence of the Spirit of God, both parent and child alike are left free to choose whom they will serve. In the change that takes place when the soul surrenders to Christ, there is the highest sense of freedom. It is true that we have no power within ourselves to free ourselves from Satan's control; but when we desire to be set free from sin and in our great need cry out to God, we are imbued with the divine energy of the Holy Spirit to obey. To become one with Christ is the way we enter into that union and have power.

THE LONE EMBRACE
A SPECIAL WORD OF ENCOURAGEMENT FOR SINGLE PARENTS

You want your "Cruel Cleo" to become "Caring Cleo" and your "Depressed Dorothy" to become "Delightful Dorothy." First, let God have your imbalances. Then cultivate the opposite trait in Jesus' power, under His direction. As you gain this experience in the struggles with your own thoughts and feelings, you will know how to direct your children out of their jail cells of sin.

Discipline may necessitate bringing them to a decision and giving a consequence. This process may need to be repeated four, five, or more times. In the beginning, children are not motivated to surrender those familiar, wrong problem-solving techniques and to try new ones in Jesus. But persevere with God in the right spirit, and your pay will be worth all the heartache and hardness of gaining those first experiences of surrender and cooperation. The next encounter will be easier. This is the pathway to complete freedom from self reigning and ruling in your household. God will now be enthroned on each heart, and its heavenly influence will be sweet. God is there for you. He awaits your requests to overcome self.

Chapter 8
HABITS

"To him that overcometh will I give to eat of the hidden manna, and will give him a white stone, and in the stone a new name written" (Revelation 2:17).

*S*ome cultures have had a tradition of naming their children according to their predominant character trait. Would you like to be called "Valiant"? "Honest Henry"? "Generous George"? "Vivacious Vicki"? "Tender Heart"? "Purity"? "Serving Sarah"? If these were our predominant character traits, we'd likely all be pleased with our names.

But what if you were named "Blind Judgment"? "Hotheaded Hubert"? "Envy"? "Conceit"? "Murderer"? "Gossiper"? "Harlot"? "Vanity"? "Prideful"? "Dishonest Danny"? "Mistrust"? "Airhead"? "Greedy"? If one of these were your predominate trait, how would you feel about your name?

To a great extent, our habits determine what name will best describe who we are today. We'd like to hide some of our habits so that we would not be named by them, wouldn't we? As parents we need to eliminate, not hide, the negative character traits in our children and in ourselves, gaining us a fitness for heaven. Through restraint, discipline, and communion with God we can address the problem and plan to reconstruct our characters. We want to replace wrong habits with the right ones, giving our children a goodly name that honors God. By our parenting practices we can largely mold our child into a child of God if we will put forth the effort and understand the process of reaching that objective. If we neglect this work, however, Satan will keep them in his camp.

God wants to give us a new name as the text above indicates. To him that overcomes, Jesus will give a white stone with a new name written in it. That new name will show that we have forsaken the kingdom of Satan and self and have chosen Christ's kingdom and character to be ours. Our choice is confirmed by cooperating with Him to let Him create this new trait in us by His power. As we learn how to let Jesus be our God and as we become His people, we are changing masters—and thus changing our names.

Then "Dishonest Henry" will be renamed "Honest Henry." "Harlot" will be renamed "Purity," "Ignorance" renamed "Wisdom," "Sassy Susie" becomes "Sweet Sue," "Worldly Wiseman" becomes "Godly Wiseman," "Prideful" becomes "Humble," and "Despair" has the new name of "Hopeful." God can accomplish this transformation of character down to the core of our being, if we *let* Him and cooperate with Him. "Behold, as the clay [is] in the potter's hand, so [are] ye in mine hand, O house of Israel" (Jeremiah 18:6). If we let Him work our clay, we can become a fit vessel for His service and for His honor.

We have the privilege of representing Christ in our habits. With proper parenting, under God's watch care, we can raise a "Helpful Hannah" and not have to manage an "Unhelpful Hannah" and all the baggage that goes with that negative character trait.

Parents, we must come to see that we are responsible for our children's negative character traits. Christ knows. He also knows that unless there are decided changes in our principles and purposes of life, all will be lost—not only our children, but we who have raised these unruly children, for the child's character demonstrates they know not God. If we neglect changing our children's habits, we neglect changing our own.

But, praise God, we can change that! We all have habits that need changing. We need to admit our lack of understanding, our need for a power outside of ourselves, and our need to give top priority to addressing this lack of character building. Seeking God to mold our clay and that of our children must become our preeminent purpose in life. Everything else must become secondary. Satan has distracted us, deluded us, and kept us preoccupied with everything but character development. Let neither wind, nor rain, nor sleet, nor snow, or any combination of distractions keep us from this work of molding the habits of our children under Christ. Let's look at how habits begin and can change.

"I ain't going to do it, Andrew!"

Mother interrupts the boys' discussion. "Matthew, you can't say *ain't* any more. That is not a good word; it isn't even a real word! It's slang."

"Mother, I like the word. I don't want to stop saying it."

"God wants you to say only good words. Satan wants you to say words that aren't good. Which habit you choose to repeat will show whom you are serving. A habit is created by any act or thought that is repeated until it becomes instinctive. Your habits reflect your choices and formulate your character, which Jesus is trying to make upright.

You've used this word only a few times, so it will be easy to eliminate with Jesus' help. You just have to put your will to it. In Jesus, a strong six-year-old can do this in one or two days. That's fast!"

"Really, Mother? Do you think I can?"

"Yes, son, because Jesus is *really* strong."

Matthew was inspired by this discussion and put forth his best effort. And sure enough, in two days it was done. Truly as a man "thinketh in his heart, so is he" (see Proverbs 23:7).

But his next experience didn't prove to be such an easy solution. Matthew enjoys fun, and one day he changed the word "coconut" to "canokanut," repeating it often to his brother in a singsong fashion. At the time I was either inattentive or unwilling to deal with this "little thing," but as a result it grew to a "big thing." After about a month or so, I became aware of the power of habit even over the short term.

"Mother, pass me the 'canokanut,' please," Matthew, aged six, asked, unconsciously using the wrong word. It had become a habit right under my nose.

"Matthew, that isn't a proper word. Please say it properly," I corrected.

He playfully tried to obey but said "canokanut" again and again. He was getting frustrated with himself because he couldn't say "coconut" as he wanted to. I thought he was playing and gave him a work consequence to enlist his will to obey me. Then I realized he was honestly trying but *could not* say it correctly. This is a good lesson of how any wrong habit, allowed to grow in childhood, begins. I sought God for wisdom!

I kindly tried to help Matthew overcome it. "Matthew say 'co—co—nut.' " I had to say each syllable slowly and decidedly for him to copy me. Over and over it went. I couldn't believe how tenacious a simple thing like this could be. Habits are just that way. Many habits came up in my boys because I didn't understand the importance of this early training.

"Matthew, I don't want you ever to say 'canokanut' again. The wrong word has control over you; you don't control it," I explained nicely. "A lie is just like this. If you say a lie often enough, you will soon believe it is the truth. It will lead you down a wrong pathway. When a habit becomes comfortable by repetition, we don't want to change because it takes effort. But we must. All our habits are important, son. Any act or thought repeated becomes a habit either for good or bad. We need to remain on God's side."

Over the next six to eight weeks, "canokanut" would come out unexpectedly and the right word would have to be said in its place. Conscious efforts were made to speak it carefully. Periodically, Matthew wrote the word ten times to put it into his brain by sight. He needed more drill, so I had him say the word ten times out loud before breakfast when coconut was on the table. Still "canokanut" influenced his life. He had to submit to discipline, consequences, and pray often for help before he overcame this habit. Truly, bad habits are more easily formed than good ones and are given up with much more difficulty.

Admittedly, this was an innocent habit. But it taught me the strength and tenacity of habits learned young. Weeds will grow in my child's tender heart-garden if I am not watchful and careful. I will be rewarded for neglect or diligence in this warfare against bad habits.

So how important are habits?

Extremely important! If I let *habits of sassiness* be spoken, repeated, and exercised for the first four years of life, how difficult will it be to get that habit out of the child's character and life? Compare the strength of Matthew's five-week habit to the strength of a four-year habit! What is sassiness doing in the mind? Sassiness can be an attitude of the mind that says "I'm in control, and you must do what I say." It can be a negative attitude of looking at life. Or it can be just a habit that says, "This is how I talk, and this is how I respond." Should this character trait be corrected when the child is still small and the habit weak? Or should we wait to address these weeds in the life until the child is older, can reason better, and the habit is well grounded and rooted?

Parents who permit the use of unbecoming language are more worthy of blame than their children. In this way wrong habits are confirmed, and the child grows up to be an object of dislike to all around him.

The earlier we begin a good habit, the better. A little child of two or three can be taught to pick up a piece of string from the floor and throw it in the wastebasket to be helpful. He can be told how helpful he is. And so, in little ways, we sow seeds of helpfulness very young. We cultivate this goodly plant by having the child help clear the table after meals. He can help make bread. At age four, he can be given a sharp knife to cut vegetables responsibly, under supervision, in preparation for supper. These little things are each exercising the habit of helpfulness. When a child is five, he can have a disposition to help do the dishes, vacuum, or whatever. Establishing attitudes and habits of helpfulness are up to us—so cultivate them in your children.

If a little child is told he cannot help mommy, that he's too little, that the work is too hard, that this is mother's job—if, instead, he is left just to play and play—what will his attitude be toward helping? Will he be inclined to work when he is older? No! He will want to play, play, and play as you have habituated him. All work will appear unfair to him.

When you finally give him a little work to do, he will think it is a lot of work or that it is too hard. After all, isn't that what you have taught him? At five or six years of age, many children who could be good helpers-in-training to relieve mother of some work, are, instead, trained in evading work. You can give them a task, but they don't stick with it. They whine, ask for help, or want you to do it for them. They act so pitifully about this little amount of work. Can you see why they aren't good, helpful workers at five or six years of age when we have trained them this way in their younger years? Their habits are established, and now you will have to work against not only their habits but their heart, their attitude, and Satan who is pushing all their selfish buttons to resist. What will they be like at thirteen or fifteen years of age—a bigger, stronger plant of the former.

This is the price of neglecting to correct bad habits when our children are young. God considers this criminal neglect! As soil once overgrown with thorns can be reclaimed only by diligent labor, so the evil tendencies of the heart can be overcome only by earnest effort in and with Christ.

The habits formed in the first three years determine the foundation of your child's character. The first seven years of a child's life have more to do with the formation of character than all that he or she learns in future years. What is the character? It's the thoughts, feelings, dispositions, habits, and responses. All the training done after these first seven years will have to work against great odds to change the habits already formed.

Can you see why Satan has promoted the lie that letting our children grow up unrestrained in these younger years and free to follow their own inclinations is a demonstration of love? He wants to be able to cultivate self to grow unhindered. Unaided by God, your children can only be selfish. We have only two masters to serve—God or Satan. There is no middle ground. Satan wants you to believe the lie that young children do not understand correction. He wants them to be under his authority as much as possible, so that he can form their habits and characters after his likeness during these formative years. And his lies are so well received that unsuspecting parents do little to resist him or to restrain the evil habits in their children. He works his will freely in the minds and hearts of our children, cultivating the noxious seeds of selfishness.

What if your children have already passed seven years of age? It is not impossible, *with Christ's help,* to change their habits now, but it will take more effort than if it had been done earlier. If this is your case, you need to go back to pick up the dropped stitches by cultivating the goodly habits of abiding in Christ as soon as possible. Begin by teaching them to know the voice of God; present Christ as He truly is so that your children may fall in love with Him and talk with Him. Establish your-self under Christ's authority and from this position regain your proper authority to redeem your child.

You will need to use very firm measures with love to bring them out of Satan's service. Satan has spoken his lies to the mind of your child for so long that the child believes him and is inclined to listen to his voice above all others—just because it's so familiar. How sad that we have not taught our children to recognize God's voice sooner. God wants us to speak the truth often, until our children finally believe it instead of Satan's lies. Jesus must become our child's best Friend. Train your child to follow Christ by developing right attitudes, thoughts, and concepts to replace the former wrong ways. God will inspire you with ideas of how to do this. Give Him time and opportunity to talk with your child. Starve the wrong habits by restraint, while cultivating and watering the right—led of God.

The habits of our children tell us who is their Master, their Lord. It tells us who they are inclined to listen to. For example, if they are lying, are they listening to God or Satan? If the child is sassy and unreason-able, are they listening to and obeying God or Satan? (See Romans 6:16.) If the child is helpful and honest, are they hearing and heeding God or Satan? (See Galatians 5:22.) If they posses love and gentleness, where do these traits come from?

The "Habits Chart" on the next page will help you evaluate whom your children are following and serving—based on what they are doing, not what they know they should be doing. Name your child according to his or her predominant character trait. If that trait is against God's character and way, learn and plan to cultivate the opposite trait under God's tutorship. God is our Redeemer, longing to redeem our children—and us—from Satan's service and bondage through His sufficient wisdom and power.

During a typical home-school day, I multitask my duties. One day I made bread during parts of English and spelling class. I didn't have enough time to wash up the dishes, so I set them aside in order to correct the boys' spelling lessons right away as was my habit. Matthew, age twelve, had finished early and had gone to his room to do some recreational reading with his free time. Then I heard the dishes rattling.

I looked up. "Matthew, you are washing the dishes without me asking you?"

"Yes, Mother," he said.

"That is so sweet of you. Can I ask why you're doing that during your free time?"

"Sure. God asked me to. I was upstairs reading, and I came down to use the bathroom. As I walked through the kitchen, I saw those dishes sitting there, and God asked me if I'd wash the dishes for you. At first I reasoned I didn't need to do it because you hadn't asked me to. God worked on my heart a while before I came out of the bathroom, and I decided I could do that to help you."

"Oh, you make me so very happy, son!" And I went over to give him a kiss on the cheek out of gratitude. He snuggled down shyly like he didn't want that kiss, but the smile told me he liked it.

Was that the voice of God or the voice of his flesh, putting this act of kindness upon my son's heart? It is the character of Jesus that would do something like that. Matthew was listening and heeded His suggestion to his soul. Through repetition of these thoughts and actions a new habit was formed, bringing joy to all. In due time this helpfulness became the norm rather than the rarity. Everything good comes from God.

Years later, both Matthew and Andrew were known to say with a kidding glimmer in their eyes, "It's dangerous to go through Mother's kitchen. You never know when God will ask you to do something good for her."

HABITS CHART

Any act or thought that is repeated becomes a habit.
Habits can be for good or evil—a blessing or a curse.
Habits and behavior are outward evidences of which kingdom rules us.
Habits = Characteristics = Character (Spirit) = Mark (of Cain or of the Holy Spirit)?

Which "garden of habits" is your government growing in the heart and life of your child? **A fruit garden or a weed garden?**
Which kingdom am I of? Which kingdom is my child of?
Whatever habit we allow—or cultivate—will determine whom our child is following!

PERSONALITIES/NAMES "Characteristics" 1 John 4	FOLLOWS CHRIST "Trained Up" Orderly Gardens **Cultivation Takes Effort**	FOLLOWS "SELF" & SATAN "Come Up" thistles of arguing / anger **Allowing the thorns of disobedience to grow**
Sassy Suzy → Sweet Sue	Strong in self-control	Strong in self-indulgence
Angry Aaron → Amiable Aaron	Strong in integrity—do right	Strong in display of anger—do wrong / justify it
Deceitful Danny → Honest Henry	Strong in self-denial	Strong in getting his own way
Lying Loud Larry → Calm Curt	Strong in honesty	Strong in lying / foolish / deceit / excuse wrong
Overbearing Orville → Kind Karl	Strong in courtesy / kindness	Strong in being over-bearing / bully / ruling
Disorderly Dora → Orderly Dora	Strong in order / cleanliness	Strong in disorder / excuses herself
Lazy Lucy → Lively Helpful Lucy	Strong in persevering in doing right	Strong in persevering in slothfulness / slow
Persnickety Paul → Polite Paul	Strong in serving others	Strong in "What's in it for me?"
Fretful Florence → Rested Florence	Quick to come when called	Quick to excuse herself from coming
Faithless Felise → Faithful Felise	Offers to work willingly	Excuses herself from service for her own interests
Fearful Frank → Courageous Frank	Ruled by God—seek His will	Ruled by feelings / emotions / carnal bent

Sit back . . . watch . . . analyze your child . . . Whose character traits dominate or rule? Selflessness = Christ . . . or . . . Self and selfishness = Satan
My actions often repeated → form habits → habits form character. Characteristics like: Polite / Impolite Paula . . . Honest / Dishonest Henry
How do I know if my child is a Christian . . . a follower after Christ? . . .
"By their fruits . . . ye shall know them" (Matthew 7:16) . . . Not by what we say or profess . . . Examine my child's fruits?

We must come to see the importance of habits in our developing children. Overseeing, restraining the wrong, cultivating the right needs to become pre-eminent in our parenting. Let's not let Satan mold our children any longer!

If you want to change your child's disposition, thoughts, attitudes, or habits, you need to bring him or her into association with Christ. Only by acquaintance and association with Christ can we become like Him. Our children need Christ as their constant Companion and familiar Friend. They need to be in constant communion with Him habitually, for this is what will change them to be Christlike to the level of their thoughts and feelings. (See 2 Corinthians 10:5.)

If our children do not know Christ personally, they can change and come to know Him as their Friend and Savior from self. We can do our part by bringing them to Christ, through consequences if necessary, to bring them out of this or that bad habit. We need to teach them what God thinks of them, how He wants to help them leave off the unhappy habits that give them grief and sorrow and put on the opposite traits through faith in Him. They, too, will fall in love with Him through repeated experiences of His delivering them out of their thistlelike habits.

We must realize how simply habits begin and how Satan will nurture his evil traits right under our noses. Any thought or action repeated becomes a habit.

"Flowery Florence" began fussing about doing the dishes—at first in jest and fun initiated by her sister "Grumpy Georgette." They play-acted about how hard the dishes were to wash; the two sisters seemed like Siamese twins whining the same words. Mother sensed a warning to correct this, but she shrugged it off, erroneously attributing it to innocent child's play.

The first time, the girls still did a good job of washing the dishes as was "Flowery Florence's" habit then. But as time went on and this distaste for washing dishes was expressed and repeated, it became a real issue and a trial both to the girls and to their mother. First the dishes weren't getting done—the girls would sneak away from the dishes when Mother would get on the phone. Then they'd be unwilling helpers when she would come and get them to return to the undone dishes. The lying thought of how hard it is to do dishes influenced poor washing habits and engendered more frequent corrections. The girls would say over and over, "There are so many dishes to do. Mama must use every dish in the cupboard when she cooks, and she expects us to do all 'her' work." Thus their resentment grew.

What was happening here? The good thoughts were being starved or replaced by the negative thoughts, which the more they were expressed, the more they were eventually believed by both sisters. Satan is always hard at work promoting wrong thoughts and thus influencing wrong feelings, which together are strong influences for wrong responses. Thus habits are born and character is formed.

Satan is permitted to set up his hellish banner in our families, making his power felt through our children. Satan's voice is expressed in the unsubdued will and warped characters of our children because we parents are uneducated in Satan's devices, hold misconceptions, or know not a personal God that can help us.

Parents, are we missing something important in our concepts of training our children? Are we neglectful of governing their thoughts, feelings, emotions, and attitudes? Are we unmindful of God's warnings? Do wrong concepts hinder right parenting; do we think that these things are of no consequence in our children's young years? The truth is that these negative attributes are what drive and create the habits and responses we know are not right. Without addressing their thoughts and feelings or connecting them to Christ to empower them, our efforts to change our children's behavior are all vanity. It is like treating the leaves on the tree without addressing the nourishment necessary to the roots which are transmitting the diseased sap to the leaves and creating the disease problem.

Look at the fruit of the Spirit chart on page 104. Evaluate your child's fruits. Which Lord is leading your child—God or Satan? To get to the root of the issues with our children's bad habits, conduct, and manners, we need to help them change masters. Addressing their thoughts and feelings, focusing on whom they are connected to and listening to—that will bring true success to character development.

Don't you want good manners in your child? Don't you like them to say, "please," "thank you," "I'm sorry," "Can I help you"? Don't you like them to be courteous, friendly, and social? Don't you want them to have high standards so that they lead other children higher rather than being lowered by their associations with others?

These characteristics need to be cultivated, for they will not come up by themselves. Planting these traits firmly in your children will tax you. At times you will war against opposing forces, habits, and natures inspired of Satan. But don't be discouraged. God is big enough. He has won the victory. He knows everyone's weaknesses, and by His grace we can override all hereditary tendencies to evil. His power is sufficient to lay in the grave even hereditary and culti-vated tendencies toward evil. Seek His face and grasp His enabling hand so that you and your children can walk in the freedom to serve Him and right!

Often it takes the lower motivation of consequences in order to restrain wrong choices, and it takes inculcating right choices so that our children will have the opportunity to taste the grace that can change them. These good experiences inspire courage and hope to change in Jesus. Their natural bent is to be selfish, and until they experience the real God changing them, they will not want to go there. Once they experience God giving them power to be happy instead of sad and they become familiar with the process, they will want to repeat it.

As parents, our duty is to teach them of this personal, loving God. Discipline is discipling my child to Christ. Consequences are to moti-vate them to come to Him to be changed and to experience His love transforming their character and life.

Andrew became a cute little "Pillsbury doughboy" as a toddler. Due to his colic condition as an infant, I had begun the habit of overfeeding him—wrongly thinking his difficulty was insufficient food. The colic was corrected, but the habit of overeating remained. Satan began his program, using this perverted eating habit to instill other undesirable habits in Andrew as well. As a toddler, Andrew was inclined to be sed-entary. I unwisely cooperated with this tendency by carrying him when the family went on a walk and he got tired. I was cultivating and nur-turing these wrong habits. He didn't have perseverance in working, play-ing, or enduring any hardship. When he wanted to eat, impatience would rule.

After we moved to Montana and began seeking God's will for

Which Spirit Do We Bear Fruit To?

Matthew 7:16 — "Ye shall know them by their fruits."
Manners . . . Conduct . . . Habits
Proverbs 20:11 — "Even a child is known by his doings."

Fruits of the Spirit	**Fruits of the Flesh (Self)**
= following after Christ (self-less)	= following after Satan's character
Galatians 5:22, 23	Galatians 5:19-21

Fruits of the Spirit	Fruits of the Flesh (Self)
Love	Hate—given to anger
Joy	Quarrelsome—Strife / Murmuring / Complain
Peace	Envy—Foolishness
Longsuffering	Impatient—Without sympathy / compassion
Gentleness	Dominant—Uses physical force
Goodness	Unkind words / deeds—Pride
Faith	Unfaithful—Believes and speaks lies
Meekness—Self-submission	My way—the only way—Whines / fusses
	Difficult to entreat to right
	Self-exalting
Temperance—Self-control	Intemperate in food / drink / work / play
Obedience—Self denial	Disobedient—Large or small
"Not my will but Thine be done."	"My will be done. . . my feelings are supreme"

Works of the Flesh
Galatians 5:19-21

Names → that make practical application of their character
Repeated actions form habits, and habits form character.

Adultery = Dishonest Danny—Not faithful in his house chores; lies begin small and grow
Anger / Wrath (Matthew 5:21, 22) → Angry Aaron → Wrathful Wendy
Emulation = Crazy Karen—Follows trends however ridiculous—hair / dress / deportment
Envy / Jealousy = Thankless Theo → Faultfinding Florence
Fornication = Untrustworthy Eunice
Hatred = Hotheaded Henry—Sees only injustice to himself—doesn't see his wrongs / reform
Idolatry = Selfish Sam—"My thoughts and ways are supreme"
Lasciviousness = "I Want" Ivy—Follows her own feelings / passions, doesn't care right or wrong
Murder = Complaining Critical Cleo → Angry Al
Reveling = Foolish Frank → Vulgar Vera
Strife / Sedition = Arguing Ann → Excusing Ed → Fretful Florence
Uncleaness = Disorderly Dora—Her room is messy—won't submit to parents' counsel
Variance = Warring Wendy
Witchcraft = "My Way" Miriam—Independent of proper restraint

Galatians 5:21—"Doers of these things . . . shall not inherit the kingdom of God." ! !
Psalm 55:19—"Because they have no changes, therefore they fear not [know not] God."
There is no excuse for not having the character of Christ.
Evaluate: What are your children's fruit? → By their doings, not what they know!

parenting, I started to see many things I was doing wrong and that needed changing. Although this was hard, it was good for both my children and me. I began addressing Andrew's slothful work habits. I insisted he walk longer than he wanted to, and I restrained his overeating. Still, change was slow. God then impressed me to change my management approach to training my child in self-government.

In this process, God led me to use the following consequence when Andrew was not being responsible for his few personal care chores within the appropriate time allotted—he would miss a meal. Now that was hard on this soft mother, but God knew best, as I learned later in this lesson.

Andrew did surprisingly well with this consequence. So I felt God was there working with us. On these occasions, Andrew would go to weed in the greenhouse while we ate breakfast. He was learning and had chosen to talk with God while he was working instead of fighting and fussing how unfair all this was to him.

"Andrew, you will do just fine without breakfast; I am here with you," the Holy Spirit impressed on his mind.

Andrew was listening but asked, "Lord, this work is hard, and I'm so hungry. I want to eat. Maybe I'll die!"

"You wont die, son. That is a lying thought. It's just hunger pains. This will pass in a little while. Trust Me! I want you to go get some more water to drink like your mother suggested. Fasting is good for you; it won't hurt you. I had to fast too."

Andrew took his glass and got some more of that fresh mountain spring water from the garden tap. He was pleasantly surprised how the groaning in his stomach soon ceased.

"You know, Mother told me that my stomach was stretched too big and that is why I want more food than is good for me. She also said that by not eating it would shrink to a more normal size and that I'd be satisfied with less. Well, maybe not eating can be good."

"Yes, that is true. Those are good thoughts to think on when you miss a meal by choice or by consequence. Have you thought that weeding could teach you interesting lessons?"

"Mother has told me that, but her lessons aren't very interesting."

"You have to change your attitude; then weeding can become interesting."

And so Andrew, age five, and God talked together out there in the greenhouse. God gave just the reasoning that he needed according to his age. Andrew did cooperate to think on God's thoughts by picking those weeds, with courage, labeling them as his weeds of complaining and murmuring. "Out of my heart you go!" He said to himself. His desire for this work to be pleasant became a reality as he cooperated in this way.

They talked more about fasting, and Jesus encouraged him how good it is to fast for a meal or a day. If he would persist in this discipline, it would help him say "no" more easily to extra food at mealtime. And so God helped me to restrain the wrong habits and cultivate the right habits beginning with Andrew's thoughts and progressing to his feelings and responses toward his consequence. That is why he took the discipline so well, and by repetition of talking with God, his habits began to change just as they had talked about.

So it can be with you and with your child's wrong habits, in your home. Jesus is there to make your desires and choices real as you seek Him to be your Helper and Savior. The Creator God wants to re-create all of us into His image, and instilling good habits in us is part of His program.

THE LONE EMBRACE
A SPECIAL WORD OF ENCOURAGEMENT FOR SINGLE PARENTS

Take courage that through parental consistency, under Christ, you can take your child up this pathway and exchange bad habits for good. Christ will be your spouse, nurturing and encouraging you in your pathway—giving help as He helped my Andrew. Your child can be redeemed from whatever habit he has that wars against God. You are not alone!

Let no habit develop or continue that will need to be changed when your child gets older. Deal with all you see in order to give them a heritage of good habits after God.

God has designed that through consistency you can regain your child's heart and habits. Follow your Shepherd and become the undershepherd He designed you to be. You, too, can overcome, and this will excite your courage that your child can do the same. You will be able to tell your child of God's love and power. You will be able to present obedience to God in the fear of the Lord as a desirable thing. Only in this way can our characters become Christlike.

Good habits will not be developed by a casual or superficial approach. Good habits develop by a choice, a connection with God, and a will to do battle against wrong thoughts and inclinations.

You can be blessed of God because of your faithful work, and your children will receive their white stone with their new name—"Amiable Aaron," "Helpful Hannah," "Faithful Felice,"—and they each will have won the battle against self through surrender and cooperation with Jesus. Through the blood of Jesus Christ they receive their new name and freedom from self.

No greater joy is there for a parent than to see their work pay off with such wonderful dividends. The hardness of the way is forgotten when your home is heavenlike because your children know and want to be like Jesus and are in the process of reforming. But joy inexpressible will overflow when Jesus places that crown upon their heads in the end. Be faithful and enduring, dear parents. Instill those godly habits in your children, for their habits will determine their destiny!

Chapter 9

BRINGING OUR HABITS TO CHRIST

"He hath chosen us in him . . . unto . . . adoption" (Ephesians 1:4, 5).

Jesus created us, and thus we should serve Him as our Creator. But we have gone astray from Him to serve another Master—Satan, sin, and self. So Christ Himself has paid a high price for our adoption. He wants to give us another chance to choose to serve Him of our own free will, to choose to be His child and not another's. That is a great love—to pay the price for our waywardness so that we need not die the eternal death. So we can choose to be adopted back by Him and re-created into His image in this life.

As a result of our being under Satan's servitude, serving sin and self more naturally than God, we have a problem: our habits, by nature, are against God. Adam and Eve sowed the *habits of disobedience,* and we are the inheritors of their choices. Thus our nature is independent of God. The Bible calls this our carnal nature. Adam and Eve made bad choices that have brought us into our unenviable position—being under the servitude of Satan. But, like Adam and Eve, we too, have a choice. We can continue in the path they passed down to us, or we can choose to be adopted of Christ and serve His character and will instead.

How do we change to serve God instead of our flesh? I'd like to illustrate that using a banana and a cup.

We all have habits that need changing, don't we? Of course! Well, a banana with lots of spots illustrates our character dilemma. The spots on the banana represent our self-directed life and the habits learned there. We are the one in charge, not God, when we allow the natural spotting of the banana to occur. We are doing our will! Our character is being spoiled or marred, just like the banana. It's the natural trend of decay! We are not consulting what God would have us to do. The spots, therefore, represent wrong habits inherited and cultivated in this self-directed mode. There is no hope, in ourselves, to stop the banana's spots from worsening.

A banana with both large and small spots on it represents the parent's character. The large spots represent the well-ingrained, well-exercised, long-term *wrong habits* that we parents have allowed to stay. The smaller spots show further decay encroaching. This state of decay will continue until the banana eventually turns all black and dies. We can change our spots if we change our present course and become God-directed.

A banana with *little spots* can represent our child's character dilemma. Our children haven't exercised their bad habits—their unrighteous practices—as long as we; therefore, these spots are not as ingrained nor as ugly as those that have grown through the lifetime of a parent. These spots can be changed through a vital connection with Christ our Savior.

A beautiful blue cup represents *the solution*—the Spirit-directed life—and the upright habits that are available to both the parent and the child in Jesus. Getting into the cup is God's program *to erase* the old spots, the wrong habits, and our history of poor problem-solving techniques, regardless of whether they are big or little. Praise God we have a way of escape *in Him!*

To change our spots, we must come to understand and experience that we need a power outside of ourselves. Of ourselves we cannot wrestle down Satan or self, nor erase our habit spots. Scripture says in Ephesians 6:12, "For we wrestle not against flesh and blood, but against principalities, against powers, against the rulers of the darkness of this world, against spiritual wickedness in high [places]."

The power to change is found in Jesus Christ Himself. It is not found apart from Him. John 1:4, 12 says, "*In him* was life; and the life was the light of men." "But as many as received him, *to them gave he power to become* the sons of God" (emphasis supplied). Christ wants to adopt us for sure! We are told in James 4:7 that Christ can subdue the devil and send him away. "Submit yourselves therefore to God. Resist the devil, and he will flee from you." God has put all things in subjection under Christ (see Hebrews 2:8). Therefore, when we place ourselves in Christ, we are choosing to be God's child by adoption. This represents getting into the cup. The blue cup represents obedience to God instead of obedience to my old habits, my carnal nature, or myself.

In bringing our habits to Christ, we want to exchange bad habits for good habits, which requires not only an intellectual surrender to

God ("This is best for me.") but also a physical cooperation with God (to do His will in place of my old ways). We must choose to obey God in the moment with a free-will choice. How does this work?

At nine years old, Andrew was inclined to be slothful and sloppy at times. His schoolbooks just happened to be left out here and there instead of in the place provided for them on the bookshelf in his bedroom. He was reasoned with and given consequences when he did not get them into the right place following school. I tried to teach him to exercise self-government. He agreed it was a good idea for everything to have a place and everything to be put in its place, but it wasn't done consistently. Sometimes he'd choose to do so, while other times he didn't see it as important.

"Lord what shall I do? He has been spanked for his sloppiness, he has had extra chores to do because of his lack of follow through, we have talked and prayed to You often over the past several weeks. We have discussed the value of neatness and orderliness, and he agrees with it. I believe he really wants to do better but just doesn't do it. So what do I do now?"

"You have taught him what is right, but you haven't trained him to do the right. He must exchange good habits for bad habits. I will take the bad habit that he voluntarily gives Me, but he must perform the good habit in place of the bad habit in order for Me to expel it. It's the replacement principle. He needs to know what to do instead of the old way.

"Your approach will help or hinder his choice. Tell him what you want him to be in an encouraging, positive way rather than railing on his failure, which will discourage him. You want to correct him, but you also want to nurture his courage and cooperation so that he can change. There is power available, with his hand in Mine."

A sweet idea dawned in my mind. "Andrew, your schoolbooks have been disobedient again today. You need to discipline them so that they don't stop short of getting to their proper resting place."

Andrew giggled but looked close into my eyes to see if fretfulness and faultfinding would follow, as was my former, common response. So I assured him. "Andrew, I'm not going to be harsh or fretful as I have been before; that's not God's way. I've given that to Jesus to take away. And I'm choosing to be helpful and kind instead. God wants us to be doers of His word and not hearers only.

"And that is just what you need to do, too! You need to give Jesus your habit of coming short of fully putting your books away and cooperate with Him to supervise over those books that they get all the way back to their resting place. Without your cooperation, all the power of heaven is neutralized and God cannot help you. But cooperation with Jesus changes bad habits into good habits. I know you want to do right—so please discipline those books like a good parent."

To my shock Andrew took up the cause and spoke cutely to his books about how they were naughty and how he was determined to watch over them better so that they always got back to their spot on his bookshelf. He would take responsibility for them.

Andrew turned to God this time without my impetus. Walking upstairs, he cried out to God, "Lord I do want to do right. Help me do right not only this time but next time as well. Mother says that Satan wants me to be unhappy by clinging to bad ways, but You want me to be happy by following Your better ways. I give You my habit to forget and my habit of not wanting to put away my books. I want to live like Jesus did. You have the power to change my ways when I cooperate!"

"Andrew do you recognize the joy in your heart right now?" God asked.

"Why, yes, I do! Why is it so easy this time?"

"Because you have set your will to do the right. You are not fighting against the right; you are cooperating to do it. When you put your hand in Mine this way, I can change you inside. When you are stubborn and unwilling to give up your old ways, I will not go against your will. But when you give me your heart—your thoughts, feelings, and habits—I can recreate them into a good heart—My heart! Do you like it?"

"Oh, yes, Lord! I want to do this again."

For the next several weeks, Andrew was very responsible. Repetition made the new habit stronger and stronger with each choice and action. His will was in gear, and his cooperation with God's still small voice was consistent. How much easier life is when we let God lead and direct us! And it works reform in our child.

This kind of response can be the response of your child if you will consistently exercise the watch care over your child's thoughts, feelings, and responses that God wants you to exercise. Teach your children that God is a personal God. In our day-to-day life we can point out how God communicates to their minds so that they can recognize His still small voice. It will not be an audible voice, but a reasoning voice, the voice of their conscience. It is so important for our children to come to see that it is better to face our fears and weaknesses than to remain in bondage under their servitude. You must also let God have you first so that you will not hinder your child's decision to follow Him through harsh or unkind correction. This ideal example can be your experience in your home with your child.

"Hitting Henry" came to visit, and shortly after his arrival, he hit my son because he wouldn't do what "Hitting Henry" wanted him to do. Henry seemed to be lashing out at the whole world, trying to control everyone to do his will. When they didn't, he'd become so distraught that he would frequently hit his mother—unprovoked. She was the receiver of his unresolved feelings and emotions through the expression of hitting.

The mother spoke with me of her frustration. This had been going on for years. She admitted how she would become so distraught that she would hit him back. She described herself as showering a pitiless hail of fretfulness and faultfinding upon her young son of five. She'd become this way because neither spanking, talking, nor praying with him seemed to make any change in his behavior. Hitting almost always became an issue when they would go visiting friends or relatives "What am I to do?" she asked.

"You need to bring your child to Christ," I replied. "A personal touch with God will heal him of his bad habit of hitting just as the woman who touched the hem of Christ's garment was healed. You need to teach him that Jesus said, 'Suffer the little children to come unto Me.' Let him know that God wants to help him out of all his troubles. Encourage him to enlist his will and cooperation on God's side. Explain how he needs to give his ill feelings to God, think good thoughts, and respond better. Then God can work the miracle of heart transformation and bring him true happiness."

"Show me how," she requested. "I need to see it to understand."

We prayed together for God to give us wisdom, for I knew the principles but not the specifics necessary for this child. God knows. So I trusted He would give me the words and ideas when I needed them. With her permission, we took "Hitting Henry" for a walk to explain simply who Satan is, who God is, and to set up a new program of coming out of wrong habits in Jesus—a program that they could take home with them to bring Henry completely out of the habit of hitting.

I began by saying, " 'Hitting Henry,' I like you very much. I have seen that you get very upset when things don't go your way. That is so sad. I can see in your eyes that you don't want to hit—it causes so much pain in here," and I pointed to his heart. "You know Satan hits, and it's his voice that pushes you to hit others. He says things to your mind, and when you think on his thoughts, emotions rise in you and you feel compelled to hit. You don't want to hit, but you do. That is nasty old Satan wanting to make you unhappy. You know you don't have to hit others or be hurt yourself any more."

"That's not so," Henry said with passion. "I've tried and tried! It doesn't *work!*"

"I know you are trying, but I want to teach you how to try with your hand in Jesus' hand. It will be different from anything you've done so far. You will find power to do the right. Jesus loves you so very much and wants to help you out of all your troubles." We talked very simply about Psalm 50:15 and Jeremiah 32:27. "God is able to change you," I assured him.

Hitting Henry's eyes showed he was listening; it appeared hope was rising.

"Henry, I want to show you how you can change into 'Gentle George.' I know you would like that. The secret to success is putting your hand in Jesus' hand for power to be re-created. But it's vitally important for you to cooperate with whatever Jesus tells you to do at the time of the trouble. When unfairness or anger arises, and you're inclined to hit, it is much better to learn to do something in place of hitting rather than just not hitting. For the urge to hit is very strong."

"I'm scared!"

"Yes, that is Satan's thought to your mind right now. He doesn't want you to know Jesus and freedom from hitting. He wants to keep you as his servant and not let you go. Life is so much happier when you have the freedom to be 'Gentle George' in Jesus."

We used the visual illustration of the banana and the cup to help him understand how to cooperate. "You have to lay down the banana— the old ways of responding. Then you choose to get into the cup— which is listening to and doing God's way instead." I further explained the process of coming out of old habits by replacing them with new ones. "Mother will ask you to be kind instead. You'll need to follow her with all your will against the thoughts and feelings from Satan. Jesus will speak to your *thinking place,* and whatever He says to you, do it. It will be a battle, but in time Jesus will show you the joy of being 'Gentle George,' and oh, how wonderful that will be."

And soon opportunity came.

Something stirred "Hitting Henry," and he raised his fist to hit. His mother saw it and was prepared. "Henry, come here first—right now." She spoke calmly to exemplify to Henry the right spirit.

Henry didn't hit, but you could see the great controversy between Satan and God in his countenance. The struggle in his little mind as he made the decision to come to his mother was so pitiful to watch. We sent up a prayer to God for wisdom in this all-important first decision.

Thankfully "Hitting Henry" obeyed his mother's call. "Sit here on my lap 'Gentle George.' You don't want those ugly feelings. We need to give them to Jesus and throw them away, remember?"

"But, Mother . . . ," Henry began to express the injustice of the present situation.

"That is the old way. Jesus has a new and better way we must follow."

Just then I returned, bringing the banana and the cup to make this next step tangible.

"What you need to do now is to lay down your banana. The banana is your anger, your frustration, and the unfairness that is pushing all those ugly feelings. Hitting is the results of those thoughts and feelings. You do not need to obey them any more." I picked up the banana and laid it down—demonstrating. "Jesus has something better to replace that ugly way and it will bring peace and happiness to your heart again." I picked up the cup—to demonstrate getting into the cup. "But you must cooperate in thinking new thoughts so that God can make new feelings. You need to pray with us for Jesus to help you right now," I said.

We knelt in prayer, and the grizzlies in Henry's heart lessened but did not go away entirely.

"Do you feel any different, Henry?"

"No! This is scary." He was panting, and fear was gripping him.

"Trust Mother and trust Jesus. This fear is how Satan keeps you doing naughty things. Trusting Jesus must be done by faith—that which is not seen and yet believed. Your feelings will change, you will see. Jeremiah 32:27 says, 'I [am] the LORD, the God of all flesh: is there any thing too hard for me?' God is able to deliver you if you trust and obey His way and will. You can do it Henry. Give the wrong to God."

Henry was hesitating, still fearful.

"Henry, you must choose to believe God. Take Jesus' hand; it's outstretched for you to take. You can't do this on your own—only with Jesus. Take Jesus' hand, and the fear will go away."

Henry clutched his mother, and she comforted him. " 'Gentle George,' you must choose Jesus in order to be what you want to be."

"Lets pray again, Mommy! I want Jesus." And he reached up his little hand to take Jesus' hand. During and after prayer, a growing peace came over "Gentle George."

"This is getting into the cup. You are in the cup now, and Jesus will work a good work in your little heart. You have chosen to trust Him, and so He can come in. This peace is what it is like when Jesus comes in. It is good, isn't it?"

"Yes, I like it."

"Now 'Gentle George' must do a gentle act so that God can complete what He has begun in your heart."

"What must I do?" he asked.

"You need to go over to your playmate and do something kind for her."

"But, Mother, she didn't do what I told her to do!" The old passion was pulling at him again.

"No, you need to give Jesus those wrong thoughts. Lay down the banana again. That little girl does not have to obey you, son. You need to bring your unfairness to your mother for her to resolve. It is not your duty to punish her. You don't want to make people hurt! How would you feel if she hit you because you didn't do what she said?"

"She can't do that!" His injustice was stirred again.

"Well, neither can you do that to her. You can trust God and your mother to take care of her. You don't have to punish her any more. Give it to Jesus."

And "Gentle George" picked up the banana, looking at the spots, and laid it down. Putting his hand into the cup, he said. "I want to get into the cup again, Mother." So we prayed again. "I don't need to hit her or control her! She doesn't have to obey me," he said. And again peace reigned in little Henry's heart.

"Now you need to go to that little girl and do something kind."

The new "Gentle George" went over as resolutely as a five-year-old can and said to the little girl, "Would you like me to show you how to make a pond in the sand? Then we can play going swimming?" And thus began the new birth of "Gentle George" in Jesus.

I spoke with the mother. "Now you want to get rid of all the tools that nurtured "Hitting Henry" to hit. If you hit your son in a rash moment of passion, that must go. You get rid of it the same way you are teaching your son to get rid of his bad habits. If your husband, uncle, neighbor, or child's playmates display the hitting pattern, you must shield him from these instances as much as humanly possible. As kindly as you can, let him know that these people do not know Jesus as it is their privilege to know Him and that they are not the pattern we want to follow. They are in bondage to Satan as Henry once was. We need to pray for them. We certainly don't want to cultivate the thought that we are better than others, but neither do we want to excuse sin or follow in its path. So teach Henry to pity the sinner and to show them a better way. Find this balance in Jesus.

"You also need to continue what we have begun here. Maintain consistency, in Christ, with no variableness in follow-through regarding this new trait of character. Gentleness will replace hurtful hitting as long as you keep the program going and alive.

"One day the new trait of character will be stronger and will become your child's habit. Until then, continue your influence for righteousness by exercising proper parental management. There will come a day when the old way will earnestly strive for mastery once again. Be willing to do whatever God asks you to do, in reason, giving your child consequences and timeouts with God. Weary not in well doing. Don't stop until your child is once again free on God's side."

God knew just what "Hitting Henry" needed to hear. He needed to experience God changing him inside until he was free to be "Gentle George," who could serve God in heaven some day. Through repetition of experiences like this, the mother learned to filter through God what to say and how to say it to her child's understanding. Through repetition "Gentle George" learned to pet the cats and dogs with gentleness instead of hitting and hating the animals. He gained friends among the animals and his peers. He was much happier being free to be "Gentle

George" than he ever was as "Hitting Henry." To God be the glory!

Next, I want to introduce you to "Insecure Ivan." He was afflicted from birth with insecurity due to his mother going through physical and emotional trauma during her pregnancy, the messy divorce that followed, and a quick remarriage. His mother's experience was his experience in and out of the womb. He partook of the trauma physically and emotionally with her as if it were done to him personally.

His anxiety and insecurity levels were very high and not easily relieved. It was extremely taxing upon the infant and the mother in those early years, not knowing how to bring these traits to Jesus to stop their influence upon his mind and emotions.

As he grew, insecurity plagued him. He would often ask his mother, "Do you love me? Do you really love me?" His mind was flooded with doubting thoughts of his inability to please others; his failures loomed up as if to crush him—even if they were of a very small nature. Even when kindly corrected by his mother with ideas of how to improve his performance, his pace would slow, his insecurities would rise, and his eyes would cast downward. Apparent failure was like a destroying giant, paralyzing his very muscles so that they could not come to action.

He would cry out over and over, "Forgive me! Do you forgive me? Do you still love me?" Amid a truckload of love and affirming words, his response was, "I don't feel loved." It was obvious that issues of abandonment and rejection were driving his insecurity and paralyzing his performance. He saw himself as always failing to please, even when he did please. Thus responsibility became a constant source of agitation and fear of failure.

When Ivan was nine years old, his overpowering insecurity manifested itself in a fear of going to sleep alone. The parents tried reasoning with their son, praying with him, quoting Bible promises, even spanking him. Nothing they did brought freedom to their son from the thoughts and feelings that oppressed him. They had allowed their son to come into their bedroom and sleep in a sleeping bag on the floor beside the mother. But even that didn't make him feel secure. He would stay awake to make sure the mother didn't go to sleep before he did so that he wouldn't be left alone—abandoned. The exhaustion of sleepless nights was taking its toll on the entire family, and a schedule and productive home-school were almost impossible.

The mother told me their story. She wanted some direction about how to help her son overcome his fears and insecurities. We discussed some ideas to begin the process of implementing *replacement* principles in his work habits through right thoughts about himself, and disciplinary measures under God to gain him independence from their bedroom to his own. God had to become his personal Friend, Savior, and Lord.

She went home to apply what she knew and understood, while battling at the same time with her own unique fears, inadequacies, and insecurities. She gained a degree of success. After five months, her son graduated to sleeping across the room instead of beside her, holding her hand. With much effort, his work habits had improved a little, but still the fear of rejection and doubts that he was loved plagued their valiant efforts for freedom.

We were at a family camp meeting, and I was going over my notes in preparation for my presentation in one hour. My prayers had been earnest for this sweet family, especially "Insecure Ivan." "How can we make God real and help Ivan over his insecurities and all the resultant wrong thinking?" I cried out to God.

To my shock and joy, God had me re-write my entire message within that hour to present the newly dawning concept of the banana and the cup.

Now let me tell you who Sally is or isn't at this time. It took me more than forty hours to write one sermon. I had my own battles with insecurities and inadequacies, hindering my sermon preparation. So this was a first-time experience—not only in writing a sermon in an hour, but also in successfully delivering this message in a logical, concise manner. "Insecure Ivan" was on the front row, and often I spoke directly to him and to his mother. They didn't know this sermon was for them, nor did I tell them.

The mother was particularly encouraged by this message, and God inspired her in applying it after she returned home. I want to tell you their story of success against strong hereditary and cultivated habits to show you the power, love, and presence of God that can help you!

"Insecure Ivan" was eleven years old now. The Holy Spirit took the vivid illustration of the banana and the cup and drove home to his heart what Jesus could do, if he would cooperate with Him fully. Hope rose!

On the way home from camp meeting, the mother was inspired by

God to take a banana left over from the camp meeting meals. She and "Insecure Ivan" wrote on pieces of paper the common thoughts and feelings of fear and insecurity that Satan would bring to his mind that kept him from being able to go to sleep alone, and taped them to the banana. These lying thoughts that ruled him, the wrong habits that resulted, represented the spots on the banana that were decaying his character.

When they arrived home, his mother was inspired to take a cup from her cupboard. She used a white cup that had these words printed on it: "As for me and my house, we will serve the Lord." White would stand for the truth and purity of Jesus. He would never lie to Ivan. God's Word could be trusted. Ivan would let the mind of Jesus be in him by consent and cooperation. The verse printed on the cup represented the decision the son was making to leave the service of Satan and begin to serve God. Mother and son looked up Bible texts of promise that matched his unique internal struggles. They wrote them on slips of paper and put them in the cup. These are the honest and right thoughts he would think on instead of his old destructive ones.

One of the verses was Psalm 27:10—"When my father and my mother forsake me, then the LORD will take me up." His greatest fear—built on his early traumatic experience—was that his parents would leave or abandon him. This verse helped to connect him to the One who would never leave or forsake him.

Ivan chose Psalm 4:8—"I will both lay me down in peace, and sleep: for thou, LORD, only makest me dwell in safety." He realized he could lay down his fear of abandonment, triggered by bedtime in his own room, and be perfectly safe in Jesus.

Insecurity and doubt, pushed by his fears, brought about much anxiety of soul, and thus he chose Deuteronomy 31:6 to cling to. When the lying thoughts of insecurity strove for the mastery, he would trust Jesus' words instead: "Be strong and of a good courage, fear not, nor be afraid of them: for the LORD thy God, he [it is] that doth go with thee; he will not fail thee, nor forsake thee." God's word would be his sword.

If God leads you to use this pattern to overcome a bad character trait in your life, it will be important for you to first name the sin that is besetting you and then replace that wrong way with the opposite trait of character. For example, you replace fear/doubt with trust, your insecurity with God's security, and anxiety with peace in Jesus.

Ivan and his mother promptly put these visual items into his bedroom, and he chose to lay down his banana the first night home from camp meeting. He had his weapons for this warfare in his white cup, and Jesus as his General in this battle! Courage with timidity rose to the occasion, looking forward to God's victory, but knowing that this would be a battle for his mind and emotions.

Before "Insecure Ivan" was tucked into bed that night, mother had him hold in his hand the banana and led him in a prayer of "changing masters." He chose against the lying thoughts and actively cooperated thinking the right thoughts from the cup. As Ivan told Jesus that he was choosing to follow Him rather than Satan, he laid down the banana and picked up the cup, saying, "I believe God's thoughts." After saying "Amen," he crawled into bed, smiled peacefully at his mother, and was not heard from again until the next morning. He reported that Jesus had given him perfect peace and that he had gone to sleep very quickly and had slept all night without one troubling dream. By faith, the truth—as it is in Jesus—set him free!

Day after day and night after night, Mother would rehearse laying down his banana and getting into the cup as his battle plan. Often they prayed to dispel the fear.

Then one night Satan succeeded in bringing "Insecure Ivan" back down that old path through those old thought patterns, and he came into his parent's bedroom for residency. His stepfather took him back to his room and through discussion and a necessary loving spanking, followed by prayer, "Insecure Ivan" again laid down his banana—lying thoughts. He picked up the cup—getting into Jesus—with such confidence that he was immediately put back on the path of victory. Peace once again reigned in his mind and heart.

Another night the devil tempted him with "It's impossible for you to sleep in your own room." He was awake until eleven o'clock, when he finally gave in to the lie and crept quietly into his parent's bedroom and went right to sleep. The next morning, Satan started telling him the next lie, "You are hopeless and helpless. You might as well just come back into this dark cave of fear. You were never meant to walk at liberty."

When Mother saw him, he was so overcome with a sense of failure that he couldn't even look at her. He fully expected a lecture, but the Lord restrained his mother, and instead she took him to viable texts on not abandoning yourself to discouragement and despair—but rather, to hope in Christ. "Insecure Ivan" recognized the lies of Satan and laid down his banana—lying thoughts. Again, he reached out in faith to enter that cup again.

Hope returned. While washing dishes after breakfast he said, "I wish it was bedtime right now so that I could go to sleep in my own room and prove what a liar the devil really is!" And for a very long time, he did this most successfully.

The emotional battles were intense and downright fierce at times, especially the first few weeks. But it was not as long and drawn out as Mother and "Insecure Ivan" had anticipated. After two months, "Insecure Ivan" was going to bed easily and peacefully. Insecurity and fear were no longer an issue. He was now "Peaceful Peter," sleeping safely in the arms of Jesus.

Then two years later he again had a hard time going to sleep because of a conversation at his neighbor's house that had stirred up those old feelings of fear and insecurity. The devil again started telling him that he couldn't sleep alone. So he decided to wage war in Jesus' strength. The next day he told his mother what happened.

"I was unable to go to sleep; the old thought patterns wanted to intrude themselves. But I was able to recognize them as lies and cried out to Jesus for help again. I laid down my banana—my old ways—and picked up the cup. I got up and read my Bible. I prayed for everyone I could think of. Then I recited Bible promises and thought about the invisible army of God that Elisha saw with the eye of faith. I didn't go down the path of fear and frustration, and after a time perfect peace filled my heart. I went peacefully to sleep. It is a wonderful freedom to know Jesus. I need never fear again."

Courageousness was another trait he added to his armor that night. The three brothers Courage, Trust, and Peace like to travel together. At present, it is five years since these experiences took place, and this wonderful young man has faced fears in other areas of his life and has been as successful in these—with Jesus—as he has been with sleeping in his own room. He has become a skillful and diligent worker carrying increasing responsibilities in the home without paralysis and slow work habits. It's only by acquaintance and association with Christ that we can become like Him. In Christ is how we build "real" men.

Isn't our main objective in parenting to get our children to take hold of God for themselves? What is God asking you to do? This story can be yours!

THE LONE EMBRACE
A SPECIAL WORD OF ENCOURAGEMENT FOR SINGLE PARENTS

As a single parent we need, above all else, to find the treasure of Jesus Christ working in our lives. As the man who found the treasure went home to sell *all* to possess the pearl of great price, so too must we learn to sell all our self, sell all our old ways, sell our independence from God—lay down our bananas—in order to possess Christ that He may possess and free us and our children (see Matthew 13:46). God wants to perform a character transforming work in our hearts, habits, and lives so that we can understand practically how to instruct our children to overcome their selfishness.

Getting into the cup is gaining that vital connection with Christ so that we have power to overcome. God can change any wrong character trait when we come under His control in this way. Child or parent—redemption begins in our thoughts. However difficult it may be to let go of our own way—it is profitable. Bring your habits to Christ to be changed in thought, word, and deed!

Chapter 10
GETTING THE HEART

"My son, give me thine heart, and let thine eyes observe my ways"
(Proverbs 23:26).

Getting your child's heart is gaining his love, his admiration, his attention, and his cooperation to follow your godly directions. If you have shown yourself trustworthy over the years, it will be relatively easy to direct your child from his fleshly ways to Christ. For you can build on his trust toward you and transfer that trust to Jesus, the Friend of his parent.

" 'Cleanly Clarissa,' you are working your play vacuum as well as Mother does her real one. You will make a very fine mother and house-keeper one day. Here, let me give you Mother's vacuum. See if you can handle this big one."

"Cleanly Clarissa," age five, was so pleased, she accepted the challenge with joy. She was happy to be working with Mother; it was always a pleasant experience. Whatever Mother was doing Clarissa wanted to do—after all, Mother appreciated her help. She wanted to be just like her.

"How am I doing, Mother?"

"You are doing quite well, my little one! That is a mighty big vacuum for such a little girl, but you are strong and getting stronger. You are Mother's little helper! I love working with you beside me. You do such thorough work. One day Mother will be able to let you be responsible for sweeping the living room because of that thoroughness you are learning. In fact, I'll let you finish right now. I'll dust instead."

Now Clarissa hadn't yet developed thoroughness, but Mother was wise and skilled to inculcate right attributes by telling her child what she can be and will be, beginning by putting this goodly quality in her mind as something to be desired.

Shortly, "Cleanly Clarissa" became distracted, looking at the toys in the corner box in the living room. She began longing to be building a house with her blocks instead of vacuuming right now. Turning to Mother, she said, "I'm real tired, Mother. I'm going to play now." And she turned off the vacuum.

Mother sent up a little prayer to God, "What should I address and what should I let go?"

"She needs to live out the thoroughness you attributed to her earlier," God's still small voice impressed upon her mind.

" 'Cleanly Clarissa,' did you finish all the sweeping? A thorough girl will finish it all before she goes to play."

"Yes, Mother," she said, looking down.

"Is that the truth, dear Clarissa, or is Satan tempting you not to be truthful? Listening to Satan brings sadness, you know. You can still choose the right."

She got that shy, self-protective look, and Mother knew Satan was out for her daughter's thoughts and feelings, making sin look enticing and the truth look more like a burden. "Lord, what would Thou have me to do?" (See Acts 9:6.)

"Bring her to Me. Have her give Me her heart so that I can cleanse it and implant upright thoughts and thus change her feelings as well."

"Clarissa, do you trust Mother?"

"Oh, yes!"

"Then I want you to tell me the truth. Good or bad, the truth is the best way."

A pause of decision. The struggle to trust was difficult in light of her confused emotions right now. But soon forthright confession came. Surely God was talking with Clarissa; she understood and heeded His voice as well as Mother's.

"Mother, I wanted to build with my blocks." And tears began to flow. "I didn't finish the floor. I'm sorry."

"You have chosen well to tell the truth. I'm proud of you, my dear little one. Now you must ask Jesus to forgive you, too. We'll pray to Him. He loves you more than I. If you give God your naughty thoughts and feelings, He will clean away all that badness, and you can finish sweeping the floor and be happy. This is what you want. You will be happier building with your blocks in honesty than in dishonesty. Jesus spoke to your little thinking place, encouraging you to tell the truth—didn't He?"

"Yes!"

They prayed together. "Cleanly Clarissa" yielded her mind to Jesus' way of thinking and gave Him her bad feelings! She said her own sweet little prayer of confession, asking for forgiveness with tears.

"Now, what do you need to do, Clarissa?" Mother asked, rather than telling her daughter what to do. This is a good exercise in helping children make their own decisions.

"Finish the floor. I want to be thorough like Mother."

"Good girl!" A sweet hug and a kiss on the top of her head sent "Cleanly Clarissa" off with a better heart and better thoughts to think instead of the selfish "I want" thoughts. As she cooperated with those upright thoughts, her feelings were transformed, and she was happy vacuuming until it was done—and done right.

That was a great victory that day. Clarissa added the beginning exercises of the adult muscle of thoroughness. This little influence went far in her life thanks to Mother's watch care and sensitivity to her thoughts and feelings. Mother had Clarissa's heart and wanted to transfer that trust to Jesus—and so, too, must every parent.

Getting the heart is building on the trust factor between the parent and child and extending that trust factor to Jesus—whom the child cannot see with his eyes. This choice against strong fleshly feelings takes an act of faith. In trusting Jesus at the recommendation of her mother, Clarissa allowed God to transform her thoughts and feelings, making them upright. This is what God is asking when He says, "My son, give Me thine heart" (Proverbs 23:26). God wants to redeem and re-create us into His image in thought, word, and deed.

In contrast, if the parent has been inconsistent, indulgent, and indecisive, if he or she can't be counted on—or if the opposite is true, and the parent is dominating, unfair, scolding, flammable, coldly indifferent, intruding, or unpredictable—the child will have difficulty learning to develop trust or transferring trust toward Jesus. Trust is earned!

The untrustworthy parent—and there are many—must come to Christ to find redemption from the flesh ruling over him or her and then ask forgiveness of the child. He or she will need to show the child that he is now trustworthy because he is denying self in Jesus. Under the lordship of Christ, a parent can regain his lost trust factor.

You see, getting the child's heart is the parent dealing with the child's bad habits and misbehavior by dealing at the core of the wrong. Proverbs 4:23 says, "Keep thy heart with all diligence; for out of it [are] the issues of life." God wants our mind and our heart. Therefore it is our children's thoughts, feelings, and emotions that are the core of their responses, wrong habits, and behavior. Redemption begins in the heart!

"Faultfinding Florence" and "Dominating Duke" were the parents of "Rebellious Rufus." Rufus was nine years old and had developed some survival tactics to be his parents' son. When his mother went on a fretful, faultfinding rampage, Rufus was able to tune her out by going to an imaginary place in his mind with turbulent ocean waves crashing or the noisy swishing of downhill snow skiing. These imaginary noises effectively tuned mother out. Rufus went there to survive rather than to be crushed by thinking there was no good thing in him. When her passion heightened to critical screaming, he'd tune in enough to know what she wanted him to do and then do it grudgingly to avert the heavy hand of punishment he knew she was capable of when she got angry enough. Life was miserable for everyone.

When Father came home and heard mother's story of Rufus' misbehavior, insensitivity to her needs, and unwillingness to listen to her, he would come to push Rufus around harshly. He did so physically, but even worse, he did so in a Bible-thumping manner, threatening Rufus with the loss of heaven if he continued in this way. If God was like his parents, Rufus decided, he wasn't attracted to Him.

"Dominating Duke" let Rufus know with certainty that whatever Father said, Rufus must do. Father wrongly thought he was a Christian because he'd read Bible texts to Rufus about how he should obey his parents. Parents can wrongly use the Bible if they use it like a club with a compelling and forceful spirit. This is not of God—although it uses His Word. Father demanded that Rufus should honor and do whatever his parents tell him to do if he was to be happy. That was God's commandment, Father assured Rufus! Then came the painful words, "You are so rebellious! God cannot love you."

Rufus felt lost! Again, he responded to this rejection with an attitude of "you can't hurt me." His reply? "If you and mother are what heaven is like, I don't want to be there!" And that would only escalate the harsh, ugly words between parent and child, leaving lots of hurt, heavy hearts, and evil emotions to wound them further.

Parents, to a great extent we make our children what they are. Rufus's parents made him "Rebellious Rufus." "Fathers, provoke not your children to wrath" (Ephesians 6:4). Where is God's love here? Pitiless hail breeds discontent and self-protective measures.

Rufus's parents used consequences—taking away privileges, making threats, and carrying out those threats—in the flesh, often and consistently.

This spirit of the devil only confirmed Rufus that he was not loved nor appreciated, but hated. Tears in his bedroom alone and unanswered prayers to God almost erased any hope he had of a God in heaven who could do anything to make his home life better. Thoughts of running away from home, giving up entirely on God, or taking his own life were common, but as yet he was too young to carry them out. He'd just have to wait until . . .

When a parent such as this finally spends some time with God, letting God touch his heart, their wrongs, and his sensitive nerves instead of focusing on his child's faults and failures, God can give him an honest picture of himself. If you have a willing mind and heart, God will take you to Galatians to see the fruit of the Spirit in contrast to the fruit of the flesh. You will be appalled at what you see in this mirror— if you are honest. If you can trust God, and cooperate with Him, He will lead you to forsake the old ways. The truth will not crush you but will give you wings away from those devilish destructive traits of dominance and overcontrol. Christ will adopt you and empower you as you give Him consent to work in harmony with your free will.

Cast your helpless self on God. You cannot change your thoughts, feelings, or habits as you may desire, but you can control your will and place yourself on the Lord's side. Christ can subdue all the selfishness your flesh holds and show you the course of freedom when you will come to Him. Give Him your wrong thoughts and feelings; let Him cleanse the selfishness from your heart and soul and give you Jesus instead.

"My son, give Me thine heart!" Jesus asks of you. "Let My mind be in you."

If you do as He directs you in cultivating the opposite character traits in the power of Jesus—not yourself—you will find the sweet victory you long for. God wants to transform your all. Won't you let Him show you what He can do with your cooperative heart? And in this way, you will be able to show your child an attractive, powerful God.

Realize that you have passed down to your child the same inheritance your parents passed to you. Control issues, self-protective responses, walls, and put-downs make for a miserable experience, a disheartening life. You can choose to give your child a better inheritance. That goodly inheritance is Christ in you evicting Satan's character traits from ruling in you any longer! Restrain the wrong through faith in Christ and cultivate the right by connecting and communing with Him. In Christ is freedom to serve Him.

"Fretful Florence" saw who she really was one day and at first turned to denial, trying to push unwelcome thoughts out of her mind as she had done countless times before. In the end, she turned to God, asking, "Why Lord? Why am I this way?"

"What is your first memory of being fretful?"

She recognized fretfulness as a self-protective measure developed in childhood. Her parents had harped on her until she thought she'd die. She retaliated by pointing out everyone else's faults so that she wouldn't look so bad by comparison. By controlling others and putting them down, she felt better. Providentially, God had her discover that Satan used her tendency to dwell on the faults of others—or even on her own faults—as a means of separating her from Christ, her source of strength. Thus, she had remained Satan's servant and served him faithfully for all these years.

The Holy Spirit also impressed upon her mind, *"Your history need no longer dominate you this way. This is a bad problem-solving technique you can choose to abandon. You can cast it away as chaff. If you do not, you will perpetuate Satan's torture upon your child whom you claim to love— the same torture you received as a child. Do you want to do that?"*

Florence decided to change and took Christ's loving hand to show her the way.

"Dominating Duke" had a similar experience and chose Jesus although the emotional battle felt like severing a limb from his body as he struggled to do God's will instead of following his old dominating, critical, hurtful way of thinking. The wrong way was still so comfortable. Although the beginning was difficult, it got easier as he persevered in holding Jesus' hand and didn't try to change by his human willpower alone.

Mother apologized to "Rebellious Rufus" of her fretfulness and fault-finding, admitting it was not God's way but the devil's. Rufus listened but remained at his usual distance for some time. "Fretful Florence" was seen less and less. When she reverted to the old ways, it was for shorter periods because she would now go for a walk with Jesus.

God prompted her to tell Rufus he was a good boy in certain areas. He didn't believe it. She told him she loved him. He received it as mockery, thinking "How could you treat me the way you have for so many years if you truly loved me? True love would not do this!" The old ways, attitudes, and spirit were still so vivid in Rufus's mind, and pain came with their memory. But still he had to admit that his mother was different. This brought confusion. He didn't seek God and for a time continued in this unsettled way.

One day Rufus verbally attacked his mother in a tirade of fretfulness and faultfinding, which he had never done before. Then, in this fit of rage, he took hold of his mother, grabbing her by the throat. She broke loose, and rage flashed back out of her eyes. Flashbacks of her mother doing something similar drove her feelings and emotions to new heights of anger she had never known. Just then, God called her to leave the scene and let Him calm her anger. She chose to follow His leading, give Him her emotions, and let Him calm her angry seas as He had done so many years ago to the storm on the sea of Galilee.

"Peace, be still!" These words, spoken by God, work miracles on our thoughts, feelings, history, and old habits. Florence returned to the house calm and peaceful with her hand in Christ's hand, her ear tuned to heaven to know how to gain the heart of Rufus. She was finding peace after so many years in bondage to her old ways. Perhaps, just perhaps, she could spare her son those many years of torture under this fretful servitude. She entered his room with a gentle knock. She was prepared to say whatever God impressed upon her heart. She wanted her son to come to know Jesus as she had.

"Rufus, I love you! I know you don't believe me yet, but I'm determined to show you it's true. Jesus is changing me inside in my mind—my thoughts, attitudes, and concepts. Jesus is changing me in my heart—my feelings and emotions. I was fretful and faultfinding toward you, and for that I am very sorry. That was very wrong, and both your Father and I contributed to creating you into 'Rebellious Rufus' by our actions. We are changing. It's none too soon, son. You are following in the pathway we created for you.

"I deserved your anger to be poured out on me. I forgive you for what you did, and I take the entire blame on myself! If you had killed me, I would have deserved it for what I have done to you all these years. Killing is what you were trying to do, son. Do you know that?"

Tears were welling up in Rufus's eyes. "Yes, Mother! Yes, I was. I vowed I'd never be like you, and I am! Mother, I don't want to be that way any more. You are changing! How do I change? Is it possible for me?"

"Oh, yes, yes, most certainly, son! Jesus loves you and wants to free you from your hate, anger, fretfulness, and faultfinding. We don't have to stay Satan's subjects. All you have to do is surrender and cooperate with God. Give Him the wrong feelings, and He will take them away as you follow wherever He leads you." And they talked through the process in simple detail.

Her son knelt down in her arms and prayed the surrender prayer with a full and free will. Mother cried. Rufus cried. God worked repentance in his heart—his feelings and emotions. It all began at the level of his thoughts.

To hear Rufus tell the story, the change came when he was able *to believe* that his mother *maybe* really loved him. This truth cracked the dike of his unbelieving thoughts. Hope sprang up that maybe, *just maybe,* God was real and could answer his prayers to mend his family. He also feared the rage that overtook him that day; he knew he was out of control and needed help. It was his mother's courage from God that inspired Rufus to be courageous and trust Jesus, his mother's Friend. Trust is the foundation of all correction.

Every child wants to be loved, to belong, and to be accepted and properly appreciated. When your children are secure in your love, your correction, reproof, and consequences will take on a new perspective. You and your children become a team on the same side— instead of being on opposing sides. When you gain their trust and you are *truly trustworthy,* you can influence them to come to Christ and be changed. Then they will long to please you, to obey you, and take your counsel. Children are much like rubber bands—very flexible. When they have sufficient evidence that you are different, they will forgive heaps and heaps of wrongs for the privilege of being secure in the genuine love of their parents!

When we let God work on us and develop a balanced approach to life and parenting, we can regain our child's love. God sees *free-will obedience* as a very valuable commodity. A forced obedience, dominating obedience, or guilt-laden obedience looks good in the short run, but obedience out of fear is all vanity—it isn't real or loving. You do not have your children's hearts as you may think! Love cannot be commanded; it must be earned.

When forceful, dominating obedience is gained, it's like tying the apple onto the tree branch. It looks good to the casual observer, but it isn't real fruit, is it? A fearful or forced obedience is an outward obedience that bypasses the heart. Outward obedience has no value whatsoever; it creates only whited sepulchers—with a lot of death, darkness, and ill will inside. It is the best that humanity can produce apart from God, but it's false and empty. God wants a true heart-obedience with a free will. It is of the greatest value. That is what we parents want for our children!

If we can connect our child to Christ so that he or she is communing with Him, then God and parent together will nurture right thoughts. As the child chooses freely to cooperate with right thoughts, God will immediately take possession and create right feelings to match the right thoughts—and in this way right behavior is born.

Getting the heart is filtering out *my* irritation through Christ and speaking His way, not mine, in a hot situation. Thus you demonstrate to your children that they don't need to get upset and irritated in a conflict, but can work through it calmly. Then when you kindly entreat them to a better way, they will respond more positively to you and seek to connect with your God. Being treated respectfully is the desire of every child, whether he is pleasing or out of control. Jesus is your most powerful tool to mold, shape, and refashion your child's heart, character, and life. Go for the heart.

Practically, parents must deny, restrain, and starve traits like passionate screaming, envy, jealousy, anger, rage, hate, being mean, being a bully, dominating others, or hitting. These character traits are Satan's and show us that Satan is on the throne of their hearts directing their responses. These emotions demonstrate to the parent the child's thoughts. The child has accustomed himself to listening to Satan's voice; he feels Satan's feelings and follows him. We have left our post of duty unmanned, and, thus, Satan gains his strongholds in the mind and heart of our child.

We want to replace these ugly weed plants—under God's direction—with the goodly plants of self-control by surrendering our children to Jesus. God's ways need to be made attractive, and they truly are, and Satan's way needs to be seen as ugly, as it truly is.

Getting our child's heart into Jesus' hand is our most important goal in parenting. As parents, we must cultivate an ear sensitive to the Spirit of God speaking to our minds and offering us an alternative plan to get our child's heart out of Satan's control and in touch with God. We are God's mouthpiece to call our child out of serving sin and self. Then we can be Christlike. God must have *our* heart in His hand before we are prepared for Him to be the General in this battle to gain the heart of our children. This is a warfare, and Satan is our foe!

Getting the heart is putting "Angry Aaron" on your lap, taking a moment of silence to pray for God's presence and wisdom, then looking into his eyes sympathetically as Jesus looked at Peter, and speaking the words God puts on your heart to reach his heart with an understanding smile and no condemnation. "You don't need to get angry like that, 'Angry Aaron.' Jesus can take away those bad thoughts and feelings. You don't like them, anyway! Here is all you have to do . . ."

Now you can walk the child through the process of surrender and cooperation with Jesus, helping him to see God as his Helper, not as an all-punishing, hateful God. Children don't enjoy being angry; they are waiting to be shown what to do instead. They do not know any other way except what you show them. Make following God attractive and beneficial. You can show your child a better way to react to disappointment and frustrations.

If your child is angry because of fear, you need to approach the emotion of fear under Christ. Teach him to give Jesus his fear and to do whatever Jesus tells him instead of being afraid. Reason with him. "You don't need to fear the dark; let's face the dark together, and you will see this fear as Satan's lie. You can trust Jesus that you need not fear. He can remove that fear from your heart and give you His courage. Let's pray."

Now you take him out to face his fears. The child needs to experience the reality that his feelings can lie to him. Again, attribute his distasteful fears to Satan and show him that his safety comes from Jesus.

If your child is angry because you have modeled anger for him, how can you help him? You must commit to letting God have *your* emotions of anger and show you how to overcome. Evaluate why you respond the way you do and make a plan with Jesus how to overcome your anger. Plan what you will do the next time instead of getting angry. Show your child self-control in Jesus. Point your child to Christ as his source of self-control that really works.

Getting the heart is getting wrong feelings and emotions into Jesus' hand and helping the child cooperate in cultivating the opposite traits. Under the generalship of Jesus, cultivate love and appreciation in place of anger. Displacing anger brings love and security.

Perhaps the child has been the one in charge; you have wrongly allowed him to be in the ruling position. Anger can be a form of control. Your child should get nothing for which he cries; otherwise, you strengthen selfishness. Anger can be a form of crying. The bottom line is that Satan has your child and is torturing him through his lying emotions—stirring up anger. It's up to you to set your child free in Jesus. Tell him what God will do for him. Tell him that he is not the one in charge and how he should respond in love instead of anger. Have him act it out.

Your approach and course will vary according to the cause of his behavior. This is why you need Christ. He is the Great Physician and will help you diagnose the *real* problem. He will help you to do spiritual surgery that will remove those harmful character traits, to apply the healing medicine, and to feed and nourish the right. Through your consistency *in Christ* your child can come out of anger. He will love you for it.

If your "Angry Aaron" is already twelve years old, what will you do? If we let this trait grow as your child grows and strengthen as your child grows in strength, you will soon be fearful of his anger, which will grow into uncontrollable rage or a lashing out for your life. The older the children get, the stronger their passions become and the more out of control they will become—under Satan's generalship. Our "Angry Aarons" need Jesus as their Counselor, Friend, and Savior.

"Son, you don't like what you are becoming," Father said lovingly. "Jesus loves you as do I, and we want to help you out of those rages. Satan says you'll be happier expressing your anger, but you aren't; it only gets worse. Jesus, on the other hand, tells you the truth and wants to help you out of all this trouble. He is strong enough to keep you. I haven't always been able to help you myself; I've been angry, too. Let's make a pact, son, to lay aside all anger. You and I will learn together how to do this. Put her there, son!" And Father holds out his hand to seal a pact to follow God together out of anger and irritation. They kneel in prayer.

Soon afterwards, Father said, "Son, when I'm getting angry, you have my permission to get my attention and not let me go down that all-too-familiar pathway of harmful venting. I promise by the grace of God to turn to Him and do something better in place of anger. God will deliver us, especially if we are a team together."

And the son mirrors the commitment of the father. "Will you help me not go into my anger and rages, Dad?"

Under God, and in His power, they can never fail. They become skilled with the weapons of spiritual warfare through repetition. They find the pull of inclination and habit to be serious warfare, but victory comes when they persevere with Jesus directing their thoughts and feelings. The first moments of decision are difficult in the war against old thoughts, feelings, passions, and habits. But, in Christ, they find the power of true self-control. The next battle is much less severe in intensity and duration. Both father and son fall in love with Christ as *their* Redeemer, and thus a genuine love toward each other develops!

Getting the heart is gaining the love and confidence of our child. It's becoming a team together fighting against the common foe. The sense of belonging and being on the same team is a strong bonding experience. What a thrill when Father tenderly calls his son to put aside his anger, and he responds. Or the son successfully calls his Father out of his anger, and he responds! Is there any greater thrill for father or son? Jesus wants to bind us together in Him.

THE LONE EMBRACE
A SPECIAL WORD OF ENCOURAGEMENT FOR SINGLE PARENTS

Getting the heart is playing with and enjoying the children honestly—and telling them so. It's working side by side together in a sweet spirit that draws companionship. It's showing an interest in what interests them—even if it doesn't interest you. It's saying endearing words of affection to them. It's expressing appreciation and teaching them the art of this expression. It's enduring difficulties being a single-parent family and accepting the additional responsibilities well.

As each learns how to express genuine love, it draws the hearts to one another with strong ties that bind. Getting the heart is being a workforce, a family, and a team. Home is a pleasant place to be. All our hearts are knit to serve Christ. Love is not letting your children disobey or remain in bad habits but showing them deliverance in Jesus. You will have their hearts and service for life, through thick or thin, through prosperity or poverty.

Getting the heart is yours for the claiming, and Jesus will show you the way.

Chapter 11

CONSEQUENCES

"Because sentence against an evil work is not executed speedily, therefore the heart of the sons of men is fully set in them to do evil" (Ecclesiastes 8:11).

Consequences are not to be looked upon as punishments nor to be done in the spirit of the flesh. God doesn't approach correction in this way. Neither should we as His representatives here on earth to our children. Consequences are lower motivations that we use to bring our child to Christ. We are endeavoring to connect our child to God to be changed in heart, habit, and life. Consequences are used to motivate the child to let go of sin, self, and Satan's way in order to grasp Christ's way—a better way! True happiness is found only in Christ's *true* way, not in Satan's *false* way.

We need Christ as our General in this warfare against the flesh and the devil. The devil uses unfair tactics that we must not use. He uses force, compulsion, guilt, harshness, anger, oppression, and lies. None of these have anything to do with God. He wants us to use reason and positive entreaty to gain a free-will obedience from the child. When that doesn't work, God wants us to use firmer measures. I encourage you to study those measures in the way God expelled Satan from heaven. See how He deals with his disobedient children in Leviticus chapter 26. This is an eye opener of the right use of firmness.

The indulgent parent, who comes from the too-soft side, needs to see that firmness is love or he will never balance out his too-soft approach. But the parent who is already too firm doesn't need this counsel. You need to consult God's Word to find balance in exercising the softer virtues. You need to add some love and reason to bring balance to your approach.

Now, firmness is not force. To see the proper balance of firmness and love, notice how God uses both. The tender child sleeping on His lap is love. The way He handled the woman at the well—a harlot—was soft, tender, and loving. Then there is the cleansing of the temple—an example of very firm measures against evil. The opening of the earth to swallow Korah, Dathan, and Abiram was very severe consequences that followed soft entreaties at first. When Aaron and Miriam committed the same sin of envy and jealousy, God, in His wisdom, gave her leprosy—a very firm consequence—followed by mercy and healing. We must come to see that the wisdom of heaven uses both approaches. For us to have such wisdom, we need to commune and connect with God to learn which course our child needs in each given situation.

For, you see, God was after the heart in each situation in the Bible. He reads hearts rightly. Some responded more quickly and easily, while others responded more slowly, more arduously, over longer periods of time. Whether it was a Peter, a Judas, a King Saul, or a Paul, God labored for their hearts. If He could get their hearts, miraculous changes could occur. That is why God calls for our hearts until the day we die. To become God's child requires a heart surrender of our thoughts, feelings, ways, and will to Him. God is after free-will obedience in His service. So please read Leviticus chapter 26.

A mother with two young boys, "Tumultuous Tommy" and "Whiney Willy," asked me for help. Her dilemma was a lack of obedience and angry outbursts. Her children would not do what she asked them to do even in little things like washing dishes or in cleaning their side of the room. Spanking did nothing more than increase the tumult. And their home-schooling was a disaster.

We discussed her need of Christ as her own personal Savior in order for her to have the right approach in correction, instruction, and reproof. She needed to understand and recognize His voice directing her soul. This would take time. She was too soft in her correction, wanting her boys to obey out of love. So she would ask them repeatedly to obey and then swing into severe anger and frustration when they didn't listen. She would then discipline in harshness and anger. She did see the need for drastic changes in her parenting practices, but she couldn't grasp giving discipline or consequences in a different way. She had come to the place she was by tolerating disobedience in the little things, by her inconsistency in denying her children wrong traits, and by her failure to train them in good habits.

Sitting in her backyard, we were discussing a plan of action for the next time a situation like this occurred. She was taking notes when "Whiney Willy" came out, pouting and unhappy.

"What's the matter, Willy?" Mother inquired.

"Tommy did . . ." And Willy went on to complain bitterly and passionately. She didn't correct his exaggerated views or restless spirit, but gave him sympathy instead.

"Why don't you just sit down here by Mother," she consoled.

"Whiney Willy's" pouting increased to moans, groans, and scuffing his feet in the dirt. He wanted her to bring justice upon his brother!

"What should I do?" she asked me.

"He needs to obey you. He needs to let go of his grumbling, either by prayer, instruction, or being occupied in something better. You need to ask God what He would have you to do."

So Mother bowed her head to pray while Willy kicked up more clouds of dust right in front of us. " 'Whiney Willy,' come here." She sat her six-year-old in her lap and speaking very nicely, suggested, "You need to do something rather than moan and groan and make dust clouds in our faces. Why don't you go pick a bouquet of flowers for Mrs. Hohnberger or go for a swing?"

"Whiney Willy" resisted, chose not to decide, got up, and continued to scuff the ground. Mother repeated her entreaties for a time until she was at the point of exasperation. Then she said, "This is just what happens every day. I get nowhere. I'm frustrated. What am I suppose to do?"

"You do not have his heart," I replied. "He needs to be taken to Jesus for power to change. You *ask* him when you should be *telling* him what to do. You give no deterrent or restraint on the wrong; he keeps doing it over and over. You need to call sin by its right name, restrain it, and not sympathize with it. He isn't deciding to do the right, which means he has decided to do the wrong. And you are too soft on his indecision. You allow him to remain bitter and passionate. Without a decided decision for God, you will get no change. He will just delay the decision forever, for there is no motivation or consequence for his wrong actions. [See Ecclesiastes 8:11.] Without choosing to do right, coming to God, and connecting with Him, there will be no hope of a change in his disposition. He is very accustomed to you not expecting him to obey."

"Can you show me how to do that?"

"If you want me to do this, then you need to tell Willy that I am the authority right now and that you expect him to obey me. He needs to know I have your permission."

And so she did.

" 'Whiney Willy,' you are so unhappy right now. And the reason is because you are not listening to Jesus, who loves you and wants you to be happy. Instead, you are listening to Satan, who hates you and wants you to be unhappy and miserable. He pretends to be your friend, but he really isn't. To change, you need to give up on your old way and be willing to do what is right. Jesus will come inside of you and create happiness again. You need to be willing to learn. Do you understand what I am saying?"

He was disinterested, unwilling to listen or answer. His mother got involved, and he began fighting with her. We prayed with him and for him. He was fully uncooperative.

"Lord what would Thou have me to do? How can I get this stubborn heart out of Satan's hands and into Yours?"

"Don't give him another chance. Begin with consequences for motivation."

" 'Whiney Willy,' I am sorry you are so uncooperative. By not cooperating you have earned a consequence. Now the purpose for a consequence is for you to see that your bad choices are not the way to go. After you complete the chore of my choice, you will have another chance to choose to do the right instead of the wrong.

"I'll be praying that you'll make the right choice next time. I love you too much to let you disobey this way. You are hurting yourself and us as well in your present course. I am different from your mother, and you need to do what I say so that you can put away all these unhappy feelings you have. Jesus will help you if you cooperate. So you will need to sweep a portion of the garage now. Come, I'll show you." I said all this calmly, but decidedly.

"Whiney Willy" continued his old technique of being obnoxious and uncooperative. I continued to pray to God to know how to get Willy's heart to choose God so that a miracle could happen. My goal was to get him in touch with God.

He was a very poor sweeper. He bent over the broom and dragged it slothfully. He had never been taught how to use a broom precisely because of this attitude he was displaying. He usually got out of it entirely—his mother would sweep the floor, thinking it was easier than trying to get him to surrender and do a decent job. These bad habits were strong. But God gave me an idea.

"Use the law of the mind to show him that his hands can hold a broom properly and that it's easier to obey than to disobey."

The law of the mind is that when a desired object is so firmly denied that the child loses all hope of gaining that desired object, he will soon yield up his will and cease to long for it. Then he will cooperate.

Well, for Willy this desire was to get out of work, consequences, and obedience to mother. If he was obnoxious enough, he usually won.

"Now, Willy, I'm your friend. And Jesus is a better Friend than I. We need to pray again." And we did. "Now Jesus is with you because we prayed for that. He will come into your life and give you power to obey when you cooperate with a will. I need to show you how to hold that broom and how to sweep so that you can do a good job. You want to do a good job; it's quicker and better than what you are doing." I showed him simply and then returned the broom to him with a smile. "Now you can choose to cooperate with me in sweeping the best you can. If you do not choose to do so, I'll have to add another strip of this garage floor to sweep. It's entirely in your control how much of this floor you'll need to sweep. It's easier to obey than to continue as you are."

He pouted, grabbed the broom, and I was surprised at how well he could hold that broom and sweep compared to what he had done thus far! "We have part of his will; thank You, Lord," I prayed. I continued to ask Jesus for Willy's entire heart so that he could taste grace evicting those ugly thoughts and feelings in proportion to his cooperation.

"Address the pouting attitude," God impressed upon my heart.

I gently turned his head up to my smiling face and said, "Willy, Jesus wants you to be happy in your heart—your feelings—but you need to cooperate by good sweeping and by putting a smile on your face. Your pouting and grumbling affects your attitude, making you think the work is harder than it really is. By smiling you will allow God to change your attitude and realize that this is actually easy. God will make it real inside as you do your part. I want this to be easier for you."

He pulled roughly away and continued pouting. His sweeping, which was already slow, slowed further.

"I feel so bad for your choices, Willy. You have added another strip of the garage floor to be swept. Choose Jesus' way, not Satan's way." I said sympathetically.

This is a battle between Satan and God for Willy's heart. Do you see how Satan has stepped up his efforts to keep his captive? He pushes those emotional buttons to retaliate and be in control. He also suggests lies to Willy like, "This lady hates you. She's making you do unfair work. She is a hateful woman; you don't have to obey her." And Willy cooperates with what is familiar. This is what he has been exercising for most of his six years of life. Satan's voice is a familiar voice, although it is a harmful voice to listen to. But Willy doesn't understand this yet. Willy's countenance made me assume this was going on in his heart and mind.

"Willy, is that nasty old devil telling you lies about how unfair this is for you?"

He looked at me in astonishment as if I had read his mind. I hadn't. His countenance revealed this likelihood to me, and I just know the devil and how he commonly works.

" 'Whiney Willy,' God is just waiting for you to try Him so that you can find out that what I've told you about Him is true. He loves you and wants to help you, but He can't help you until you freely choose to follow His ways instead of your old ways."

"Whiney Willy" threw down the broom in disgust. "I'm not sweeping the floor no more!"

His mother came in and gave him another consequence and returned him to me. "Willy, I'm sorry you are choosing to be so stubborn and to believe that lying old devil instead of God and me. The way of the transgressor is hard [see Proverbs 13:15]. Because you got upset and aren't willing to yield to what you know is right, we have to add another strip of this floor to be swept. Now you have this much to do." And I moved the stick to show how much of the garage he had to sweep. "Choices; it's all about choices."

Mother was ready to give up, and we talked on the side. "Don't give up until he has fully surrendered his heart to God or it's all for naught. He has to be convinced by experience that there is no other way! If he thinks there is any hope for his desired end, he will make superhuman efforts to obtain it. He must be convinced there is no hope for his way. Let's persevere in trusting the Lord." And we prayed again.

" 'Whiney Willy,' at the slothful rate you are sweeping this garage, we will be here all night. But I'm willing to stay here however long it takes! Why will I do this? Is it to punish Willy? Oh, no! I know how wonderful it is to be on God's side and how miserable it is to stay on Satan's side. I want you to come to know Jesus. I want you to experience this. I love you too much to let Satan tie you up in unhappiness."

Willy broke down in tears. "I'll never get all this finished. You gave me too much. It isn't fair! I can't!"

"At the rate you're sweeping this is true. But, Willy, you are a big boy, strong and able to sweep lots faster and still sweep well. I won't accept sloppy work. But if you put your will to it, this can be done in ten minutes. Jesus can help you sweep faster—and being happy will help that. Let's pray for Him to help you do that.

"Every need is a call to prayer. Jesus is always right there to help us if we call on Him. Jesus can chase away that nasty old devil so that he can't hurt you any more. Let's ask God to chase away the devil. How about it, 'Whiney Willy'? "

And we prayed just that. Jesus met the awakening need in his heart. He asked Jesus to chase away the devil from talking to him. And Jesus answered that prayer.

"Whiney Willy" started really sweeping. He put on a smile. I encouraged him in his good choices. He fell two more times and had to have sections of the floor added to his task. Then I tested his spirit by pointing out a missed leaf, and he received it as help, not as a condemnation. "Ah," I thought, "his attitude is changing. God is getting inside." Soon the miracle was very evident. "Whiney Willy" was smiling bigger. The sweeping was taxing him, but he was persevering until the job was completed. With an accomplished attitude, he put the broom away without being asked.

A hug and congratulations was a sweet reward for a job well done. Now he went back to his mother, and they re-enacted his original situation. She gave him two options of what to do instead of whining. He chose to go swing willingly, and off he went.

His mother and I rehearsed why our attempt had been successful. God was involved, we used a Christlike spirit and approach, and we continued until "Whiney Willy's" will was in God's hands. It took consequences over and over to motivate this choice. It took perseverance to win against Satan, his imps, and Willy's history.

Simply said, our child must be brought to a clear decision. When he is indecisive or uncooperative, he has by default chosen a consequence. Following the consequence, he is to be brought back to the opportunity to decide to follow your directions this time. This cycle continues until he touches Christ and experiences being changed on the inside like "Whiney Willy." Going over the decision-consequence circle often tests the mother's faith, endurance, and perseverance with God. When Willy yielded his heart to God, Divinity changed his disposition. Only God can do that, so persevere with Him.

What if we had not seen it through until the end? Often, about the time a mother feels like giving up is when victory is near. Weary not in well doing, parents!

"Whiney Willy" tasted grace that day, and that made tomorrow's choices easier. If his mother does not continue going to God and restraining the wrong, Willy will revert to patterning his tastes and character after Satan and allowing Satan to be his master. Why? Because it's easier to go with the flesh than against it. It takes consistency and being in Christ for good to prosper and grow. It doesn't just happen.

If Mother continues to keep Willy's heart in Jesus' hand, Christ's character traits will grow until they are stronger and more preferable to the child than the way of the flesh. So the destiny of our children is largely in the hands of parents—whether they serve God or their flesh. Our children are a product of our parenting for good or evil.

That night, after sweeping the garage, Willy was inspired of God to do a very sweet thing. He chose to go swing and play, but after a little while, he wandered over to some wild flowers and picked a nice bouquet and brought them to me.

Willy didn't feel controlled or forced to pick me that bouquet. It was an expression of gratitude that he was free to obey the right. He liked the freedom in his spirit. It was in Jesus that he gained that freedom, but our children give gratitude to the one they see. Gratitude is inspired of God. So Willy heard God's voice to his conscience, and it was pleasant to obey it.

Consequences are not punishments to hurt naughty, disobedient children. They are motivations for them to try God, to taste and see that His ways are good and right. The important lesson we learn is that in Jesus we have power to live above the pull of our flesh.

How many parents let Satan hold their child captive without a fight to redeem them from his grasp? "Temper Tantrum Tammy" throws herself on the floor to get her way, and the unwise parent gives her what she desires. The selfish habits the parent has let continue are repeated and gain strength. Satan who has inspired this response is your enemy. Jesus and the redemption He makes possible through proper, God-led consequences is your true Friend. Try God to bring freedom to your poor child.

"Screaming Scrappy Samantha," led of Satan, lets out her blood-curdling scream. It negatively influences her family's home atmosphere. For without any God-led, Christlike parent to control, restrain, or use consequences to teach her a better way, this is the family's lot. Many parents wrongly think these misbehaviors are to be endured. Without the right vision of what parenting really is, children and parents perish.

"Fearful Frank" causes unrest in the home because he doesn't know how to handle his fears. He doesn't know Jesus because his parents don't know his real problem is that Satan has made inroads in his thoughts, feelings, and habits. By allowing this to continue they bind "Fearful Frank" to Satan. They wrongly think that consequences are too hard. They do not know that a connection to Christ and right thoughts and feelings are the solution. There is a cost and a battle in coming out of wrong ways.

Then there is "Selfish Sheila," "Obnoxious Ollie," "Deceitful Denny," "Shy Sally," "Hitting Henry," and "Overeating Orville." They are all captives of Satan awaiting the day that their parents will come to know Jesus, find a better way of life, and introduce their children to Him so that they can be freed from their prisons of self. Meanwhile Satan whips these children in his service, forcing them into greater bondage in their sins. Indecision in facing the child's weakness on the part of the parent is sin.

Parents won't you please arouse to help them? Won't you get on your white horse, put on your white hat—the robe of a Christlike spirit—and ride your trusty steed to go in and rescue the perishing, wayward ones in your own family? In this warfare against Satan, we must be willing, under Christ, to come to the rescue of our children. God is the General, and we need to be His soldiers on the battlefield fighting for the good against the evil. Satan has a death hold on these children. Jesus is able to save them, and He loves to set the captives free. Won't you be part of His team?

The biggest cause of failure in parenting is trying to do right without God. The parent is trying to do all that God says—but without His power! In the fleshly armor of harshness and anger, force and dominance, some parents try to expel the devil and evil. "The wrath of man worketh not the righteousness of God" (James 1:20). Other parents don't even try. Instead, they let their children come up like weeds—and then blame the child. Many parents need a personal connection with God to change them before they can be successful in changing their child's behavior under His guidance.

Many parents ask me for ideas for consequences. Consequences can be helpful in certain situations, but never depend upon them to work reformation in your child. Instead, trust in God to reform your child and view consequences as the tool in Christ's hand to bring your child to Him.

Consequences can take the form of work. Typically, conflicts occur over schoolwork, housework, or outside work. Children do not do neat, orderly, attentive, or thorough work. What better consequence than one that exercises the weak muscle needing correction? I also like consequences to accomplish something good rather than having them keeping me from what needs to be done. This way, you don't lose time giving consequences.

We want to give our children time to think, time to talk with God. God is able to soothe the upset feelings they are struggling with right then—if they yield those feelings to Him. I've found that while their muscles are at work doing something productive and they are directed to talk with God, then arguing or fussing are crowded out. It's substituting good for evil.

Scrubbing the kitchen floor, scrubbing the tub or toilet, washing a wall, scouring the kitchen sink or the stove are all good activities that take energy. Natural consequences may involve redoing the dishes that were not cleaned well the first time, or doing extra dishes. You can have them clean or organize a drawer, a closet, or multiple cupboards. Make the consequence proportionate to their offense and age.

Outside work can include sweeping the garage floor, cleaning a messy area, pounding crooked nails straight, or organizing the workbench. We have garden or greenhouse work; double digging a row in the garden in the spring is excellent hard work for especially stubborn hearts. Lawn work—raking, digging dandelions, weeding flower beds, or hoeing—keeps the hands busy while the heart and mind reach out to God. Remember these consequences have a purpose—spending time with God, putting upset energy to good use, and then bringing the child back once again to the decision that needs to be faced.

When a child's pent-up energy results in arguing or being unreasonable, a "grizzly run" is an excellent option. It gets rid of the "grizzlies," as I call them. We would send our boys out for a long run to get rid of that energy, and they'd return better equipped to talk or discuss the issue. We have a driveway that is almost a half mile long—one way. We would have them run half the driveway or the whole distance—whatever we judged best for that situation. They had to do an honest run. If they didn't, they had to run it again. We could reason much better with them after this consequence.

Jesus needs to be the Pilot directing our steps of what consequence will work best for a given situation and for my child. I had to learn to be the co-pilot, filtering what I would do through the Pilot of my life. God knows just how to gain my child's heart.

Another form of consequence is when you use the consequence to cultivate the opposite of the offending trait. For example, having the child write a love letter to the one he has hurt. If one of our boys skipped one of his own chores, he had to do two of his brother's chores for him as well as his own. If a child thinks a small amount of work is too much, then you need to give him more work until you correct his misconception. For slothful work habits give him work consequences that require diligence. For unkind behavior, his consequence should be to do something genuinely kind. For anger, give a consequence to show and express love. For uncooperative behavior, cultivate cooperativeness in his consequence. For unclean offenses, cultivate cleanliness. For lying, cultivate honesty. For fearfulness, cultivate trust. For shyness, cultivate friendliness. For disorderliness, cultivate neatness. For intemperance, cultivate temperance. Every good trait must be cultivated in Jesus.

Let a dirty or undesirable job be motivation for your child to restrain his wrong ways. Let your Spirit be right and remain under God's guidance yourself. Bear in mind that the consequences do not move the child's heart; God does. If we depend upon the discipline to change our child, we will fail of obtaining our desired goal. If we depend upon God to direct our discipline or consequence to bring about change in the heart of the child, we will succeed. Consequences are motivators, getting you one step closer to Jesus until the child connects. When the child connects, miracles happen.

If one consequence does not motivate a change, talk to God about it. Consider adding to the consequence to increase the motivation—maybe you are too soft. Or give a different, stronger consequence. Perhaps your child needs something else. Perhaps you are too hard, and your child needs more mercy. God will direct your steps. God is the great Physician who heals broken hearts, minds, and souls. The healing of our physical bodies after an injury requires physical therapy (consequences) and a soothing balm (love). We are the nurses under the divine Physician, following his treatment program. So use consequences wisely.

CONSEQUENCES

When Andrew was twelve years old, he was in the habit of grumbling when it was his turn to scrub the tub on Friday. In previous years, I had avoided giving him consequences, thinking it was not important and that he would outgrow this as he grew older. What a lie that is! Well, God had convinced me to reform, and I began giving consequences, but they were too soft for a thorough reform. They still allowed self a place to live and be expressed without restraint. Thus I was to blame for the fact that Andrew still grumbled periodically when it was his turn to scrub the tub.

"Mother, I need some soft scrub to finish scrubbing the tub," he said with a grumble.

"Sorry, Andrew, we're out of soft scrub. Here is some cleanser to finish the job," I responded tenderly, not wanting him to get irritated so that I'd have to discipline him.

"How could you do that? You always have backup stock! I don't like powdered cleanser; its awful stuff to work with. The smell . . . " And he went on and on.

"Andrew, you need to make the best of it. I'll get some next trip to town. Talk to God and make it the little thing it is. Don't let your grumpy nature have life," I stated.

I returned to my cooking in the kitchen, which is just on the other side of the wall to the bathroom. My heart was sad.

"Lord, here he is grumbling again. I'm so tired of dealing with this spirit. I wish it would just go away!" I cried out with a heavy heart.

"Sally, to let this continue is not love nor is it easy. What were you planning to do the next time this occurred?"

"Oh, that's right!" I responded in apprehension, remembering my earlier resolve.

God had convinced me that my inconsistencies and insufficient consequences were the reasons that there had been only small improvements over the years in Andrew's grumbling and complaining. If I wanted him to truly get over this, I needed to implement the consequence that he alone would scrub the tub for an entire year! I had had to do this with Matthew. Oh, I didn't want to have to go through this again with Andrew! It seemed so hard and cruel to my too-soft mind.

God's still small voice interrupted my thoughts. *"Is it love to help him out of this bad habit or leave him in it?"*

"To rescue the perishing is love. To motivate him to turn entirely away from grumbling will serve him—and the rest of the family—well.

He will gain one more experience of Your leading, and he will change one more trait of character into one of Christlikeness. It will help him prepare for business life. If he grumbles as a salesman or a clerk, he will be most miserable."

As I thought all this through, I could hear Andrew's grumbling through the wall. I could discern only a few words, but the spirit was most assuredly one of complaining and bitterness. I was inclined to ignore it, to just pretend it wasn't happening. The thought of implementing such a strong consequence was painful to my heart and emotions. Why hadn't he learned by watching Matthew go through this? But I knew what was right and what God wanted me to do.

"Okay, Lord. Give me the strength. I've just got to do this." And I walked into the bathroom.

"Andrew, you are grumbling again. We have talked and talked about putting this bad habit away, and yet you continue to grumble. Because you have failed to choose to do the right, you have chosen, as your job, to scrub the tub yourself for one year rather than taking turns as we do now. I'm sorry you have chosen this, but I can't ignore your continued grumbling."

Andrew began to argue and justify himself. When that didn't change my mind, he said, "I'm so sorry, Mother. I promise I'll never do it again."

"Lord, what shall I do? Must I give him another chance?"

"Has he promised this before during the last four years?"

"Yes, several times each year. But he never can keep that promise."

"Then explain that to him," God directed.

And I did. "Andrew, the consequence stands. Begin right now by being content instead of grumbling. Talk with Jesus about it. Every week, this job will give you an opportunity to choose and make your commitment real. Remember, if at any time during this year you revert to grumbling, your year starts over on that day."

It was a terrible struggle for me to tell him his consequence sweetly and then to be willing to follow through for a year as I promised. We parents need to be strong and follow through until success is gained to help our children get over their bad habits.

Recently, I was reading in Deuteronomy how parents are to teach the fear of the Lord to their children. It says that our children must not go after other gods. "Other gods" include serving the spirit of grumbling and complaining. This is against God's way and will. Deuteronomy

7:2 states, "And when the LORD thy God shall deliver them [the giants] before thee; thou shalt smite them, . . . utterly destroy them; thou shalt make no covenant with them, nor shew mercy unto them."

Aren't wrong thoughts, concepts, habits, or attitudes "giants" in the land of our character development? Giants they are. God wanted Israel to fight the giants and evict them in order to redeem the land and live uprightly for God in their stead. Is Israel's battle any different from mine with Andrew?

I got into the spirit of a soldier in the matter of Andrew's scrubbing the tub. We talked together about warfare; I encouraged Andrew to slay "Giant Slothful Habits," as well as his brothers "Giant Grumble" and "Giant Complaining." We talked about Andrew's weapons in this fight— prayer, surrender, and cooperation with God as his General. We talked about how he needed to be a valiant soldier when he faced "Giant Grumble" in battle. He had to say "no" to him by saying "yes" to God. Andrew was learning to commune with heaven and yield the old ways in order to cooperate with God.

After about six months of this process, Andrew fell into a despairing attitude about himself and life. Once more, he began indulging the grumbling mode while scrubbing the tub. It started small at first. Instead of a smile or pleasant countenance, he was sad and became sadder. Then I'd hear him in the bathroom muttering under his breath. I began to squirm at the thought of following through with starting his year-long consequence anew. He'd been so good for six months. Could I do it?

"Lord, what shall I do? This is hard." I reasoned with the Lord on the side of mercy for Andrew. Another week passed, and it got worse. Satan was regaining the ground.

"Sally this is a warfare with Satan as the foe. Do you want to be soft on Satan and let him have your Andrew?" God brought that Deuteronomy text vividly to my mind. *"Utterly destroy the giants in the land,"* He counseled. *"Show no mercy to them. Smite them. If you don't, these giants will revive, grow, multiply, and kill you and your family."*

"You are right, Lord. It's not love to let this grumbling attitude live. Be with my words and give me wisdom and courage to do this battle for my son's sake. I love him too much to let Satan have him."

I peeked around the bathroom door and saw Andrew with a sour look on his face. "Andrew," I said, "you're restarting your year-long consequence today. The last several weeks, your grumbling has gotten only worse. You must slay this giant in the land of your character development. Jesus is able to help you. I'm sorry you chose this."

After a little while, Andrew accepted this consequence very graciously. But something happened as a result of this situation. He took personal responsibility for his spirit and cooperated more consistently with God. God was becoming a personal God to him. Slothful habits began to melt away in every line of work in the home and school. God had taken the throne of his heart and was subduing and slaying the giants.

During the next couple of years, faithfulness in diligence and industry grew steadily so that by the time Andrew was fifteen years old, Jim and I were counseling him in the opposite direction, suggesting that he not work so hard! His habits had shifted to a tendency to overwork and overdiligence in his hired carpentry jobs. God is able. God is good.

Don't show mercy to your child's besetting sins or weaknesses. Rather, take them to Jesus and do as He shows you to do. You don't have to be an indulgent parent any longer. You don't have to be ineffective in bringing your children to experience a change in their characters. You no longer need to raise children for Satan that are indignant, slothful, indifferent, and rebellious to right principles. You have Jesus, who can make your way clear if you follow Him.

THE LONE EMBRACE
A SPECIAL WORD OF ENCOURAGEMENT FOR SINGLE PARENTS

Take courage from God's promise for your children that He will be the father of the fatherless (see Psalm 68:5). Take courage from His assurance that He will defend the poor and the fatherless (see Psalm 82:3). You can count on God to help you overcome any and all character weaknesses in your family. Are you willing to use consequences to bring your child all the way to God to be changed in heart and life? You can be His disciple, under His guidance, and therefore a recipient of His divine grace and wisdom. The choice is yours, to be in Him—and then, through Him, you can slay all the giants with power. God's presence be with you!

Chapter 12
POSITIVE AND NEGATIVE MOTIVATIONS

"Even the captives of the mighty shall be taken away, and the prey of the terrible shall be delivered: for I [God] will contend with him that contendeth with thee, and I will save thy children" (Isaiah 49:25).

To be a Christian requires a battle to come out of self and into Christ. That battle is depicted well in *Pilgrim's Progress,* the story of valiant Christian seeking after righteousness. He saw the cost and went forward to do whatever was necessary to secure Christ within!

Interpreter took Christian by the hand, leading him to a pleasant place where there was a stately palace—beautiful to behold. Christian was delighted at the sight. He noticed certain persons walking on the top wall of the palace who were clothed all in gold.

"May I go in?" Christian asked.

Interpreter then led him to the entrance, where there was a large company of men—all desirous of going in, but not daring to. And Christian saw why. Staunchly barricading the doorway to the palace was a mob of large, muscular, heavily armed men. Their very countenances threatened hurt and mischief to any that might venture to enter in. Christian stood amazed at the scene.

Then he saw a man that sat at a table a little distance from the door. A book and inkwell were before him on the table. He invited all to enter their names and go into the palace. But all those desiring to enter stepped back for fear of the armed men. Then Christian saw a valiant man come up to the one who sat at the desk to write.

"Put my name down, sir," he commanded firmly. This done, the valiant man girded himself with armor and a helmet provided for him from the nearby armory, drew his sword, and rushed toward the door. The entire body of scoundrels lay upon him with deadly force. But this valiant man was not at all discouraged; he fell to cutting and hacking most fiercely.

Although he received many wounds, this valiant man also gave many wounds to his opponents. He appeared not even to notice the hardship of the way nor his own wounds. The Lord of this place was surely in his mind (see Philippians 2:5). What a focus! With one more lunge forward, he cut his way through all those trying to keep him out and successfully got into the palace. From within, Christian could hear pleasant voices from those that walked upon the top of the palace wall. "Come in, come in. Eternal glory thou shalt win." So Valiant went in and was clothed with golden garments like theirs.

That is how John Bunyan pictured it in his famous book. How many of us are desirous of letting God have all of us, but fearful of really entering in? We thus give opportunity, by our hesitancy or lack of decision, for the men at the door to go to hacking, hurting, and wounding us halfhearted Christians. Often our fears, our history, and even the knowledge of the strength of our old habits are like the giants at the door, causing us to doubt that we can enter.

If we fear to do battle with self, or if we are not willing to do so, under Christ's direction, we are pulling back and will never be able to enter the palace. How many of us let our children come up like weeds, not training them in the art of battling against their lying thoughts, wrong problem-solving techniques, or bad habits? When they are not taught when young how to fight, in Jesus, then in their teens they throw out that kind of religion, for it is powerless! They have tried to change in their own strength—as we have shown them—but it didn't work during their younger years. Then in their teens they see such a religion as hypocrisy—talked, but not lived. We all desire it, but many of us do not truly enter in.

We need to change, friends! We need to be like Valiant, decisive and confident in God. We need to make every effort with all our hearts and minds to get into the palace. Through Christ, we can find that power to live our desires! To be a parent for the Lord takes the courage of a valiant, determined soldier to win entrance. We, too, must put on the helmet of being under Christ's control, letting Him manage our thoughts, feelings, and reactions. If we follow Him, we and our children can enter in, as did Valiant!

Why is such a battle, such focus and determination, necessary?

Interpreter took Christian by the hand into a place where was a fire burning against a wall. A person was standing by the fire, casting much water upon it to quench it and put it out.

"What means this?" asked Christian.

"The fire is the work of grace that is wrought in the heart," Interpreter answered. Remember our heart represents our feelings, emotions, inclinations, inheritance, habits, etc. Hope and power are available to all to do what is right in Jesus—if we will not only believe and surrender, but also cooperate with Him.

"He that casts water upon the fire to extinguish it—is the devil," Interpreter continued. "The devil is always suggesting doubts and fears to our minds that God won't be there for us. He wants to separate us from the source of our strength through suggesting doubt and unbelief. By stirring up negative emotions to match our negative thoughts, Satan is most successful in separating us from God. If we cooperate with thoughts of unbelief, we will stand outside the palace—hoping and desiring to enter, but never actually coming inside."

Interpreter went on to say, "But do you notice the fire, notwithstanding, burns higher and hotter? Let me show you the reason for that."

He took Christian to the backside of the wall, where he saw a man with a vessel of oil in his hand. The man continually threw oil on the fire, but he did so secretly.

"What does this mean?" Christian wanted to know.

"This is Christ," Interpreter replied, "who continually, with the oil of His grace, maintains the work already begun in the heart." God's grace is His unseen presence, making available to us His wisdom and power through the Holy Spirit who speaks to our conscience. We must cooperate by believing, choosing, and following God's way rather than our fleshly way. It's up to us to choose to avail ourselves of His unseen power because God never forces His will upon us. It doesn't matter what Satan does to us, he cannot harm or extinguish our connection and communion with God unless we cooperate with him to believe his lying thoughts and doubts. Christ's grace is more powerful than Satan's power to hurt or discourage. We must be like Valiant and enter in with focus and courage.

"Because the man stands behind the wall to maintain the fire," Interpreter told Christian, "this teaches us that it is hard for the tempted one to see how this unseen work of grace maintains us. Especially when our eyes see the devil's hindrances so vividly. Keep your eyes on Jesus, not on your difficulty. Look to His strength, not your weakness. It is a step of faith to trust and follow Him."

"I see now how the valiant man was enabled to go into the palace," Christian responded. "It was Christ in him, casting oil that is unseen to keep the fire of his mind, heart, and desire alive and undaunted to enter in even against great odds. He fought that good fight of faith and won." Then Christian smiled and said, "I want to go in."

How about you? Will you pull back from fear of the armed men? Or will you say, "Write down my name, sir!" The choice is ours—to enter in or to remain outside.

In the work of parenting, the devil will oppose you as he and his imps oppose all those desirous of entering into the Kingdom of God. But we must see that Christ will work for us behind the scenes to show us how to gain the hearts of our children and place them into His hands. Our dear little ones will have to wage the same battle of faith against the seen and felt desires that are not God's will. It's love to have them sign their name at the door and valiantly fight their fleshly thoughts, feelings, inclinations, habits, and ways in order to *come in.* Yes, it is love, whatever their age!

We have a heaven to win and a hell to shun! To be redeemed from serving sin and self requires a battle to evict the giants in the land of our characters so that we can possess the land of promise—Christ within. We want to shun the giant's rule, dominating us and compelling us to do evil and to follow our old wrong ways. The Lord of this place (Jesus) has given us the right to serve Him without fear; we no longer need to serve the giants. In Christ, we can live uprightly and have peace in our soul. Isn't this what you want for yourself and your children? I do!

To fail to choose to enter the palace is to choose to follow the many who desire to do so in their hearts, but who draw away from going in for fear of the armed men. Desire is not enough; we must be willing to fight the fight of faith and actually enter in, not considering whether it is difficult or that we might get hurt in the process. The difficulty only demonstrates the value of the prize on the other side! Friends, the many never sign their names to be on God's side because they choose to believe Satan's lying doubts and intimidations. They fear to face their old ways, and thus they stay outside the palace! To which group will you belong?

To bring our children out of self and into Christ requires a battle. It takes skill, courage, fortitude, and perseverance in and with Christ Jesus as our General in the warfare. It matters not if others misunderstand us. It doesn't matter if we lose sleep over making plans to make our lives and the lives of our children better. It doesn't matter if we get hurt in the process, if, temporarily, we are not appreciated by our child, are misunderstood by others, or are attacked by those who tell us that our views are all wrong. All that really matters is *Am I following God as He is directing me?* Parenting is not a popularity contest. We cannot please everyone with what we do. I want to please God. I want to enter into that doorway to heaven. "Put my name down, sir, for I'm going in by the grace of God."

Some see consequences as negative motivation because they call for firmness, decision, and positive requirements—often in opposition to the child's will. It's not easy to be consistent in the face of "Whiney Willy," "Obstinate Ollie," "Mean Mark," "Slothful Sonya," or "Disobedient Dorothy." For some time I found it difficult to be firm with my children. But God was patient with me and encouraged me to balance my softness with upright firmness under His generalship.

"Lord," I prayed, "coming up with consequences is so difficult for me. Jim helps me to try to make standard consequences for wrong behavior or habits that are repeated. That has helped in a couple of areas, but there are a dozen areas we need to work on. I can't face another day under the stress of coming up with consequences ten times a day for little and big issues. For me it's a big stressor, and I'm sure my indecision makes it stressful to the boys! Whatever can I do?"

"How would you like to try using a consequence jar from which you could draw out a consequence when the boys misbehave? It would be similar to drawing lots, like you have recently read about in your Bible."

I pondered the idea a little, and it grew. Excitement and joy to continue my post of duty in this way heightened my hope for a better way than I was presently following.

"Jim, I'd like to call a family council tonight. I have an idea I'd like us to discuss regarding consequences." Jim agreed, and that evening we came together to talk.

"You all know how difficult it is for me to come up with ideas for consequences and what a stressor that is for me." All agreed. "God gave me an idea for a jar into which we can put written consequences. Boys, we can pray to Jesus to guide your hand to the right consequence for you in each situation. Then you will draw one from the jar and do what it says as your motivation to change. What do you think?"

"Mother, I think it is a good idea. I'll cut out the pieces of construction paper and write the consequence on it for you. I can fold the papers so that we can't see what the consequence is; that way it will be fair," Matthew, aged nine, offered. Then he asked,

"What will the consequences be?"

"Well, I don't know what they will be. I'd like everyone's input."

We began to discuss various ideas. I was surprised that most of the ideas came from our boys. They were harder on themselves than I would have been.

"Mother, you don't look happy. Isn't this what you want?" Father asked.

"Well, I'm thinking about what is involved in implementing this plan. I'll still have a hard time deciding in each situation whether to have the boys draw a consequence from the jar or not. If I think the consequence they might draw is too hard for the offense, I won't want to use the jar. Then I'll be back into the stress of coming up with a consequence at that moment."

"Mother, why don't you have two jars—one for easy consequences and one for hard consequences? Maybe that would help." Andrew, aged seven, suggested.

"Let's call them the 'major infraction jar' and the 'minor infraction jar,' " Father put in.

For the *major infraction jar* we included such consequences as "One chore for the one you've wronged," "Write a love letter to the one you've wronged," "Write a thankful list," "Write one full page of 'what I did and the evils of it,' " "One dollar to one you've wronged," "Double school work with A+ work," "A half day of extra school work," "One hour of work extra—Mother's choice," and "Grizzly run to the mailbox and back" (about two-thirds of a mile, nonstop).

For the *minor infraction jar* we included consequences such as "A half hour reading a spiritual book," "Fifty cents to the one you have wronged," "One reasonable favor for the one wronged," "One chore for the one wronged—I pick it," "Lose one-half hour of free time," "Write a half page of 'what I've done wrong and how to correct it,' " "No dessert," and "Grizzly run to the gate" (about a quarter mile).

As we closed our family council with prayer, Matthew got up, all excited. He went to get the construction paper, took my list, and began writing the consequences. Andrew went to get two peanut butter jars to put the consequences in. I drew a pretty label for each jar. Within the hour the jars were up and operating. We all looked forward to the improvements these would make in our home life.

Within the next several days I had an opportunity to use these jars for each boy. Matthew accepted his consequences better than ever before—perhaps because he wrote out the consequences. This was great. Better cooperation and a better spirit in correction was balm to my soul. Andrew's experience was similar.

But one day Andrew got real stubborn. Originally, I had decided it was a minor infraction, but his resistance and bad spirit made me consider changing it to a major infraction. "Lord, should I make this a major offense? He is so stubborn and willful."

"I will lead his hand. Can you trust Me?"

I struggled, but surrendered to what I perceived as God's will. Andrew prayed for God to guide his hand to the correct consequence. He pulled out "Write a half page of 'what I've done wrong and how to correct it.'"

"Lord," I complained, "that isn't strong enough for his resistance and attitude problem right now. How can such a little thing ever help him to face his problem or to correct it?" I cried complainingly.

No answer came. So I went through with the consequence without saying a word to Andrew.

The outcome was marvelous. God used this consequence to help Andrew see his wrong in a very special way, and it made lasting changes for the better. A hard consequence would not have worked this reform. The wisdom of man is foolishness next to God's. I'm so glad God is willing to help mothers in the management of their children, aren't you? God can use "consequence jars" to help mothers today.

This change really lessened my stress and my apprehension of giving consequences. Now, I could simply decide if an offense was a major or minor one—and then pray for God to lead us to the right consequence and follow through. It transformed my attitude toward my correction processes. It also helped my boys very much.

If you choose to try this "jar" approach for consequences, make up your own ideas—or use some of the ones we used and also some of your own. It is very helpful to vary how you implement the consequences in your home. One approach will usually lose its effectiveness if you stick to it without change for a whole year. Use it for several months, then leave it off and return to it at another time. If everyone's attitudes are good and the approach is working successfully, continue with it. Let God direct your steps and depend on Him—not on a particular method.

Consequences are to be motivations for the child to cooperate to do right and leave off the wrong. It's to encourage him to realize that it is easier to do right than wrong, that putting forth effort to do right and come out of the wrong is desirable and that God is there to help. It's to encourage them to enlist their will and desire to do right. Consequences should *not* be used to punish them, crush them, or show them how bad they are.

For some problems, consequences work easily and give a quick reward. Others are more difficult, long term, and need additional approaches in order to be successful. It's much like Valiant doing whatever is necessary to enter the palace. A problem may be too big for you. That's all right; it is not too big for God. If we are unaided by God, the sight of the giant may daunt us, but with God all things are possible. Draw close to Him.

One day I became discouraged again about having to implement so many consequences each day. I complained to God, "Lord, I'm so tired of being the ogre in the home. I'm the one who has to dole out the consequences, and I'm responsible for coming up with the idea of what is fair, right, good, and motivating—hour after hour. I'm weary of this *supposed* well doing. The jars have helped, but still I'm tired of only this negative approach. Can't I give privileges for being good rather than just giving consequences for being bad?"

To my surprise, God was leading me through the very question I was asking Him. Isn't He wonderful? "That's it," I said. "How can I give the boys a privilege—a reward for choosing to be good? Can this help enlist their will and cooperation?"

The idea flowered into a lovely bouquet. I got excited, talked with Jim, and then we had another family council that evening to present this wonderful idea to our boys. We like family councils because they engender communication both ways. The boys feel a part of the family government. Explanations are given for why we are doing what we are doing, and seeing that we are giving consequences in love, in a desire to help them, enlists the boys' cooperation and plants better attitudes in them. I recommend this program.

"Well, boys," I began, "I'm very excited. I'm so tired of doling out consequences to you for wrong behavior or wrong habits that we are trying to correct. I feel like an ogre, and perhaps you feel I am, too."

Both Matthew and Andrew expressed their frustration. "Mother, sometimes we feel crushed to the core when we get so many extra chores. So many consequences make us not want to try."

"I want our home to be happy, and yet we do need to change our attitudes when they need changing. There needs to be more cooperation from you boys."

The boys agreed.

"I've liked the major and minor infraction jars," I continued. "They have worked well." They agreed life was much better with the jars. "But surely we can learn from positive affirmation as well as negative consequences. By that I mean, why don't we incorporate a privilege jar as a positive reward system for being good. We can write rewards on pieces of paper and draw one out at the end of the day. I'd like to see what adding positive rewards would do."

"Hey, I think that is a great idea! What would we have to do in order to draw a privilege?" Andrew asked.

Father answered, "Well, I think you have to be without correction that day. You need to be sensitive to God's leading you, and you need to choose to do the right instead of the wrong. There is a battle to fight against self, and you need to be willing to enter that battle yourself—not just having Mother managing you. You have to exercise your own self-government. This will make home happier for all of us."

"Yes," I added, "a privilege is a reward for being good and for not needing correction. But I think you should still be able to draw from the privilege jar at the end of the day if you have had a temptation and struggled with it, but you have taken advice and instruction and have chosen willingly to change your course easily. Doing that is a victory, too. We will have temptations, but I want to reward you for choosing to do right, even if you had initially given in to the temptation. Of course, if you are stubborn and resist reformation and doing right, I think you don't deserve to draw a privilege. What do you think?"

We discussed it, sharing various ideas among ourselves, and concluded that the boys could still draw from the "privilege jar" if they turned a temptation into a victory with relative ease. All agreed. "So what would you boys consider a privilege that would motivate you to change your wrong ways?" I asked.

Thus the contents of our privilege jar became "A foot or back massage for fifteen minutes," "One-half hour walk with Mother or Father," "Picking a dessert for tomorrow," "Receiving $5.00," "Picking activities for family fun for the night," "Receiving $1.00," "Having evening chores done for you," "Picking the meal menu," "Choosing a hiking, swimming, skiing, or canoeing outing," "Having parents do a reasonable chore for you," and "Having morning chores done for you."

It amazed me how such simple things excited our boys. Our children really want only us, don't they? It was cute when Matthew suggested receiving five dollars as a privilege. Jim responded that we needed to also include a one-dollar privilege slip; otherwise, he would go broke giving out ten dollars every day. It was good, natural humor and a great natural encouragement to the boys that we were expecting many victories.

God uses every member of the family as a team. Father is the head and has the final say, but everyone's input is heard, considered, and weighed, and has influence on the final outcome. God gives His input through every family member. Let God lead your family in a fair balance of justice and mercy in your family government.

If you'd like other suggestions for consequence or discipline alternatives, I have an article titled "Fourteen Discipline Ideas" that lists other ideas.[1] My source of all these ideas was God. I was an idea-less person at this time. So if you need more ideas, consult Him; He has a thousand of them and is happy to share more with you.

The very next day after we instituted the privilege jar, Andrew was corrected and became very stubborn as before. I called for his cooperation, reminding him that he wouldn't be able to draw a privilege from the jar if he continued in this way. In relatively short order he put forth his effort to cooperate. And through submission and cooperation with Christ, he turned his temptation into a victory.

The warfare against self is the greatest battle that was ever fought. The yielding of self, the surrender of all to the will of God, requires a struggle; but the soul must submit to God before it can be renewed in holiness. God cannot accept homage that is not willingly and intellectually given. A forced submission would prevent a real development of mind and character.

That evening Jim asked me if the boys deserved to draw from the privilege jar. After considering for a few minutes, I said that both boys deserved a privilege. Matthew reminded me of Andrew's need for correction, and I was pleased to report that he had turned the stumbling block into a steppingstone. The privilege jar isn't for perfect children; it's for children striving to say, "Put my name down, sir" and who then do battle against the foes at the entrance of the doorway to the kingdom of God. Turning to God and doing the right deserves the reward of a privilege.

Adding the privilege jar to our character development program especially nurtured and encouraged Andrew. He made wonderful strides, victories, and changes in his responses to despair by this positive reward. It motivated him so much more than all the negative consequences alone. It enlisted his will and cooperation, and he discovered Christ as his Friend and Helper. Through this approach he felt more positive about himself rather than beaten down and discouraged by the negative alone. Areas that we had been working with for a long time were gaining notable ground week by week and month by month.

In this way our children come to discover by experience that putting forth effort in the warfare against self isn't as hard as Satan has implied with his lying thoughts to the child. That even though it may be a hard work for a time, it is well worth the rewards on the other side of the battle. It's rewarding to learn how to be good in Jesus!

Positive and negative motivations are character development tools to enlist our child's will and efforts. Use them in Christ Jesus our Savior.

"The son of God was manifested, that he might destroy the works of the devil" (1 John 3:8).

Those giants, great and tall, that stand before the door, armed to hurt and impede our entrance, are nothing but paper giants. When you wield the sword of right doing decisively in Jesus and when these giants are challenged sufficiently, you will see them crumble as paper giants. God will work in you to will and to do of His good pleasure. We must come to know Christ savingly. Our human choices must be carried out in cooperation with Him and by His power. In this way we cross over

161

from the self-directed life to the Spirit-directed life and find power to become that living, vibrant Christian we desire to be.

THE LONE EMBRACE
A SPECIAL WORD OF ENCOURAGEMENT FOR SINGLE PARENTS

God wants single parents to come up to the man at the desk at the doorway of His kingdom and say, "Put my name down, sir." Trusting in Jesus, let us put on the whole armor of God (see Ephesians 6:10-18), which is faith, truth, righteousness, and peace. Let's put on His helmet of salvation, and the word of the Lord, our hope of salvation (see 1 Thessalonians 5:8) and have the mind of Christ working in us (see Philippians 2:5). Then, ready for battle, let us charge all our spiritual foes who think they can keep us out of the kingdom, and we will discover they cannot keep us out. Under Christ's banner, God will see us through. Every giant will fall before you as long as you are connected with Christ and remain in Him (see Exodus 14:14).

Jesus will be a father to your children, a spouse to you, and a Savior for all in your household. No matter what your circumstances, your complicated messes, God is big enough for all of it. Come under His banner, and He will direct you out of all your troubles (see Psalms 25:22; 34:6, 17).

---

[1] See the appendix on page 288 for a list of these fourteen discipline ideas.

Chapter 13

POSITIVE ENCOURAGEMENT

"And, ye fathers, provoke not your children to wrath: but bring them up in the nurture and admonition of the Lord" (Ephesians 6:4).

A father came to pick up his little girl after a visit at our house. "Papa I didn't need a spanking. I was a good girl," she reported excitedly. Her father had made it a point at the beginning of her stay to give me permission to spank her if she was naughty. He implied she'd likely need it.

"She surely was a good girl," I confirmed. "You have a lovely daughter. She has a love for the Lord and a love to please."

"Well, I hope you can be that way when you come home!" her father said with a stern, disapproving, doubtful look.

The little girl smiled, trying to speak nicely and be brave. Obviously her father's attitude was a common one in her home. She suddenly broke down into uncontrollable sobbing. I drew this little child into my arms and let her sob out the pain she felt from her father's hurtful words. I tried to soften the undeserving, evil blow by speaking reassuring words to her. I was praying that, by the grace of God, the father could see what he had just done. But he stood nonresponsive to this pitiful scene.

Gaining control, the little girl looked again into her father's countenance, hoping to see love and acceptance. But again his face spoke only of denunciation and rejection. Tears again filled her eyes. The hope for positive communication was fully dashed.

Is this how Jesus would respond to a striving, openhearted child? No! It is said of Jesus that He would not even quench smoking flax (see Isaiah 42:3). And He admonishes parents, "Provoke not your children to wrath: but bring them up in the nurture and admonition of the Lord" (Ephesians 6:4).

Knowingly or not, this father was provoking his child to wrath toward him—and toward God—for the miserable, unfair life she had to live. He was goading her to give up on herself, to think that she couldn't do anything right or good enough. He was so exercised in put downs and criticisms that he had no sense of his daughter's need for encouragement, tenderness, and compassion. This is the *worst cruelty* we can do to our little ones—to represent Christ as cold, heartless, and undesirable. This father quenched the smoking flax of love and hope in his daughter once again. He neglected nurturing her honest efforts to please and do right.

He could have apologized on the spot and gained back his daughter's heart, but he didn't. She just wanted to be loved or appreciated, or at least respected. She would have responded positively even then. Instead, she had to steel her affections from him to protect herself from any more hurt and rejection. As her parent is, so she sees God. If the parent is stern, unjust, and unloving, that is the conception the child will form of God. Why do our youth give up on God? Are they really giving up on Him or just on your version of Him?

This happens to our precious little ones all too often! This is why our children and youth do not want to be hugged. This is why they appear to be indifferent or rebellious and have no incentive to personal worship. We make them rebellious by our treatment and attitude toward them. God will hold us accountable.

Is this you, dear parent? There are thousands of parents just like this who are discouraging and disheartening their children day after day and year after year. This must change! This is not Christlike, nor does it recommend any child to come to Jesus. This is cruelty!

This "little girl" actually wasn't so little. In reality, she was well into her teens. Yet she responded to her father as a small child still striving for approval. How much longer will she try?

How much longer will you make your child wait for the needed changes in you? You can redeem and regain those lost years of pitiless hail, fretfulness, and faultfinding. "Come out of her, my people"—God admonishes us. Parents, we need to look into the mirror and begin the needed changes for our home—beginning with us! Become Christ-led and Christlike and empowered from above.

Friends, I've seen this destructive manner of correction carried out even in prayer. Using prayer as your pulpit to tell your child how bad he or she is, how rebellious and how needy of change, engenders hopelessness. It squelches all attempts to please you, because you cannot be pleased. If the child tries, it is never good enough or long enough; something is always wrong. Moreover, prayer which should be a key in the child's hand of faith to unlock heaven's storehouse and connect him with the One who loves him and is able to make him truly successful, is seen rather as a destructive weapon in the hand of the parent. Prayer like this is the devil's tactic—not God's.

A demanding, denunciatory attitude destroys cooperation and love. Why would you serve someone who hates you? Only from fear of punishment, and what good is that? Our deportment and countenance—both verbal and nonverbal—speak volumes to encourage or discourage our children in the path of right. If they are trying to do right, and you are still indifferent and denunciatory, what does that do to their will and heart? Perhaps your parents treated you that way, and you clearly understand its ramifications. Then you must stop perpetuating this heritage to another generation. Turn to God and let Him re-create you right now!

God will have pity and compassion upon you. He will draw you in and put His loving, character-transforming arms around you. You can come out of self.

This girl had made honest efforts to be good while at our home. We nurtured and complimented her, and she thrived under this positive nurturing; it was such a different kind of parental government from what she was used to. We did not force or compel her; we just loved, respected, and appreciated her, and set before her an attractive example. In her short stay of two days, she fit in instantly. She had exercised self-government, timidly reached out to God, and even took responsibility for her own personal worships. She saw God as desirable, and she responded to Him. She wanted to come to know this Jesus. "He can love hopeless me?" she wondered. "He can help me?" And fresh hope arose in her heart!

She had a strong desire to please, yet she found simple compliments hard to accept. Why? What are we doing to the children God has loaned to us? Where is nurturing? Where is a sense that they are loved, that they belong, and that those to whom they have been entrusted are there to help them?

Parents, we all need to be more like Hannah, the mother of Samuel, in the way we train, nurture, and admonish our children in God's way. Hannah was sweet, kind, and modeled an attractive God. Everything about her directed Samuel's thoughts and feelings to be in line with the

Word of God. Fear was not to rule over him; God would help him out of that. Sassiness was not to be tolerated, but that doesn't mean Hannah scolded or showed any harshness or anger. Rather she demonstrated a calm spirit inside and out—one that her child could imitate. She took young Samuel to prayer and told him of her love for him. She told him that he did not need to be sassy or angry, for Jesus would take that away. In a loving, Christlike way, she showed him how to do right instead of wrong.

Hannah was a very special mother. She named her son Samuel, which means "asked of the Lord." She had been barren for many years, and when God answered her prayer by giving her Samuel, she wanted to keep her promise to raise him to serve God. To do that, she had to be focused, determined, and faithful. She made God real to her son from his earliest moments. I'm sure she prayed and experimented with all sorts of ways to do that practically. She took advantage every day of her opportunities. She appreciated Samuel; he was special, and she told him so often, which endeared his heart to her.

She was truly dedicated. She didn't allow tasks, jobs, or other distractions to keep her from her first work of raising her son to serve the Lord. She cried out to God for guidance and listened for His voice to her conscience throughout the day. She was a woman of prayer.

Hannah also made every common object of their home a spiritual tool to teach Samuel about God. I can imagine that when she gave him a drink of water she'd say, "Jesus is the water of life. He refreshes you, cleanses you, cools or warms you as water can." When she'd light the fire in the stove, she'd instruct him, "Jesus is the cleansing fire that burns away the dross—the bad things in our lives like anger, irritation, or an unwilling spirit. When we ask Him to, God can cleanse these things and burn them up like the fire burns the wood. The heat is the result of burning wood. And a sweet spirit like Jesus' is the result of the evil being burned away from our thoughts and feelings. Come to Jesus for Him to cleanse your wrongs away." I can imagine she rehearsed how God brought the Israelites out of Egypt and into the Promised Land. She made Jesus truly attractive to Samuel.

And so it went. Day after day and month after month, Hannah showed Samuel a desirable Jesus in her countenance, deportment, and positive correction. She restrained the wrong and cultivated the right in its place, lovingly as his helper in trouble. She gave consequences, corrections, and discipline as the Holy Spirit led her until a truehearted surrender was obtained. She took Samuel often to Jesus, and he would submit because he knew he was loved and that it was safe to trust his mother. And he came to know Jesus as his Friend as well as his Savior from self. He found power to change both within and without.

In those few years of training that she had, Hannah instilled in her son honesty, integrity, and upright thoughts, feelings, and habits. Knowing what was right and doing it in Jesus' strength—not his own—was foundational to Samuel's walk with God. He was only about four years old when his mother took him with her to the yearly sacrifice in Shiloh to give him to the priest, Eli, to serve the Lord there.

Hannah was very focused, knowing Samuel would be under her direct influence for only a short time. She understood that those early years are far reaching in character development. If you see that you have dropped a stitch, it is not impossible to change even now, with the Lord's help. Pick up those dropped stitches. Let Christ have your heart so that you can be like Hannah. When God has your heart, you will be able to show your children a religion that is attractive and has power. This is the greatest positive encouragement you can give to your child.

Andrew's greatest battles were against slothful work habits. I considered this character weakness to be like the giants the Israelites faced in the Promised Land. To a degree, we had successfully starved this giant by cultivating energetic work habits and lively diligence. I must have become inattentive, and the weed roots that were not pulled up began to regrow secretly. The little taproots of slothfulness are neglectfulness, inattentiveness, and forgetfulness. I saw evidence of these in little ways, but I excused them as insignificant. Apparently, I hadn't talked with God about it, for surely if I had, He would have revealed this to me.

One day the problem became obvious. Andrew's bed was made, but not well. His dishes were washed, but not carefully. The clothes were folded and put away, but not with care. And then he forgot to water the flowerbeds, and as a result my flowers were seriously wilting.

At last I was motivated to do something. "Lord, what do I do now? This didn't just happen. There were little steps away from diligence, and I was inattentive. The problem is with me. Now, with my failure, how do I deal with Andrew?" And so we talked.

"Do not despair, Sally. Human nature will bend to the carnal way when it is not being exercised in the way of right. I forgive you, Sally. You made a mistake, just a misstep. You didn't see it then, but now you do. Now you can make a change in your management. You need to forgive yourself so that you can go forward and help Andrew."

I hadn't recognized that my heart pain was from taking on too much blame. God is good. He saw my tendency to overly blame myself and enter into the emotion of failure, which keeps me from even trying to help. Then I recalled my recent thoughts of giving up on my son and myself.

"This is Satan wanting to keep me from helping my son. God is right! I'm not forgiving myself for failing to see this for what it is more readily. Okay, Lord, I give You my wrong thoughts and feelings and ask You to cleanse my mind, heart, and will. Return them to me purified. Lord, what can I do for Andrew to help him out of the domination of that nasty old 'Giant Slothful' and his brother, 'Giant Despair?' I know 'Giant Despair' quite well."

No answer came for some time. Then one day Jim and I were going through all of our stuff, as was our yearly custom. Each year we get rid of things we no longer need or want. We sell what we can and throw away what we can't sell. Living in a small home requires us to exercise discipline so that our stuff will fit neatly into the space we have. Jim gave me a box of things he was discarding, and I had a box also.

Jim said, "Matthew would really like to have my compass. Could we use it as a motivation somehow?"

"Why not? Let me give some thought to that." And I prayed.

Again no notable answer came.

As I looked over these discardable treasures, I thought, "Andrew might really like father's watch. It's a bit big, but he doesn't have one. Jim's knife would be a great treasure, too. Maybe I could use these for a motivation or a reward." So I set several things aside.

While I was making supper, the idea dawned. "Why not make it a fun thing? I'll use these items as an unknown reward for facing their character weaknesses and consciously exercising the opposite trait. This is another positive reward. I like this, Lord."

God led my thoughts, and I shared my ideas with Jim. Together, we began by using the lesser items as an incentive for Andrew to face sloth-ful habits and to engender faster work habits in Matthew. If they cultivated diligence and swiftness for a day, they would get an unknown surprise at the end of that day. We made it mysterious and exciting, and they loved it. The boys were about nine and eleven.

I know God was in this, for it cultivated such good things and the boys were so responsive. We had only a few items, so we used them wisely and put much thought into how best to use the two bigger items. When the daily rewards worked well, we were encouraged to require a week's worth of diligence for the knife and the compass, although they didn't know what the reward would be. We wondered if an unknown item would be sufficient to motivate their self-denial and self-control for a whole week. It worked marvelously! Andrew's "Giant Slothfulness" was being starved once again. We were on the right track. But this giant was no easy foe. He was tenacious. About the time we thought he was dead, he'd revive again. I asked God to keep me attentive to this area of Andrew's life and to stay positive in my corrections.

This was great! Life was better. I pondered on how effective these little rewards were. Each year we'd sort our belongings and have a couple more special items to use in this way. It was exciting to the boys to have a mystery incentive. It drew out their effort and cooperation, and they did not fall back much at all. They were progressing and gaining in virtuous character traits.

To encourage our children forward in the Lord is so important. To have the right spirit and vary our approaches keeps them going onward and upward. They feel a part of a positive team rather than on one that continually doles out consequences. They see correction and encouragement as good for them as they taste the freedom in Jesus.

We may not actually hear God, see Him, or at times even sense His presence with us, but according to His Word we know He is right there with us, directing our steps. Looking at the big picture, I continue to see His presence influencing our family in the way of heaven.

Paul wrote, "And I myself also am persuaded of you, my brethren, that ye also are full of goodness, filled with all knowledge, able also to admonish one another" (Romans 5:14).

Next God providentially took our use of motivations to a deeper level. One day Andrew said, "Mother, I'd really like a fanny pack like the one I saw in Sportsman's."

"You would," I replied. "Describe it to me."

"It's the one that had two holders for water bottles, one on each side of the pack. In the center was a pouch to carry other things. It rested on my hips with a buckle."

"Why do you want it?"

"Well, when we go mountain climbing, it would be much better than a backpack. It wouldn't be so difficult to carry water. It would be lots of fun with that pack!"

I felt like God had paved this road. Andrew was now eleven years old. He would climb mountains, but it was not his favorite thing. The old slothful habits of thinking and feeling would press on him the thought, "This isn't much fun. This is so hard!" So for him to say that climbing mountains would be fun if only he had this particular fanny pack was a new attitude, a new way of thinking for him.

"Well you'll just have to save the money you get working for the neighbors and buy it for yourself, I guess."

That evening I talked with Jim of Andrew's love for this fanny pack and how great it would be to encourage him by buying it for him as a motivation he could earn. "This would encourage him to face his fears, inadequacies, and slothfulness. And after earning the fanny pack, he'd enjoy the mountain-climbing outings in a new way. I'm sure Matthew could be encouraged with one as well; you know how much he loves to climb mountains."

"That sounds good! But how would we motivate them?" Jim responded.

"How about if I come up with a chart that has thirty squares on it. We can have each child work on "his" most difficult character trait because this is such a good motivator. Each day that they are successful, they can advance one square forward. If they don't cooperate, they don't just stay on that square—they have to move backward one space. This way the lesson that the way of the transgressor is hard will have a natural consequence and hopefully motivate them for tomorrow's choices. When they reach the end of the board—after at least a month's worth of daily trying—they earn this fanny pack they want so bad. This consecutive exercising is so good for them. I'm excited!

"Positive incentives work so well hand-in-hand with the negative consequences we have to give. I think it would be a good incentive and worth the investment. What do you think, honey?"

Jim thought and prayed about the idea and after a couple of days gave me his approval to go forward. We would have to save money from our budget in order to afford them. I was very willing. We called the boys together to get their response, which was gleeful enthusiasm.

"Matthew, we want you to work to slay 'Giant Foolishness.' Be attentive to God leading you to cultivate thankfulness instead. And, Andrew, we would like you to work to slay 'Giant Slothfulness,' cultivating diligence. In Jesus you can do this!"

"Everyone can be a winner. It doesn't matter who finishes first. It only matters that you keep your attitude right to finish the race and get to the end. Then you, too, are a winner! And Jesus is your coach. Keep your ears tuned toward Him."

"We will, Mother!" Both boys expressed their enthusiasm.

"Matthew, I'd like you to use your artistic ability to make us a spring picture." And I showed him how I'd like the squares, like a boardwalk, put onto this large piece of white cardboard I had bought for just this project.

He drew the boardwalk and made a lovely spring scene around it. We put it up on the closet door in our kitchen, to be a constant reminder. Each evening I would judge whether they had earned a step forward because they cooperated with God, or a step backward because they cooperated with their flesh. We applied the same concept we used with the privilege jar. If they'd struggled but were easily entreated to turn the temptation into a victory, they advanced. But if they were stubborn, they lost ground that day. We did not use the privilege jar at the same time we used this thirty-day game board. I recommend using one at a time.

And so we discovered that a known incentive worked ever so marvelously. For well over a month, Andrew worked earnestly against slothful habits, cultivating diligence, faithful work habits, and thoroughness. When he was rewarded with his fanny pack, he was excited to enjoy climbing those mountains—doing hard things! Andrew exercised these qualities to earn the fanny pack, and the fanny pack exercised more of the same qualities. How providentially wonderful! God is so good!

Encouragement was a key factor in this success. Andrew felt loved, and "Giant Slothfulness" fell at long last like a paper giant! In Jesus, this can be your story in battle against the character weaknesses in your children. God requires human effort before His divine power does the work of cleansing and finally achieving total victory. Andrew had to relinquish his wrong thoughts, feelings, habits, and responses by the faithful exercise of the opposite trait, and one day the lethal blow brought that giant to the ground. Your child's hand in Jesus' hand, led by a faithful, Christlike parent, will do the same. You can be next. What do you say?

I want to encourage all parents. There were many times during the period that Andrew was eight to fourteen years old that I was ready to give up fighting "Giant Slothfulness" on his behalf. The giant seemed to be an unconquerable foe. I'm so thankful that God and my husband kept encouraging me to go forward and try again and find another approach. I'm so thankful I chose to trust the unseen God instead of my tangible eyesight. The continual efforts to encourage Andrew to exercise diligence, skillful work habits, and healthy thoughts about himself eventually freed him from the tyranny of "Giant Slothfulness." As Andrew learned to cooperate with the many different approaches to restrain the wrong and cultivate the right, God worked a mighty change in his character. Andrew could not be the man he is today without this perseverance. And I am so properly proud of him.

God is the victor. Gaining our child's heart, thoughts, and habits is a very important and far-reaching work. It's a difficult work at times, but the difficulty is insignificant compared with the reward—the reward of seeing your children set free from their captivity. It's worth every bit of effort.

I wish my mother had understood this when I was a little girl and that she had worked with Jesus to bring me out of my extreme shyness. So often this type of child is excused or petted in their shyness. This is not love! My shyness kept me in bondage to Satan. By his hurtful lies, he kept me thinking and believing so many negative thoughts about myself. Fostering these habits formed an unbalanced character that God had to work to correct in later years of my life. It is much harder to overcome these deficiencies in adulthood than it would have been in childhood. Whatever you do not overcome will overcome you, and the more familiar it is, the more difficult it is to go against it. In Christ, success is possible, and we shall see in the life hereafter how close to the precipice of being lost we were by remaining under these imbalances.

Mothers, help your "Shy Sally" by restraining her shyness and cultivating her boldness to speak and to answer when others speak to her.

Mother says, " 'Shy Sally,' I want you to say hello to 'Mrs. Neighbor.' "

"Shy Sally" turns her head away from Mother, nonverbally saying it is too hard to speak to the neighbor.

Mother prays and calls Sally again to a decision, " 'Shy Sally,' you can say hello to 'Mrs. Neighbor.' You need to do that right now. You may not be shy now."

"Shy Sally" steps behind mother's skirt, hoping to be forgotten.

"Come with me, Sally." And Mother steps away a little distance, gives a loving spanking, cuddles Sally, and prays that Jesus will give Sally strength and courage.

Mother waits to see Sally's decision. Indecision is still strong, so mother nudges Sally gently toward "Mrs. Neighbor."

"Hello, 'Mrs. Neighbor.' " Sally says shyly and softly.

Mother smiles at Sally and says, "That's very good."

Sally smiles back, feeling better about herself although this was a hard thing to do.

Mother is wise because she has committed herself and her daughter to Jesus each morning and cultivated an ear sensitive to the Holy Spirit. God was faithful to prick her conscience when Sally needed attention in this area. He posed ideas of what to do in each instance. Mother followed God's guidance and found success through repetition.

When "Mr. Visitor" asks Sally how old she is, she recoils into silence as is her inclination. Mother, prompted by Jesus in her thoughts, knows she must work with this situation. Making connection with God, she asks, "Lord what would Thou have me to do?"

"She must answer the question. I am with you; follow your reasoning."

"Sally, you must answer 'Mr. Visitor's' question. That is being a lady. You want to be a lady, so you must say, 'I am five years old.' "

Sally struggles in her heart; her feelings and emotions incline her to believe she cannot speak. She struggles in her mind; her thoughts are fearful thoughts creating fearful feelings to match them, which is a compelling influence against God and right.

"You must choose the right, Sally. Don't believe those lying thoughts and feelings. You can do it, if you choose. Jesus is here to help you."

"I am five," Sally responds timidly.

"Mr. Visitor" asks her another question, and this one is answered with greater ease. The third question is even easier. And the door of victory in Jesus is opened, never to shut again. In time, Sally will come to have a love for visitors and neighbors. Although she will have a nice reserve, she will be interactive and overcome her fears, finding them to all be lying thoughts as Mother said.

Mother's horizon enlarges after these few victories, and she has "Shy Sally" say "Hi" to the grocery man and the clerk before they speak to her. She has Sally talk with Grandma and Grandpa on the phone. And soon Sally is a pleasant, outgoing little girl!

True love prays with the shy child and encourages her to trust Jesus rather than her feelings. True love shows her in a practical way how to cooperate with God's will and believe in His power to free her from her fears. True love requires her to face her shyness and talk with others. Love also disciplines when she is unwilling and takes her around the decision-reward cycle until she surrenders to freedom. In this way she develops good habits to speak when spoken to. She will come to know Jesus personally changing her inside, instead of remaining boxed up in her bondage of shyness.

"Boisterous Billy," on the other hand, has a frustrated mother that can't rein him in. From the time Billy was very little, Mother has let his outgoing nature be exercised to excess. He is six years old now and causes embarrassment multiple times a day. This mother wants to follow Jesus but doesn't know how. After reading a book, she is inspired that there is hope for her Billy. She realizes it will require a battle of natures, that a new course has to be enlisted to restrain his boisterousness and to replace this response with a better one.

She begins by trying to have an ear tuned to heaven for heavenly guidance in her own life and character. After some missteps, she learns that God's voice is simply a thought in her mind amidst other thoughts and that she needs to determine if a thought is from God or not by judging the truth of the thought and its spirit. She asks God to be in her and she goes forward, experimenting on Billy to help him learn this new way, too.

"Billy," she tells him, "we are going to a meeting at church, and you may not be loud. If you forget, I will have to take you out and give you a consequence for forgetting. We will pray and then return to the meeting. It will be just like the quiet times we are cultivating at family worships or the meal table at home. You can do it!" she encourages him enthusiastically. "Just keep your hand in Jesus' hand and your ear attentive to Him. When God calls for your heart, give it to Him. I will be right there with you."

After a while at the meeting, "Boisterous Billy" wiggles a little and says in a more-than-boisterous tone, "I want to go home now, Mother!"

"Come, Billy," Mother says quietly. She takes "Boisterous Billy" outside and talks to him briefly about what has just happened. "I want you to run around the church parking lot three times and then return to me."

Billy does. He feels frustrated with himself. He wants to do better than this. While he is running obediently, he cries out to God, "I want to be quiet in this meeting; please help me, Lord. I just forget!"

"Boisterous Billy" returns to mother. "I'm sorry, Mother. I'll try to listen to Jesus better."

"Son, if you ask God to keep you and give Him permission to interrupt your thoughts, He will be faithful to remind you before you speak. Let's pray and return to the meeting. You can do it with Jesus; I just know you can."

Mother, and then Billy, says a prayer, and they return to the meeting. Billy is obviously trying, but it is a difficult test. Satan is pushing so many of those old buttons—those old thought patterns, feelings, and responses. "Lord, what shall I do to help him other than prayer?" Mother asks.

"Try the replacement principle," the still small voice impresses her mind.

As she applies her reason led of God, an idea dawns. "Yes, I'll have him be attentive to the meeting by listening for key words. He can put a mark under each word I write down. That will crowd out the wrong thoughts and, by the grace of God, dispel the wrong feelings and responses." She prays quickly, "Okay, Lord, I think this is You, and I will follow to see."

Billy does very well with this. It takes only a few such experiences to teach him, and it works wonderfully when he applies himself. A couple of times during the meeting, Billy gets very excited about listening for these words and blurts out a word or two. But he catches himself and silences himself quickly. Mother responds with a smile of success and gratitude for God, for she is seeing her son change before her eyes.

Soon "Boisterous Billy" begins to become distracted again and starts to wiggle. "Choose, Billy. Choose again to say "yes" to God and "no" to the old ways," Mother says, smiling.

And he does.

After the meeting, the adults socialize, and Billy is again tempted to his old ways. Mother puts her finger to her mouth, "Shhh." She winks at "Boisterous Billy" and pulls out a color book and crayons to occupy him.

Billy is beginning to see that Mother's way—God's way—is better than his old way; he likes all this special attention from Mother. Having self-control is a wonderful experience.

Mother restrains the wrong way by consistently saying no to the wrong in a sweet spirit and following through with replacement activities that foster better response patterns. She began this process in her home at family worship, at the meal table, and in daily play activities, and now, in situations outside the home, she builds on what Billy is learning at home. The positive direction, prayer, and a Christlike spirit encourages "Boisterous Billy" toward self-denial and self-control as it can be in Jesus. His character, his disposition, and his responses are changing, and soon he deserves a new name! In Jesus, and under Mother's God-led hand, he becomes "Mild-Mannered Billy." What a testimony to the grace of God and proper parenting!

Then there is "Argumentative Abe." Mother had tried all the above on her "Argumentative Abe" with no notable results; she came to me for some additional ideas. Because of her own feelings of inadequacy and unworthiness, her personal walk with God was not what it needed to be. These feelings stirred doubt in her mind and caused inconsistencies in her parenting. I worked with her to encourage her that God is with her and that she needs to depend not upon her feelings but, rather, on the truths that are in the Word of God. We discussed Jeremiah 32:27; Jude 24; John 1:4,11, 12; Psalm 91; and other texts. She needed to cry out to God and believe that He was there for her.

"You need to model to your children a calm, trusting spirit in Jesus, and in time, they will imitate it as they learn the new program. Are you argumentative like Abe?" I asked.

"Yes, I am," she admitted. ". . . So, I am the one he learned it from?" The idea dawned in her mind.

"Yes, you need to cultivate and encourage the opposite trait in yourself at the same time that you're teaching your child. In place of being contrary and quarrelsome, cultivate being peaceable, being content to let others lead and decide, and enjoying harmony in the home at the cost of not having your way."

"Oh, I desire peace in our home!"

"It will cost you letting go of the wrong spirit of control through arguing. God must have your wrong feelings, and you must take His right feelings in their place. Your son recognizes the argumentative spirit and absorbs that spirit like a sponge. He returns this spirit to you. If you want to get rid of it in your son, you must let God take it from you and work redemption from sin in you. Then you can portray the right, Christlike spirit of peace inside and teach your son how to imitate that."

"Oh, that sounds so hard, so complicated, and so impossible!"

"This is a good thing; it is not as difficult as it may seem. You can't trust your feelings or your past experiences; instead, you must trust the Word of God." And we rehearsed the texts we had just read about the peaceable fruits of right doing.

She took courage from these texts and the hope that doing it *in Jesus* would be much different from when she tried the same methods and approaches in her own strength.

We played Mother, may I? to encourage her and as a way of helping her to gain a foothold of respect and obedience in a playful way. In turn, she could build on this experience to show "Argumentative Abe" that peace and harmony were more desirable than arguing. And Mother would be personally familiar with the steps of overcoming these negative traits in Jesus. This would help her make it simple, practical, and consistent for her dear son to overcome, too.

"Argumentative Abe" argued that he didn't have to say "Mother, may I?" before he took the steps she told him to. We prayed that he would listen, and then we began to teach him the new way things would need to be done.

First, the spirit of arguing must be given to Jesus; this was the problem in their home that was creating unhappiness. In place of arguing, Abe would yield his will to that of his mother and God, which would bring about peace and harmony. He would be happier for this change if he would just trust us and cooperate.

Second, we explained how to play the game. "Argumentative Abe" would be asked to take three giant steps forward. He must say, "Mother, may I?" before he took the steps. If he didn't ask permission first—the cost of not filtering—he must remain where he was until his next turn.

Abe understood, but he failed his first opportunity to think and talk with God before he acted. He argued and fussed and exhibited the wrong spirit. Mother could not reason with him, so she asked God, "What shall I do?"

"Let go of your argumentative spirit, your ill will and aggression. Give it to Me."

Mother sensed that God was with her, for this was true about her. She trusted Him to redeem her from this spirit as she consented for Him to take it away. She decidedly put her will on the side of cultivating the opposite trait—a peaceable spirit.

She turned to her son in a sweet spirit, saying, "You need to deny your arguing. Give it to God and let Him take it from you. He will," she encouraged him. "Face your fears and try Jesus. God's way of peace is so much more desirable."

His spirit of argumentativeness remained.

"Son, you'll need to sit on the sidelines now. You may not argue. To fail to decide for Jesus is to decide against Him. When you are ready, let me know. I'll help you find your peace."

He pouted and went to the sidelines, watching the rest of us have fun for some time. Mother and I prayed for "Argumentative Abe," and soon he yielded up his spirit to God and asked, "Mother, may I have some help now?"

Mother halted the game and took her son aside to pray a sweet, simple surrender prayer, after which Abe returned to the game.

We encouraged him that *in Jesus* he could be different and find a happier life. We told him that we would help him find that joy, that he could choose peace to rule in his heart. In a reasonable time, "Argumentative Abe" began playing with the other children, following the rules and enjoying it immensely.

Mother went home to continue to experiment with God's principles and her son. As God freed her own argumentative spirit, her son gained freedom by imitation and exercise. Mother began to be consistent because she saw the love involved in helping her son overcome this attitude and habit. She also found power in Jesus that she had not found in herself or methods without Christ. When Mother was fully free, her son followed. Mother, may I? was only the beginning. God gave her other ways to exercise the positive traits, and she followed them as well.

In place of the contrary, belligerent "Argumentative Abe," she began to see the fruit of the Spirit—love, joy, peace, and patience. Mother inherited "Amiable Abe" as her son and thanked God for all He can and is willing to do in any heart that is surrendered to His molding, fashioning ways. Truly God is the Creator and willing to help every mother that is encouraging her child to come to Him to be changed.

THE LONE EMBRACE
A SPECIAL WORD OF ENCOURAGEMENT FOR SINGLE PARENTS

Yes, the greater share of the responsibility of raising children for God typically rests upon the mother in the home. It's her sphere of influence, her duty under God. The father is out of the home making the livelihood while the mother forms the child's character at home. Take courage, because many mothers who have spouses also feel alone in this responsibility of character development, just like you. But whether you are the single mother or the single father, the principle is the same— you are the single responsible party for this task.

God will be there for you! His power awaits your request and cooperation. You need never give way to despair again for the hardness of your life. For God will supply your needs in your character, in your health, in your attitude, or even your disposition in the moment. He can cleanse away the evil and implant His good.

He can and will help you with your finances if you cooperate. Didn't He provide never-failing oil for the widow and her two sons? Notice, the blessing didn't come until they did what He asked them to do. Truly, He is there for you! When you are at your wits' end, He will give you strength and wisdom for the task of nurturing and admonishing your children in a Christlike spirit—if you cry out to Him. He will bless all that you put your hand to. And He will make up the difference where you lack. God can be a Parent to you, encouraging you forward. May you look to Him—the Author and Finisher of your faith—and encourage your children as Christ encourages you!

Chapter 14

MY CHILD'S WILL

"A new heart also will I give you, and a new spirit will I put within you: and I will take away the stony heart out of your flesh, and I will give you an heart of flesh. And I will put My spirit within you" (Ezekiel 36:26, 27).

For parent and child alike, walking with Christ means letting Him get down to the heart of the matter, which is our thoughts, feelings, emotions, motives, and dispositions. Jesus wants all of our heart; He is knocking at our heart's door. Our *will* is the doorway that gives Him permission to enter. God will not force entrance; He wants to be invited into our lives through our free-will choice.

When Matthew was about eleven years old, we had just completed a math lesson on the conversion of English measure to metric and metric to English. The textbook taught a formula to use in making these conversions, and I spent extra time explaining the importance of following this formula. At first, the exercises were easy in order to develop competency, but more difficult problems would soon follow in the next lessons. Matthew went upstairs to my bedroom to do his written work.

When he brought me his lesson for correction, I saw he had written down the correct answers, but there was no work using the formula. "Matthew, did you use the formula or just your head?"

"Just my head, Mother; they are so easy."

"Matthew, you don't understand how important it is to gain the habit of using the formula. You need to use the formula with the easy problems so that you will be comfortable using it with the difficult problems later."

He didn't look convinced or interested. "Trust me that this is so! I want you to redo these last ten story problems showing me the conversions using the formula written out each time. I need to see you using the formula," I said with a kindly smile.

He redid the work, but his heart was obviously not in it.

The second day was similar. He resisted using the formula because he knew the answer without it. "Mother, it's easy! I don't need that silly formula."

"Matthew . . . " I reasoned with him as I had the day before, but he didn't really surrender. "Son, you need to pray to Jesus to ask Him what He'd have you to do. You must surrender to do what is right. Let's pray."

We knelt and prayed to Jesus. Matthew said all the right words but *without a will*. Outwardly, he was complying, but inwardly he was not agreeing nor surrendering.

Hindsight showed me that he was verbally inviting Jesus into his heart, but he was holding the door closed with his unsurrendered will. He was still going to do it his way. And thus Jesus could not come to reason with him or to clean up and change his thoughts. Jesus will not come in against our will or force His reasoning upon us. He wants us to make a free-will choice to seek and serve Him. I could only conclude that Satan had Matthew's heart since God did not!

"Lord, what will Thou have me to do?" I inquired (see Acts 9:6).

No clear answer came. So, I decided there was nothing more I could do for the present.

The third day things got more intense. Without asking Jesus, I tried harder to convince Matthew of the need for using the formula. Exasperated in the flesh, I gave up trying, not knowing what else to do. How sad that I left God out!

The next day was different. I prayed, and God calmed my emotions as I yielded them to Him. All fretfulness was gone! I cooperated by being willing to do whatever He might ask—to be used or not used. And God reasoned with me thus:

"Don't help him figure out his problems and get into an argument about the formula. Let experience be his teacher. Let him wrestle through correcting the wrong answers. Don't be anxious that he is learning wrong methods. When he is ready to learn the right way, you will have his ears and his heart. Then you can teach aright."

I concluded that Matthew would just have to learn by experience. "I'll give him room to do that," I said. "It'll only be a matter of a little time." Since this seemed all right with God, it was all right with me. In this way God gave me a clean heart and took away my stony, fleshly heart. I had an unusual peace although my situation was as yet unresolved. I was trusting in God to work it out and willing to be used when He called me. It took several more days before the problems became hard enough that Matthew's mental math was insufficient. His work became increasingly more frustrating. He worked hard and long, and his answers were most often wrong, and correcting them seemed impossible with the mental process he was accustomed to using.

Frequently, I had to reaffirm my commitment to God to be silent until He called me to speak. When the temptation came to be frustrated, I'd submit it to Him and gain peace in my heart and emotions again. It wasn't easy, but in hindsight I see how good it was for me.

Sure enough, Matthew's frustration at not being able to solve the problems accurately finally peaked. Now he *wanted* help. God restrained me from saying "I told you so." Instead, I took him back to the formula and in a kindly manner explained the process simply. He tried to apply it to the present problems, but it was confusing.

I was talking to God while watching him grimace, and the answer dawned in my mind. I responded, "What we need to do, Matthew, is for you to establish the mental habit of using these formulas. So you'll have to go back to the beginning of this new section and do each lesson using the formula in order to gain that habit."

"But, Mother, that will put me behind my schedule! I've already done all those lessons," he replied anxiously.

"You haven't learned the lesson, though, Matthew. I looked over your entire schedule, and you will finish your math earlier than your other subjects, so it will be all right for you to take more time in math. This won't delay your completing your schoolwork for the year. In fact, if you want to, you can just do an extra lesson here and there and make up your time. Look at it as a little thing."

I saw Matthew struggling with his thoughts and emotions, so I responded with encouragement. "All you have to do is give those nasty feelings and frustrating thoughts to Jesus. He will clean up that room in your heart. When you invite Him in, He will take away that stony heart and give you His heart and His spirit of courage. Just yield your will, giving God free entrance into your heart, then freedom is yours! It's simple."

How lovely to watch him reach out to God and yield his will to God's will. Then he reached out for my hand. I took it, and we walked over to the couch to kneel down to pray. He said a lovely simple surrender prayer with a commitment to cooperate with God to redo each math lesson properly, using the formula.

What a blessing is ours when God is our Guide and General in this warfare against sin, self, and Satan! I cannot judge aright if my child needs a challenge now or if an issue needs to be left alone for a while. But God knows! I just need to seek and follow Him.

It is through the will that sin retains its hold upon us. Therefore our efforts to develop the character of our children need to focus on the will and the heart first of all. Through Jesus we will label or diagnose the problem more accurately. Then as we deal with the thoughts, feelings, and attitudes of our children through Christ, we will gain their right behavior and habits in the end. This heart work goes far deeper than just outward compliance and brings lasting changes.

Our children hear the voice of their flesh casting its vote of what they should think, feel, and how they should respond. They hear the voice of God casting its vote in similar fashion. These two votes oppose each other. The exercise of their will is casting the deciding vote of which way they will go. Our children have a bundle of choices every day, showing their choices to follow in God's way or the way of their flesh in their thoughts, feelings, responses, and behavior.

Walking with Christ means to give wrong thoughts, feelings, habits, and inclinations to God for Him to cleanse and return them to us purified. We need divinity to make our human effort effective, and yet, God cannot change us without our cooperation. All the power of heaven is neutralized without our cooperation, for God never forces us. A free-will obedience is the only valuable obedience.

For example, if we frown and yell at our child for him or her to sit down—and they sit down—what have we gained? Obedience? No! This is not God's free-will obedience; it's Satan's blind obedience. It says the child has no choice! This is forceful compulsion. It is Satan's form of parental government and not God's at all.

Have we gained their heart? Or are they sitting down out of fear because we are bigger and stronger? Have they exercised their will to God, surrendered to reason of their own free will? Have they cried out to God to change them inside? If not, Christ cannot change them inside because God never forces us against our will!

So what have you done? You have raised up robotic tin soldiers that follow your demanding commands outwardly while inwardly they are disobedient. In their minds they are standing up, not sitting down. You have lost love and trust! You have gained outward compliance without their heart. You have pushed them from you and from your God. The only god they know is you. You have usurped God's position. Jesus would never treat them this way. So they long for the day you—the Hitler—can't push them around anymore. Resentment for your unfair treatment is planted and growing. So what have you gained? Nothing! You have lost much!

Let's look at two more views of what blind obedience looks like.

"Dreaming again!" Mother says with disgust. "Well, you will just have to sit here until you finish your schoolwork. You will miss out on evening family time if you continue this way. You have the laziest brain of anyone I know. I have done everything I could to help you! And look at you, sitting there with no reply. Ugh! There is no hope for you! I'll just leave you to yourself." And she leaves, slamming the bedroom door.

Think emotionally. If you were talked to like that, what would that do to you? The one who supposedly loves you doesn't see you have a problem and are struggling. She doesn't want to help you. You are just a bother! Fretfulness and faultfinding ring in your ears.

This does no one any good—neither the parent nor the child. It demeans the child and pushes him into a hopeless condition. Hearing your denunciatory labels is like an emotional scourging. The child takes it in and is compelled to live it out as though it is true—even if it isn't! This cripples your child, paralyzing his decision-making processes. You think you are working for God, but the truth is you are assisting the devil, using his tactics of force and violence (see Matthew 11:12).

Instead of enlisting the will of the child on the side of Christ, this mother is aiding the evil angels in their work of shutting the child in a poisonous, stupefying atmosphere. She is pushing the emotional buttons of fear, defiance, or stubbornness, yet expects to see results in good behavior. How unreasonable!

Now Father comes in with yet another negative approach.

"You lazy-brained Lucy! I want you to stop that right now!" Father demands. "If you don't get that lesson done in the next ten minutes, I'll give you a good tanning with my belt! If you have any sense about you, you'll get it done now! Mother is so distraught about your slowness; you ought to be ashamed of yourself." And out he storms.

Lucy finishes the lesson in a hurry. She is so nervous her numbers are sloppy, but it's done. Her heart is beating fast for fear of the whipping; she remembers the last one and how she vowed she'd never get another. Hate and fear are compelling her. She delivers her math book to mother, and after she stepped into the kitchen for a drink of water, she overhears her father say, "Mother, you aren't firm enough with her. I always get obedience from her." And he lays a heavy guilt trip on his wife, not to mention his daughter.

The truth is, Lucy doesn't understand her lesson. All her answers are wrong, and so she has to face this lesson again the next day compounded with a sense of painful hopelessness.

Again, put yourself in her shoes and feel the emotions engendered here. Does this kind of obedience have any value? I dare to say unequivocally, no! Lucy was never asked if she understood the math concept, and she was paralyzed by fear of doing it wrong. She tried and tried to understand it herself, but couldn't. She didn't dare ask her mother a question because she knew she'd get a hammering about her stupidity rather than practical help. She feared her mother would adopt father's approach, and what would she do then?

To all outward appearances, looking at the thoughts, feelings, or emotions isn't necessary. Didn't the father gain a quick obedience? But evaluate what is developing in Lucy's heart—her thoughts and feelings, which are her character. Is she drawn to the parent or repelled? Is she drawn to know Jesus, or is He just another unloving, unfair parent? Ezekiel 34:4 says, "With force and with cruelty have ye ruled them!"

Now let's look at what exercising the will of our child looks like and contrast it to the blind obedience exemplified above. We want to see a distinction between *outward* obedience in the flesh and *inward* obedience through Christ by faith.

"Lord, my little fellow is having real trouble concentrating. His mind wanders. He thinks he can't do math or English. His despair is awful. It appears his brain is so lazy and all my instructing, praying, and disciplining seem to do nothing. A book I read recently helped me to realize that I have been doing it without You. I want to change that right now. Teach me, Lord. I claim John 6:45 and trust You will do this for me. What can I do for my 'Brainless Bruce'? "

"He needs to come to Me that he may have life and have it more abundantly. Teach him of Me in his personal worship—and you need to begin to have family worships regularly. He needs to call upon Me to cleanse his wrong ways of thinking and replace them with new good ones. Train him that when he cooperates, I will change him inside and that he will be happier than when he followed the old way of thinking. Explain to him the exercise of his will so that he will understand in practical terms how to do

that. I am knocking at his heart's door. Teach him how to come to Me and abide in Me."

The mother begins right away. Ideas flow into her mind as she puts forth effort for some guidelines for his personal worship. Bruce is eight years old. She begins by having him read a good book about the life of Jesus written for children. Then she reads to him the Bible account of the same stories.

Bruce identifies with Jesus and feels sorry for Him when His brothers treat him wrong. He sees Jesus' love for others when He comforts others that his brothers had hurt, just moments before. In his studies, Bruce recognizes more and more how much Jesus loves everyone. He heals the leper, the blind, the lame, the demoniac. From this study, Bruce's attention span increases and a longing to be like Jesus is born.

Nighttime prayers become a new custom. He likes talking to Jesus. He likes his mother or father beside his bed at night and the "tuck in" that follows. He feels secure, warmed, and loved inside. God is becoming more real. He likes the story of Samuel and hopes one day God will talk to him, too.

Mother talks with God every day—sometimes very often throughout the day as situations come up with Bruce and his forgetfulness. Another idea dawns, and she implements it right away, excited for what Jesus might do for her Bruce.

"Bruce, you are a bright boy! I love you very much. You are very special."

"I am? No, I'm not. I'm forgetful. I can't do school without dreaming or forgetting the problem I'm on. Over an over again I have to review my problems. I'm no good!"

"Bruce you don't have to stay that way. I have an idea to bring you out. Jesus gave me this idea. You can remember very well; I just have to train your brain. I need your cooperation. And Jesus will help you remember better.

"This is how it works. I'll send you into the root cellar to get three things. So I want you to raise three fingers to remember you need three things. You repeat them all the way there and ask Jesus to help you remember them. If you remember two and forget one, just stop and ask Jesus to help you remember. While you are trying to remember, Jesus will bring it to your mind. He loves to help you."

"Bright Bruce" she named him. "I want you to get me a quart of peaches, a quart of strawberries, and a can of olives. Now, say 'peaches, strawberries, and olives.' 1-2-3.'"

Bruce goes off to the root cellar about ten feet from where they stood, repeating his list out loud. He remembers two items, and Jesus does remind him of the third thing after Bruce puts in a bit of effort in recall. He returns with glee. "Mother! Mother! Jesus talked to me. I mean He thought with me. I mean He helped me remember. I didn't hear his voice with my ears, but I heard Him with my heart! Oh, Jesus loves me!"

Mother repeats the "three item recall sequence" in this fashion over and over, and when that seems easier for Bruce, she increases the items to four, then five, and six. Bruce is becoming very bright in recall. He begins memorizing Scripture and improves more. His will is decided for God, and his actions are cooperating.

Then in math class, his worst subject, he falls down. His countenance says "poor me," and "Giant I-Can't-Do-This" looms up before him to crush him. He is going down the road of hopelessness into the slimy pit of despair. He is being obedient to these lying thoughts and feelings about himself. Now his will is engaged negatively.

"Oh, Bruce, what is happening? Are you going into that nasty old pit of 'woe is me' "?

"Nothing works for me, Mother." He pours out all his negative feelings. "It's all true. I can't do math. I try and try. I'm still daydreaming. It'll never change!"

"Stop thinking those thoughts, Bruce; they are not true!" Mother says with caring firmness. "You just need to call on God, and He will help you think good thoughts. He helped you remember the items I sent you for. You can do it Bruce!"

His silence is a nonverbal way of saying "No, I don't agree." He is yielding to fleshly thoughts and feelings, and the flesh is ruling him cruelly.

"Bruce, I will not let Satan have you. Jesus will bring you out of this, but not without your willing effort. You have a choice, and you don't have to go this way. You can choose to follow Jesus. You can do your math. In Jesus, you can be that bright boy you want to be; He has all the power you need! Listen to Him who loves you."

Bruce will not cooperate.

"Lord, what shall I do now?"

"Call him to a decision and give him a reasonable time to make that decision—not too long and not too short. Give consequences as necessary."

"You can choose to be 'Bright Bruce' instead of 'Brainless Bruce.' You don't have to despair with Jesus here. Cry out, and He'll help you. Let's pray."

Mother nudges Bruce to come pray, and he resists. She nudges him again, and the resistance increases. She knows what she has to do. "Oh, my dear, sweet Bruce. I'm so sorry you don't choose to come to Jesus. He loves to help little boys, and He is so powerful. You have chosen to believe the devil and follow his lies instead. Satan is your enemy, not your friend. I'm so sorry you chose a consequence."

Bruce responds with increased resistance. You can see the challenge in his eyes. "You can't make me!" Fear engenders stubbornness and self-protection measures.

"This is a hard way, Bruce. I want you to say, 'The way of the transgressor is hard.'"

He refuses to say it.

"Your consequence will need to be a grizzly run to the mailbox. Bruce, I love you. Don't let Satan take you so easily. Satan likes to hurt you with this kind of thinking. Talk to Jesus, and He'll talk to you and help you out of all your troubles."

The rule in the home is that when sent on a grizzly run, there is to be no questioning or arguing. A grizzly run is meant to get the grizzlies out. Bruce goes.

"Lord, what should I do when he returns?"

"I will be with your mouth. Sympathize with him, but be consistent, not wavering."

Bruce returns and breaks down, crying, "I'm sorry, Mother. I'm such a bad boy. I can't do anything right."

"What happened on your run?" She puts her arm across his shoulders gently.

"I talked with Jesus, and He said He'd help me. But I don't know how to let Him."

"Let's pray so that Jesus can evict Satan from your thoughts and feelings. You will need to be willing to do whatever He asks you to do. Are you willing now?"

"Yes, Mother, I am." Bruce is sweetly repentant. He is calm, but sad.

This time Bruce cooperates, and they pray, "Take my wrong thoughts, my wrong feelings, and my will. Lord, cleanse them as only You can. I'm willing to do Your will, whatever that may be."

"Say 'Jesus loves me.' " And Bruce repeats it.

"Now, say 'I can do my math with Jesus at my right hand. I need not despair.' " And he repeats it, cooperating by thinking these good thoughts.

Mother helps him with his first story problem, and they cry out to God for wisdom. God gives Bruce the idea that provides the key to the solution of the problem. And so Bruce is like the Little Red Caboose going up the hill, problem by problem. The fuel that powers Bruce to the top of that hard hill is the grace, power, and presence of God empowering his choices and transforming his thoughts and feelings. Christ works redemption in him, beginning with his thoughts. Christ can come in because the door has finally been opened.

From that day forward, Bruce was never the same. A system was established to help him come to know God intellectually in His Word, and trials caused him to pray so that he came to know God experientially. Through the exercise of Bruce's will, God did an inner cleansing work to change his thoughts and feelings to the side of true and good. He tasted both sides and made a conscious choice to serve God in His power. It was a free-will choice. It was not forced. Mother had wisely reasoned with Bruce to incline him to God and had given him consequences when necessary, but always in love and kindness.

Bringing your child to a free-will choice may take longer at the beginning of the learning process, but you gain something of value. You gain his heart, love, respect, loyalty, and appreciation toward you. You gain a free-will obedience, and your child is coming to know a personal God that saves him from self. God is good! Bruce's memory became great; his math excellent; and his heart free! Amen!

This experience can become the experience of anyone with a lazy brain. It takes only a parent under the influence of the Holy Spirit, willing to exercise her will to do God's will that she may bring her child to God to find the same freedom against his flesh that is active in the moment. God will personally teach you. To God be the glory!

Matthew 5:13 says, "Ye are the salt of the earth: but if the salt have lost his savour, wherewith shall it be salted? it is thenceforth *good for nothing*, but to be cast out, and to be trodden under foot of men" (italics supplied). Salt without its flavor has no value. All forceful or fretful parenting is like flavorless salt.

The flavor of the salt is Jesus indwelling in us. Without Him, we can do nothing (see John 15:5). In the Old Testament ritual service, salt was added to every sacrifice. This, like the offering of incense, signified that only the righteousness of Christ could make the service acceptable to God. Referring to this practice, Jesus said, "Every sacrifice shall be salted with salt. . . . Have salt in yourselves, and have peace one with another" (Mark 9:49, 50). All who would present themselves a living sacrifice, holy, acceptable unto God (see Romans12:1) must receive the saving salt, the righteousness of our Christ. Then they become "the salt of the earth," restraining evil among men just as salt preserves from corruption. But if the salt has lost its flavor, if there is only a profession of godliness, without the love of Christ, there is no power for good. Such a life can exert no saving influence upon the world. "Your energy and efficiency in building up My kingdom," Jesus says, "depends upon your receiving My Spirit. You must be partakers of My grace in order to be a savor of life unto life." Then there will be no rivalry, no self-seeking, and no desire for the highest place. You will have that love from heaven when you ask and cooperate!

A sweet mother was sharing with me her frustration in getting her son to submit his will to God. She expressed a lovely principle we all need to see and understand."Sometimes my son is rather dead spiritually," she told me. "His behavior begins to stink, just like Lazarus in the tomb after four days. In my humanity, I grieve and try to deal with the behavior and even reproach the Savior for not intervening before my son got into this place of stubbornness.

"When I consulted with Jesus, He told me to 'take away the stone.' The 'stone' is anything that comes between Jesus and my son. It may be the fact that quiet communion time with God gets crowded out of his day for one reason or another. It may be wrong thinking or bad attitudes driving his behavior. Whatever it is, God knows what is obstructing the way between Him and my son. And He wants to use me as His instrument.

"Under His direction, I can 'take away the stone,' and then Jesus can speak new life into me, first, and then into my son, as He did for Lazarus. It really works! You have said it in so many different ways, Sally; this is just another way of picturing the truth in my mind that our goal is not mere behavior modification or outward compliance, but character development through the exercise of our child's will in cooperation with God.

"We want to bring our children into direct contact with the Creator who can change them on the inside! The secret is union and communion with God. When my son's heart is in Jesus' hand, it quickens in that new life."

Are you cooperating with God to "take away the stone" that is keeping your children from knowing Christ as a personal God?

As our wills cooperate with the will of God, they become omnipotent. Whatever is to be done at His command may be accomplished in His strength. Do you think some supernatural element will be brought into your life, lifting you out of self into a higher sphere where it will be comparatively easy work, without any special effort, any special fighting, without any crucifixion of self? All who dally here will perish. Parent and child each have a part to play in their salvation from self.

Walking with Christ is putting my will on His side, my hand in His, and doing His will in His strength. This is very different from doing it in self. Without the exercise of faith in Christ—a choice, a surrender, and a cooperation—it is impossible to please God.

We were doing math. While I was helping Matthew gain his new concept for the day, Andrew was having difficulty understanding his lesson, but I hadn't noticed, and he wasn't asking for help. After a time I looked up with a bright comment to Andrew only to see he was in discouragement and despair. His countenance was extremely sad. From experience I sensed he was putting himself down and ready to give up.

"Andrew, do you need help?" I asked.

"I can't do it. I just can't do it. Math comes easy to Matthew. Everything comes easy to him! But for me, I can't." Nine-year-old Andrew was so frustrated.

"Now, Andrew, I don't want you to be discouraged. Reread your lesson and see if you can grasp the concept better." I thought that if I could get him positively involved, the negative, lying thoughts he was rehearsing would be crowded out. I knew by personal experience what it is like to be on this path and that the battle required him to turn around his thinking.

He didn't answer me. He just put his head into the crook of his bent arm and stared at his book and his paper. He sighed.

"Oh, Lord, he is dwelling on how bad he is and how he can't learn his lesson. Whatever can I do to get his mind off this? I can't leave Matthew right now; we are very close to having him grasp his new concept."

"Call Andrew's will into action. Send him out for a bike ride. The physical can help the mental and spiritual mind."

"Andrew, I don't want you to think those destructive thoughts about yourself. You must say "no" to them and say "yes" to God, instead. Do it with a will, Andrew, like the story we read. God can't help you unless you invite Him in and are willing to do His will. Don't continue in your bent to think bad thoughts about yourself. I want you to go out for a bike ride right now. Get your mind into a positive channel. Talk with Jesus; He'll help you. It will be at least ten or fifteen minutes before I finish with Matthew. Then I'll be able to help you. So take time for a pleasant bike ride."

He dragged himself up from the table, his shoulders bent forward, and went out for a bike ride—his favorite thing to do. Oh how following the fleshly ways can take all the joys out of life! God wants to free us from this.

"Oh, Lord, he's under the spell of despair. Slay that old 'Giant Despair' from hurting my Andrew any more today. Help Andrew reach out to You and grasp Your hand and hear Your voice to his heart and mind. Take his will and make it Thine. May he choose to serve You rather than surrendering to despairing thoughts from Satan, our enemy."

I left Andrew in Jesus' hand and continued working with Matthew. Perhaps ten minutes passed, and Andrew returned. He looked better, but sadness was still there. He sat down and without a word put his nose into his book and began reading again.

"Andrew, I'll be just a few more minutes. I don't want you to frustrate yourself; I'd rather you wait for me. You are a good student, and you can learn. You will learn this," I encouraged him.

In less than ten minutes I finished with Matthew. "Now, Andrew, I'm available to help you. Tell me where you are struggling."

"Oh, Mother, it's fine. I have it all figured out. Jesus helped me."

"Well, Andrew, tell me your story of escape from the vicious 'Giant Despair.' "

"When I went for my ride, I saw only the gravel below my bike. I was cast down, as you know. I felt that Jesus had deserted me, even as I asked Him to help me. But then God asked me to give Him my will. I struggled to do that, not understanding why, but I did give it to Him. And when I'd think the bad thoughts, He'd ask me, again, to give my will to Him, and I did. Then He asked me to look up and see the beauty around me. I did that, too. He had me think new thoughts and enjoy my ride. Soon I felt much better.

"When I came into the house and you were still busy, I got sad again. I talked with God about it, and He said He could help me just like you. I tried the problem again, and that was frustrating. So I asked Him, again, what to do, and He told me to read my lesson and He'd be right beside me to help. When I read the lesson this time, I figured it out. Well, I really think God taught me. Mother, it worked!"

Yes, time with God does work!

Andrew was free. Free to serve God. "Giant Despair" fell as Andrew served the God of heaven instead of him. Andrew had a battle to fight against the lying thoughts—the old, negative, comfortable ways. But when he put his will on God's side, he was wrapped in God's loving, character-transforming arms, and his thoughts came in line first, and soon thereafter his feelings and attitudes were changed as well. Christ's heavenly influence brought peace to reign in his heart.

Do you want that peace, too? It's yours for the asking and cooperating.

THE LONE EMBRACE
A SPECIAL WORD OF ENCOURAGEMENT FOR SINGLE PARENTS

It doesn't matter that you are a single parent. To be alone with God is to be a majority. There are no hindrances under Him. He makes up all the deficiencies. God is there for you! Don't try to battle sin, self, or Satan alone. Instead, cry out to God. Listen for His voice to your mind and conscience and do as He directs you. He will redeem you and your children through the right exercise of your will. He doesn't want you to fight temptations but to submit them to Him so that He can subdue the devil for you. There comes a place in your redemption where you have to resist the devil—your old ways that are strong—but in Christ's strength you can win. And you must cooperate by using your will to open your heart's door all the way so that He can come in and fully cleanse you and give you a new heart.

God wants to save us from the sin itself, not just deliver us from the suffering and consequences of it. We are bought back to serve holiness. You are not your own; you are bought with a price (see 1 Corinthians 6:19, 20).

Chapter 15

SELF-GOVERNMENT

"Go to the ant, thou sluggard; consider her ways, and be wise: Which having no guide, overseer, or ruler, Provideth her meat in the summer, and gathereth her food in the harvest" (Proverbs 6:6-8).

*I*t was a new day, and I felt like a robot asking these questions for the umpteenth time in my sons' lives. "Did you brush your teeth?" "Did you drink your water?" "Have you had your prayers?" "Did you make your bed?" The boys were five and seven. We had been living in the wilderness for a year, and this area of my life still hadn't changed.

What is the matter with these boys?" I cried out in my heart to God. "Do they have a lazy brain syndrome that they cannot think, reason, or make decisions? How much longer before they pick up the routine of life I have demonstrated and have disciplined them in for many years now? How does one develop self-government? They do what they should only because I'm there telling them what to do and when to do it. Then I have to remind them later because they haven't done it, and I don't want to give them a consequence. Will I do this until they leave the house and get married?"

"How do you define self-government?" God's still small voice asked.

"Well, I want them to wash up without having to be told. I want them to make their beds, brush their teeth, and help around the house with chores. Is that too much to ask?"

"Your children should be members of the family firm. Caring for the house should be everyone's job. It is not good for you to do all the work while they do little or none. You hurt your children when you do all the work."

I felt that God had just put more work on me because I had no idea how to train my boys to do what they should around the house. So I went for a walk with Jim that day, taking with me all my frustration and desire to improve. Jim had part of the answer.

"Sally, all you need to do is to make a list of their chores; it's their responsibility to do them. You shouldn't be telling them over and over, day after day, like this. They aren't learning because they don't have to learn. You tell them what to do from morning until night and wear yourself out doing it. You've got to put their decisions in their lap and see to it they do it!"

"Jim, I like the idea of a chore list." My mind sparked with ideas. "I'll work on that. But the idea of seeing to it that they do their chores—that troubles my heart and mind in a big way. I don't know how to make them accept responsibility without doing what I'm doing right now. They don't do it on their own; that is why I'm like a robot, going through the same things, day after day, with each child. Can You make it practical to me?"

"All you need to do is to give them a consequence big enough to motivate them to do their chores on their own. You can't be telling them these things every day, Sally. They have to pick up the work and do it themselves."

Jim has the big picture; he is right as far as he went. But his answer was not detailed enough or practical enough for me, so I brought this question to God.

"Lord, how do I motivate the boys to pick up this work themselves?"

"Make it as attractive as possible through your chore lists."

So, trusting that God would show me the other details when I needed them, I started by doing the only thing that was clear to me—I drew a chart listing their chores and made a picture in the left column for each chore, since the boys couldn't read yet. Then I drew a column for each day of the week across the page. The squares were pretty good size. "How can they mark off each item in a way that will be fun?" I mused. ". . . Stickers . . . yes, stickers. That's it!" I had a selection of stickers portraying happy workers that were excellent illustrations of just what we were working on. My chart looked something like the one on page 196.

Making the charts was fun for me—I had hope! I got so excited drawing the pictures and imagining the boy's positive response. They'd each have their own list. I'd tape it on the kitchen door so that they could be self-governing. They would be responsible for doing these things without me having to tell them. God would speak to them to remind them of their duties, and they would cheerfully do them because I would train them to put a sticker on each item *after* they'd finished that task.

This list would include the personal-care duties that needed to be done each morning. "Lord this is great! May Your blessing be evident

Personal Care Before Worship

Name	Sunday	Monday	Tuesday	Wednesday	Thursday	Friday	Saturday
Brush teeth							
Drink water							
Pray & listen							
Make bed							
Family worship 8:00 A.M.							

throughout this process of learning. Be with me when I bring this change to the boys. Help them see it as fun! This robot mother is retiring! I'm so grateful to You and to Jim."

The boys were interested, but not terribly excited, for they sensed it meant personal effort. This didn't appear desirable to them—as yet. But God was with me, and if I remained sensitive, He would be there when I needed Him and provide courage.

The first morning was a lot of fun picking out the sticker at the completion of each little task and pasting it on the chart. They both enjoyed looking at their chore lists when they were completed. But this first day I was right there instructing, teaching, and showing them what was expected. I was by their side throughout the morning. Here I dealt only with their minds. God empowered me to do it in a very positive, attractive manner, as I remained sensitive to His voice and heeded His will in the moment.

The second morning was not as much fun for me, for it required training—dealing with their wills! This was a weak area for me, because of my own negative attitudes about myself. My will did not want to deal with the issue on this level; it was as uncomfortable to discipline myself as it was to discipline my children. I felt the robot routine pressing to be expressed once again. The Lord helped me to recognize that I wanted to resort to dealing with their minds, to *tell* them again, instead of calling out their will. They were not choosing to be self-governing. Thoughts of woe, discouragement, and "what's the matter with these boys?" loomed over my heart, mind, and countenance, bringing emotional pain once again!

"Lord what consequence do I give? I'm so disheartened! Why don't these chore lists do what they are suppose to do?"

"The chore lists themselves cannot change the child. They only make clear the expectations and provide a tool for cultivating the right use of the will—which is self-government. The next step is to call them to a decision. Bring them to Me and show them the results of their choices, lovingly but firmly. The experience of exercising their minds and wills to choose to do the right is such a vital, important lesson for them to learn while they are still young. The chore lists provide you with the opportunity to face the deeper work of training that you have left undone so far. Fear not, for I am with you!"

"They need to be trained how to make principled decisions to do right. But that means consequences, right?"

And with that thought, despair, frustration, and hopelessness came pushing for entrance. Why did I respond with such strong negative emotions? For me, giving consequences had been a negative, failing experience. Fear of failure (my own lying baggage) drove thoughts and feelings of inadequacies, which were confirmed by my history—the memory of every time a consequence I had given the boys didn't work the desired reform. I could just lie back and let these thoughts cover me up in their blanket of woe.

But God jogged my mind in another direction. *"I am the One who works the reform in their hearts and minds, Sally, not the chore list."*

This thought helped me to see that I was still hoping that the chore list would work a magical reform in my boys—so I wouldn't have to face all the hopeless feelings that seemed to accompany my efforts at discipline. I must choose whom I'll obey—my feelings or my God.

Satan had been speaking loudly through my thoughts, feelings, and emotions to discourage me from going forward. "Give up; it won't work anyway." "It's going to be very hard." "God expects too much of you!" Isn't it interesting that my struggle was the same as my children's? Neither my children nor I wanted to make the decision and put forth the personal effort necessary for the desired end. I began to realize that God was first calling *me* to trust Him and obey—to choose to go against the negative old ways that seem so comfortable. Then He could work through me to lead my sons into the same experience. This is what's behind the scene in training the will.

"Sally, you don't need to fear; I am here with you. Give Me those old hurtful thoughts and feelings. You don't have to obey them any more. You wanted the robot mother to retire, didn't you? Or maybe you'd rather continue in your old patterns?"

I had to grapple with this reality. Then I decided based on logic, not feelings. "No, Lord. The 'Robot Mother' will retire. This is just the cost of learning new ways. This is the training of the will. I need to be willing to do hard things as Jesus directs me. I do have a debilitating attitude toward consequences, and I don't need to continue there."

"When you run the program apart from Me, you miss having divine power attending your efforts. When you let Me lead you and direct your steps, the same consequences will have a different outcome. Will you let Me be your Pilot today?"

"Lord, you always make it so logical. I'm more inclined to follow my feelings. I feel I must obey them. I tend to be negative, and You want to teach me how to be positive and trust in You instead of myself. Well, I haven't done well on my own, so I may as well trust You, instead, and learn a better way. Okay, what shall I do with the boys? They are not using their chore list to guide them, and reverting to my robot instructions is not the answer. So what do I do?"

"Give them consequences in a matter-of-fact manner. You must give them the responsibility for what they do with your instruction. What they do or do not do is not in your ability to choose. It's theirs! You don't have to hurt and grimace for their lack of right choices. I want you to show them, through training and giving natural consequences, why a lack of self-government is not a good way to live. This is designed to motivate them to choose—of their own free will—the right way the next time. What have I

said about transgressors?"

" 'Good understanding giveth favour: but the way of transgressors is hard' (Proverbs 13:15). Yes, I see it in the text! It's hard for me to be firm and give consequences because it doesn't *feel* like love. But I must see the bigger picture and redefine love as connecting them to You so that they can be empowered to do the right. Then consequences would be love. I want them to choose, to decide to do the right with a will, not under coercion.

"Experience should teach them that when they do what is right, life is pleasant. But when they transgress, then life is hard. So the responsibility for whether life is easy or hard rests with them. It's not my responsibility," I reasoned. "I actually hurt them if I make transgression easy or pleasant, without any consequences. In that case, experience teaches them that if they are naughty and get their way, that this is a good thing. So they strive for more of the same. I actually am confirming them in a wrong way when I withhold proper consequences; I'm creating what I hate. Isn't that interesting? Well, then, what would be a good consequence for my boys?"

"Give them one warning, a little time for a decision, and then reward their good or evil. Do not fuss or reason long with them. Do not try to convince them. Under My direction, let their experience teach them."

"Matthew, Andrew, come here!" I said pleasantly.

They came running. "Yes?"

"I am going to remind you boys, just one time today, that your chore lists are your helpers. You need to be responsible to check your own list and complete it all without me telling you over and over as we used to do. I'm sure you would like that. Life will be pleasant when you take this responsibility. Now, if you do not get those chores done by family worship time—only fifteen minutes from now—there will be a tough consequence, not because I'm angry or upset with you, but because you are not being self-governing. I want you to learn the joy of doing right with the help of these fun charts. So it's up to you to choose a pleasant day or a less pleasant day."

"Okay, Mother." And they were off to consult their chore charts.

But old habits and distractions were stronger than this new way, and when we sat down for worship, Matthew had completed his personal care duties at the last moment, but Andrew had not. My heart ached for what had to be done, but I trusted God.

"Andrew, you didn't choose to consult your chore chart to be sure it was all done. Neither did you listen to God reminding you to do it nor to my recent reminder. I'm so sorry you didn't put forth your effort at the right time. Because you didn't get those pleasant, easy duties done, your consequence will be no breakfast this morning." I said this with sympathy and love but without lessening this consequence because of his entreaties for another chance.

He had had five years of the soft chances, entreaties, and long discussions. This approach had not trained him to do what he needed to do. So against my past experience, my feelings, and my tender heart, I enforced the consequence. I wanted to see what the outcome would be.

Very tenderly I reasoned with him. "Doesn't the Bible say, no work, no eating?" ("This we commanded you, that if any would not work, neither should he eat," 2 Thessalonians 3:10.) I continued, "I am sorry you have chosen this consequence, Andrew. This is not my choice. I gave you several chances, but you still did not choose. Determine that you will not lose another meal tomorrow over something so simple as drinking your water or making your bed in a timely fashion. It's not worth it. Remember, the choice is yours.

"Now, I want you to go clean your bedroom and make it neat and tidy like it needs to be. Think about what brought you into this uneviable position. I love you, son! Tomorrow you can decide differently with Jesus' help."

Andrew went off with slumped shoulders and did the work, admitting that it was he that had brought himself there. He drank plenty of water to curb his hunger until lunchtime. To my surprise, he did well. Both his work and attitude were very good. He accepted responsibility and put forth effort to work. It was obvious he had yielded up his will to do right—with Jesus' help. The next day, only one little reminder was necessary before his few duties were done quickly, cheerfully, and well. And he did them from love, not from duty or fear. This experience was a good teacher.

Self-government means making decisions to serve God and not my flesh. It is hearing God's voice and responding without needing another to tell me what to do. It is knowing God as a personal God.

Now God, Jim, and I had discussed ahead of time what consequence would work best in teaching our boys self-government. Our thoughts were agreed that a severe consequence would shorten the learning time in our present situation. And indeed it did. We applied consequences lovingly, without any harshness or anger. Our hindsight evaluation gave evidence that this was God's leading. Andrew's heart was made tender by his talks with God. He made good choices that were lasting. He cooperated in a loving spirit, and a reformation was begun that nothing had been able to bring about previously.

I'm not saying that the way we went about this should necessarily be a pattern for you. God must lead you to what consequences will work reform in your child's heart. Learn to follow the great Shepherd who can read the hearts of all involved and bring about a good teaching experience.

When God leads you to give severe consequences to your children and your heart is aching, let it awaken sympathy and empathy, not a denunciatory spirit. Just recall how you would like to be treated when you err, and then treat your children as you would like to be treated. Being treated respectfully and positively with consistency will awaken their cooperation. True love will draw your children; it will not crush them with undue control or pitiless hail. If the pull of your flesh is strong, driving you toward these old selfish ways, cry out to Jesus to redeem you before you work for your child's redemption. You must come out of your own wrong thoughts, feelings, and ways first. Abide in Christ and let Him abide in you, and you can be that instrument in His hands to change your home, your life, and your children in a Christlike way.

God is the Shepherd who is leading His sheep; we parents are the undershepherds, following His lead. I saw God's love in having me do this hard thing for my son. I began to see consequences as my helper, not my enemy. The benefits to my home were outstanding. "Robot Mother" did retire, to everyone's joy. The boys embarked upon a new road of self-government under God.

There were also house chores that needed to come under this program, so I made another chart (see page 202).

I had established a pattern of consulting with God and filtering my thoughts through him as I prepared the first chart, and the experience grew only deeper as I worked on the second one. Both I and the boys found that we needed to continue to make adjustments in our attitudes, deny the old ways, and exercise self-government.

CHORE PLANNER AFTER WORSHIP

Name	Sunday	Monday	Tuesday	Wednesday	Thursday	Friday	Saturday
Set table for break-fast							
Vacuum							
Collect and burn trash							
Sweep floors							
Help mother							

Again, God was the divine Shepherd instructing me, the undershepherd, in ideas for consequences. I discovered that the process went better when He was leading. Even if the process was prolonged and challenging, the outcome was always good—a real contrast with the miserable outcomes I was accustomed to when operating on my own. At times I still unwittingly assumed the leadership role; this gave me renewed incentive to be sensitive and sure that God, not self, was leading me.

Personal worship time is training in self-government because true self-government means coming under the Lordship of Jesus Christ. Parents must gain this experience first by becoming familiar with God's voice as they sit at the feet of Jesus, spending time in His Word, and allowing His Holy Spirit to apply what they read to their practical needs—until it can be truly said of them, "My sheep hear my voice, and I know them, and they follow me" (John 10:27). This is a hidden work of the heart, but it will result in our children knowing by our attitude and conduct, even under provocation, that we have been with Jesus. Do you possess this experience with God for yourself? If not, you must make gaining it the highest priority of your life. There are no shortcuts to this experience, and it cannot be overpriced. We can give to our children only what we ourselves possess.

As I yield my will to cooperate with God in my thoughts, feelings, and behavior, I am prepared to train my children to do the same. Daily annoyances are excellent opportunities for this training. When my son was sick, we talked about the need to be pleasant, not grumpy. We discussed the fact that we are not our own, that we are bought with a price to serve God's way, not our way. By surrendering and cooperating with Him, we can all be empowered to be pleasant even when we are sick. Self-government is learning to choose to do the right although it crosses my passions, selfish nature, or old ways!

Now, our children need tenderness, care, and some tolerance when they are sick. But, led of God, we must find balance and not let Satan take over their hearts and minds, making them whiney or obnoxious. Being sick does not justify selfishness, and neither will expressing self-ishness make the child happy. Self-denial and self-control must be nurtured even when it's hard. Our children will be happiest if they learn that in Jesus, they can be kind even when they are ill. We must both *teach* and *train* so that our children can do what they know is right.

When our child falls and has a little hurt, he may need some comfort or he may not. Don't train your children to require too much attention to their little hurts. It is better for them to make things little and keep them that way. You can say, "Oh, let me help you up. You look just fine." Your attitude can properly influence theirs. When they have a more serious hurt, they need to be taught to be strong and to endure bravely whatever needs to be done to care for their injury.

One day, Andrew, age twelve, had taken the car and trailer down to the guest cabin, which is not far from our house. He was clearing some trees using the chainsaw.

A short time went by, and then I heard a calm knock on the back door. To my surprise it was Andrew.

"Mother, I need help—I hurt myself."

"Where are you hurt?" I asked, looking into his eyes.

"Circumstances kicked the chain saw, and it cut my leg. I'm all right, Mother, but you need to look at it; it's bad."

"Sit down here and let me have a look."

He sat down and unwrapped a towel from his left leg, revealing a three-inch wide gaping, bleeding wound. The chainsaw had torn out a good-sized chunk of flesh.

"This does look bad. How did you get back here? Didn't I hear the car drive up?"

"Yes, Mother. After the accident, God prompted me to check out my leg. It looked pretty bad, and I knew you needed to do something with it. I asked God how I was to get home. If I walked, my leg would bleed more than it already was, but if I drove the car, I would get blood on the carpet. So I took this towel and wrapped my leg so that I could drive home instead of walking. That seemed the best to me. And luckily it was my left leg, so I could drive." He was so calm and logical.

"Son, you did very well. I'm so proud of you! We need to clean out the wound and right now is the least painful time to do that, while it is still numb." It was a dirty wound.

Andrew was very brave as we thoroughly cleaned and bandaged the wound. The pain was severe enough to make him cry now and then, and we would stop momentarily to pray. Then we would continue, and he would cooperate with what needed to be done. Then we took him to the clinic, where he received thirty stitches.

Andrew's calmness and self-control was the result of the earlier years of attitude training, of approaching hurts logically and calmly, and consulting with God. He knew he would receive proper empathy and care, but not a sentimental overreaction.

Some parents err by curtly ordering a child not to cry. "Be a man," they command. This is not the self-control in Jesus that I'm recommending. Self-control gained through fear of a dominant parent is destructive to a child. Their tears and hurts are only stuffed down to reappear at another time—even years later. Self-government is *not* demanding obedience so that a child is not a bother to the parent. True self-government is being under God and approaching a difficulty calmly together.

One of my sons was not as neat and orderly as the other. Self-government was teaching the less orderly son to be neater and not to get angry when his brother pointed out his lack of order. He had to learn to filter his attitude and spirit through God before replying and striving to be neater. Self-government for the other son was to filter his correction through Christ. Was he giving encouragement to his brother or pitiless hail? How would he like to be addressed were he his brother? He, too, needed to evaluate, cry out to God, and deal with his thoughts and feelings in Jesus. Both boys learned in these situations how to give their wrong thoughts and feelings to God and to accept and cooperate with the right. Self-government is coming under the Lordship and direction of Jesus Christ.

Once this concept is established, you will be pleasantly rewarded for your faithfulness and example to your children. The boys would come to Jim or me periodically to tell us of their joys and accomplishments. "Mother, today I was going to get angry at my brother for not being neat, and God spoke to my mind before I said it, and so I said it sweetly rather than angrily." What a wonderful reward to everyone's heart! God is real and speaks to everyone and makes life pleasant and loving.

"Mother, I was going to sneak a cookie from the pantry, and Jesus said, *'What is eaten in secret becomes bitter to thy soul.'* I thought about it and followed Jesus instead."

These are our opportunities to give proper praise to our children. They long to be assured of our love, to be affirmed, to be appreciated for doing right, and we should give them a healthy dose of these things. Praise in the Lord is not pride, but the healing balm of Gilead encouraging more exercise of self-government.

Many parents excuse sassy behavior from their child, saying it is happening because it is late in the evening when the child is tired and should be in bed because the child has missed his nap that day. These children will grow up to be adults who justify ill behavior because they are tired, had a hard day, are irritated, or whatever. God's grace is sufficient in all circumstances for us to be Christlike. Train your children to yield to Christ even when they don't feel like it, and you will give them a great inheritance of righteousness.

Even special-needs children should be educated and trained in self-government—under God. Annie Sullivan had the courage to show the deaf, blind girl Helen Keller her potential and not to accept her obnoxious behavior just because of her disability. Communication was the key. And God blessed her efforts.

A child with no hands can learn to use his feet remarkably well. If, out of unwise sympathy, you do everything for him and train him that he can't do this or that, you make the child more of an invalid than he needs to be. If, instead, you nurture his efforts to use his toes as fingers, he may learn that he can take care of himself in ways you never dreamed of. Good parenting, under God, offers any child proper autonomy. Let God lead you and your children to find the joy of being the best you and they can be!

An ADD child is still responsible for his behavior although chemical imbalances in his body drive him to be irritable or hyperactive. Train him to reach out to God, to recognize His voice, to be helped by Him, and to be the best he can be. That takes work, effort, and self-control for the parent as well as the child.

A Down syndrome child should not be allowed to develop habits of overeating or lack of manners just because that is the way he tends to be. If you let him behave wrongly, you are teaching him that it is okay. Help them, under God, to be the best they can be and don't limit them by thinking that they cannot improve. Deal with their physical, spiritual, and mental limitations, placing all under God's direction.

At the ages of eight and ten, my boys learned the art of doing the laundry, including sorting the colors, removing stains, putting in the right amount of soap, hanging it out to dry, folding it well, ironing it, and putting it all away. Letting them manage these tasks and others had many rewards. It takes only a few weeks for your child to become professionals at such responsibilities, and what they learn in faithfulness here prepares them to manage their schoolwork more responsibly and successfully.

When my boys were ten and twelve, I put them in charge of food preparation. They prepared not just one dish, but the entire menu for the day. If bread were needed on their assigned day, they made it the day before. They were expected to serve their meals on time. It is better to be five minutes early than five minutes late. Meal preparation cultivated in them organization and thoroughness as well as the principles of honesty, perseverance, and a good attitude. They were learning to plan and how to heed the voice of God prompting them with helpful thoughts. No longer were they to think that a little work was too much.

Self-government is well exercised in all useful labor. (For more examples, see chapter sixteen, "Useful Labor.") It prepares our children to be good workers in society. They are learning to operate on principles that will make them useful wherever they go. Don't you appreciate a cheerful, competent worker in the workplace?

Self-government means to train our children to be under our proper parental authority as we are under God, not under self. Our children should always first be under the authority of God, His Word, and His Spirit. They should respect and obey us when we are under God. "Children, obey your parents *in the Lord*" (Ephesians 6:1, emphasis supplied).

Self-government is training our children in the art of hearing God's voice and recognizing Him as their Shepherd who is ever present with them. It is arousing their desire to respond, "Speak, for thy servant heareth" (1 Samuel 3:10). It is giving them experience in making decisions based on principle and duty rather than upon inclination and emotion. It is making it possible for them to rejoice in freedom from dead-end thoughts, feelings, and habits. It is strengthening in them a Christlike character.

Self-government is the practical realization of the apostle Paul's counsel to "let this mind be in you" (Philippians 2:5). It's finding power to change in Christ.

THE LONE EMBRACE
A SPECIAL WORD OF ENCOURAGEMENT FOR SINGLE PARENTS

Every parent needs to enter into the joys of their children being self-governing under Christ, but how much more the single parent! You have so many duties under your solo care and responsibility. You need the joy of a family team working harmoniously together.

There is a cost to finding Jesus, a cost to yielding our self to Him, a cost to following Jesus, and a cost to bringing our children through this process so that they can learn for themselves that God's way is best. Learning how to let God be our Shepherd, leading and correcting our thoughts, feelings, responses, and lives, is true self-government. We need to be in this position in order to be the parent God wants us to be. Our children need to learn this position and how to discern God's voice in order to be the children God wants them to be. Only in this way can they obey you in heart and become the self-governing helpers you desire them to be in your home or society.

Chapter 16

USEFUL LABOR

"Whatsoever thy hand findeth to do, do [it] with thy might"
(Ecclesiastes 9:10).

Sharon, you are so slow! You make my life hard. Why don't you speed up with those dishes? Look how slow and poorly you are doing them; it would be easier for me to do them myself! Get with it right now!" Mother railed.

Poor Sharon! At age six she was trying to please Mother. She was honestly trying to go faster, but with each cutting put down, her little hands became more and more clumsy and incapable. Her will despaired. Her heart became hopeless, and her courage was squelched. Her only motivation, now, was fear! Tears began to flow involuntarily. Feelings of rejection mounted, and as she rinsed a plate and reached to place it in the drainboard, it fell to the ground with a crash and shattered to pieces on the floor. Sharon shrieked in fear of what might happen now.

Mother came in. Putting her hands on her hips, she glared at "Slow Sharon." Then, in silence, she cleaned up the broken plate. Each disgusted glare from mother cut deeper and deeper into Sharon's feelings and emotions. Mother disposed of the broken plate by slamming it into the trash can, sending shivers of uncertainty and more fear up Sharon's back. Her mind was overwhelmed with degrading thoughts of how awful she was. Her hands were crippled by those lying thoughts, and Sharon could barely get them to wash the remaining dishes even though she was willing to do so. Another disapproving look only slowed her further, to a snail's pace.

What are we doing to our children? They are God's heritage, loaned to us to nurture and admonish in the way and joy of the Lord. Mother is pushing Sharon into her own little turtle shell of protection. She is wrongly exemplifying God as a stern, unjust, unloving God—making Him unattractive. But if any parent comes to God, desiring to change, there is still hope.

That night, Mother took time alone with God to honestly evaluate her life. She was embarrassed to the point of being willing to change and ask for direction from God. The next morning she cried out again, "Lord, I must change. I'm an ogre. I want to bring the sunshine of Jesus into my mind, heart, and home, and to my daughter. What must I do?"

"Give her practical instruction on how to wash the dishes well. Be loving and sweet. You can create the home atmosphere you desire with Me in your heart. You cannot come out of that harsh and angry disposition without Me directing you what to do in its place. I am the vine, and you are the branch. I'll give you the strength you need as you remain connected and abiding in Me."

"Give me the mind of Christ. Teach me to think Your thoughts, not mine. Take my mind, my heart—my feelings and emotions, my history—and change them into Your image. Take my will; cleanse it and return it to me purified and empowered to love, instruct, and train Sharon as You would! I commit to responding to Your Holy Spirit when He calls for me to restrain the old ways, trusting You can change me inside when I give myself to You."

" *'Slow Sharon' is a byproduct of your verbal and emotional whippings,"* God said to wipe the scales off her eyes.

"Yes, Lord, this is true!" Mother was dumbfounded. "My mother did the same thing to me. I had vowed I'd never be like her, and here I am acting as she did.

"All who come to Me can be delivered from their history. I want to break those tentacles of history that bind you to such responses. Hearken unto My voice and do My will in My strength, and you shall be free," He encouraged.

"I can?" this mother responded. "You mean I can change in Jesus? Please, Lord, save me so that you can save my Sharon, too! Save Sharon from following our family's dysfunctional responses."

"Mother, your Sharon needs to be genuinely loved and appreciated by you and to know it to be true. She is hurting and being crippled for life under your present program. Tell her how valuable she is to you. Tell her what she can be in Jesus. Show her My power by the change I can make in you. Cultivate in her the trait of diligence under a loving atmosphere to replace her slow traits. She is slow because you tell her she is. She is obeying you. Encourage her by telling her how capable and fast she can become and nurture her to come to Me in order to change. I'm with you."

"I'm thankful Sharon is only six years old. Maybe I can give her the right representation of Jesus before her character is completely formed. I hope to undo the damage I have done so far!"

So Mother made a plan with God for the day, wrote it down for reference, and went out to face this day with Jesus as her Pilot, placing her hand timidly in His.

Mother had a brief and tender talk with Sharon, apologizing for yesterday's un-Christlike attitude and behavior. Sharon responded sweetly, "I forgive you, Mother." But her tentative hug showed that she was a bit doubtful.

"Sharon, let's have some fun with the breakfast dishes today. Let's play 'Beat the Clock,' " Mother said cheerfully. How much time do you need to do the dishes? Will twenty or thirty minutes be enough?"

"I don't know," Sharon replied cautiously. Children who have been dominated and demeaned often fear to make a decision because it might not please the parent. They may have good ideas but don't feel safe voicing them unless they know for a certainty that you agree with them. May God free us from this wrong kind of parenting!

"Let's set the clock for thirty minutes, dear, and see how we do today," Mother encouraged. "Does that sound like fun?"

"Maybe," Sharon said with doubtful timidity.

"Let me show you how to make washing easier." Mother wrapped her arms around Sharon, smiled sweetly, and they washed the first glass together, rinsed it, and held it up to the light for inspection. Another encouraging smile was given. "That's very good, Sharon. Now you try alone. That's excellent! You will be an excellent mother and housekeeper doing work like that." And so Mother began heeding the voice of God to her soul and began the process of change in Jesus.

The first day went smoothly. Mother and daughter had uplifting, pleasant conversation working together in this fashion. Mother was different, and thus the daughter was different. The dishes were done just before the timer went off. "We did it!" They hugged and were happy.

The second day they decided together to lessen their time to twenty-five minutes. And they beat the clock! The third day, however, thoughts and attitudes of despair and "I can't" came up in Sharon's mind. Mother turned to God before responding. God advised her, and she lovingly discussed God's power to overcome lying thoughts. She encouraged Sharon in practical terms about how to give these wrong things to God and how to be free from despair and "I can't." They prayed, and Sharon successfully took Jesus' hand; she was freed from her old paths this time. Under Christ's direction, Mother cultivated trust in place of fear and joy in place of sorrow. Sharon did her dishes successfully and cheerfully in Jesus. What a wonderful victory!

At times, mother's old way of stern justice and silence reared its ugly head. But she turned to Jesus as her General and was directed into balanced judgment. Harshness was eradicated by grace. By repetition Sharon became brave and encouraged her mother when she was down just as Mother had encouraged her. Praying together worked. They experienced helping each other on to victory in Jesus.

Sharon began getting comfortable with her *new mother*. They became a good team together in the kitchen. Sharon felt loved and appreciated; she ventured out of her turtle shell of protection. "Mother, I think we can complete the dishes in twenty minutes. Want to try?" Sharon said enthusiastically. And they did!

In Jesus all things are possible. The heart's feelings, emotions, and reactions are set free. In this loving, nurturing environment, Sharon's hands became skillful and quick in doing dishes. As she learns how to cling to Jesus and to remain free, she need never return to her paralyzed state again. God loves to set us free from our old paths.

Mother improved, day by day, in giving proper and appropriate compliments and encouragement. She took time to be close to Sharon as she tenderly taught her greater skill and efficient work habits. She also cooperated with God in her own character development and showed her love to Sharon by restraining the expression of her former pitiless hail of criticism. Mother was being freed from her history, and as a result Sharon was freed to be the faithful "Swift Sharon" that God intended her to be.

Useful labor is a tool in Jesus' hands to free us from the bondage of sin, self, and Satan. As Jesus is given access to our thoughts, feelings, and emotions—to restore them by His grace—the byproduct is a Christlike, diligent worker. The root of Sharon's freedom was the fact that she was able to come out of the bondage of seeing herself as useless, incapable, and hopelessly in the way. She was freed to become "Swift Sharon"—mother's good helper. She had purpose and value. Life was worth living. Jesus was desirable. In Christ, Sharon was free to do her work with all of her might.

In this case, the parent's imbalanced character was the stumbling block God wanted to remove to help the child be the best she could be in Him. God's power was able to free both mother and child.

But there are other reasons our children can be poor workers. Perhaps we have not given them sufficient information and demonstration on how to perform the tasks we ask them to do. If this is our lack, we need to correct it by taking them lovingly and pleasantly under our wing and showing them the right way to sweep the floor, fold the clothes, sort the laundry, cook, or whatever. Let them awkwardly try, while we encourage their efforts. They will love to be with us, to be appreciated and to please. Encouragement, balanced with firmness, increases work quality, and as children gain experience, they will become proficient.

Our children can do poorly at useful labor because they lack a good attitude. God wants us to train their minds and wills to help cheerfully. Teaching them the distinction between a fleshly attitude and a heavenly one is the first step, but training them to do willingly what they know is right is a deeper, more difficult step that brings lasting rewards to child and family alike. Make real Jesus' personal presence with them. "Whatsoever thy hand findeth to do, do [it] with thy might" (Ecclesiastes 9:10). We must teach our child, from a very young age, how to give their wrong thoughts, attitudes, and habits to God so that they can do any task joyfully. In this way, God becomes a real Deliverer. They gain experience that God's way is the way of freedom and happiness.

But first, we must teach our own mind and train our own will to be under God. To teach our children skillful, diligent work habits done faithfully, timely, and well, we must ourselves possess those same habits first. Can we teach our children how to cook if we don't know how to cook ourselves? Can we teach and train them how to be neat, clean, and orderly if we are not? Then we must first acquire cheerful, skillful, thorough work habits in Jesus. We must become structured, organized, and efficient so that it doesn't take three hours to do one hour's worth of housework. If I don't deal with myself, my inherent shortcomings will frustrate and complicate my child's life. Believe it or not, it is easier and far better to change than to continue in the old paths.

When we moved to the mountains of Montana, God wanted to free me from the endless round of household duties by incorporating my boys as my work force in the family team. At first I thought it was faster to do the work myself, for I was a very fast and hard worker. So I'd send the boys outside to play while I did the daily housework alone. Often, after about an hour or so of play, the boys would be fussing and arguing over sandbox boundaries. We thought we had made the sandbox big enough to avoid this difficulty. Settling these disputes took lots of time, for I was unskilled in how to deal with hearts by bringing them to Jesus to be changed. Thus the household duties were delayed.

"Lord, I can't get all the housework done if I have to forever settle disputes like this! What should I do? I'm tired! I'd like to play, too," I complained.

"Your boys need to be a part of your work force. Call the boys in to help you," God suggested to my heart.

"Oh, no, Lord, that's too hard!" They'll grumble. It'll be an argument. It's faster if I do it myself."

"It is not good for you to do all the work while they do none. You hurt your boys in this way. I don't want you to be their slave, but rather their teacher, mother, and role model. They have too much playtime as it is. Self gets well exercised and causes the arguments that you have to settle when self is so strong. Your boys need well-regulated employment, amusement, and some play. You must learn the right balance."

"They need daily, systematic labor? Well, that will require little attentions often. Oh that's hard! But it truly is an imbalance just to let them play and be out of my way. How will they ever learn to work unless I daily teach them? God is right," I reasoned. "Okay, Lord, I'll call them in, but You need to teach me how to teach them. My mother never taught me." So I called the boys in from the sandbox.

"Oh, Mother," Matthew complained. "it's not an hour yet. You said we could play an hour."

"Well, I just wanted you two to help me fold these clothes. We need to share in all the housework, boys. The quicker you do this little task, the quicker you will be back in the sandbox. If I do all the work, I don't have time to play with you," I explained nicely.

"Aw, Mother!" grumbled four-year-old Andrew, who didn't want to work.

"Oh, Lord, it's just like I expected. It would surely be easier to do the work myself than have to deal with this self will!"

The Lord opened my eyes to the big picture. *"Unproductive in the home, unproductive in the church and in society. You need to pick up your dropped stitches of home training for useful labor so that they can become productive in your home and thus productive in society. Begin by teaching and training them to contribute to the upkeep and welfare of their home. They can learn by faith in Me to do useful labor in the right spirit. This is every parent's God-given work."*

With my hand in Christ's hand and my ear tuned to heaven for instruction, I went forward. "Boys, let's choose to fold these clothes in the right spirit. No grumbling."

"Why do we have to fold Mother's laundry anyway?" Matthew complained.

"Oh Lord! I'm offended at this! It's not '*my*' laundry; it's '*our*' laundry!"

"Sally, give those wrong thoughts and feelings to Me. I'll redeem you from their service. Then bring your sons to Me that I may mold, shape, and fashion them in like manner. Teach them what is right, then train them to do what they know is right."

I gave my wrong thoughts, feelings, and habits to God, and He gave me His love and wisdom; this great exchange occurred by faith, not by sight. "Boys, this is 'our' laundry. I believe some of your clothes are in here—right?" I said this kindly, but firmly. "No more complaining."

Both Matthew and Andrew folded the clothes in a sloppy manner. The shirts were folded cock-eyed, and the washcloths were not corner-to-corner. Their hands were working, but their hearts were not in it.

"Lord, what shall I do?"

"Because sentence against an evil work is not executed speedily, therefore the heart of the sons of men is fully set in them to do evil" (Ecclesiastes 8:11).

"Giving consequences is my greatest weakness right now, isn't it, Lord? Okay, You have my heart. How do I get the boy's hearts into Your hands using consequences?"

God led me to send Matthew for a grizzly run, for he was not reasonable, while Andrew was more easily corrected with a simple spanking. Even though these were given in love, it still took two consequences, with reasoning and prayer between, before they surrendered to God and cooperated. By the grace of God working in me, my spirit remained firm, consistent, yet Christlike. The boys gave their wrong thoughts, feelings, and resentments to God and cooperated by folding the clothes neatly and in the right spirit. A victory was won! What a thrill!

Gaining their hearts into Jesus' hand as an on-the-job experience took me almost an hour. But this was time well spent! A truehearted surrender was gained, and the clothes were folded and put away nicely. But the greater blessing was the influence of this experience upon the boys' lives as a whole.

They returned to the sandbox and actually played together better than ever. Self was subdued by divine power. And the next day's correction was easier and quicker. When I called one of them in to get a book for Father, it was done pleasantly without complaint. When I called the other one to help set the table, it was done cheerfully and quickly. When I called them to fold the clothes, it was done with sweet conversation. It seemed that when I called them periodically and they surrendered their hearts to God, they were more appreciative of playtime and less of self arose. There was less opportunity for self to be exercised without interruption, making self weaker. It took less time for surrender after the first encounter. Daily we built on good lessons learned. God wants all parents to call often for their children's hearts in order for them to discover who God is and what He can do for them, while hindering the growth of self.

Useful labor trains our children how to be Christians, how to surrender their wills, how to distinguish God's voice and will in order to follow Him. Practical household duties exercise heavenly qualities and change the child's character if it is done in Christ and not in self's willpower alone. They also free up Mother so that she has more time for God, her spouse, and her children—a better balance.

Mothers need to address attitudes. "This is *our* laundry." "These are *our* dishes." "We need to get *our* meal ready." She needs to address the matter of developing skillful work habits to economize the time needed for different tasks. Learning how to skillfully perform all the duties of running the home is an important class in higher learning. What better way can we prepare our children for taking on adult responsibilities than beginning with these little things? Regulating their work, play, and character development is what motherhood is all about.

In time I added chore lists for the boys to help them take part daily in household chores. In a relatively short time, these chores became

PARENTING YOUR CHILD BY THE SPIRIT

automatic. They will not become automatic if you do not do them consistently. It is good for our children to have ever-increasing responsibilities put upon them—within reason. They actually thrive when they know that they are needed.

"Andrew, having you do the laundry is a big help to Mother. Sorting, running the wash, hanging it out to dry, folding, and putting the clothes away is a big job for a six-year-old. I need you and count on your faithful service. How about a bike ride before lunch today? I have time." Andrew flourished because he was needed and appreciated. What an encouragement this was for him to do his best!

"Matthew, having you prepare the meal and make dessert for us is a big help to me. Father loves your desserts, doesn't he?"

"Oh, yes! Father loves desserts just like I do!" he said with a grin.

"I don't know how I ever did it without you," I added.

"Boys, the house looks lovely. Many hands make light work of a big job." And they grinned as we clasped our hands together in team fashion. Everyone wants to belong to a team—especially the winning team. In Christ, we all win.

If you want your children to enjoy work and to be cheerful about it, you must personally show them how. If we are exemplifying what it means to be a desirable team worker, under God, our children will love to be in our company at work or at play.

"Matthew. Andrew. Let's get our housework done quickly so that we can take a picnic lunch down by the river today."

I could see that Andrew's laundry was a big task for him. So I joined him voluntarily when it was time to hang it up outside.

"Why are you helping me?" Andrew asked.

"Well, because I love you! Laundry is a big job. You were doing it so well without complaint that I just wanted to lighten your load. Perseverance is a big-boy muscle. You are going to be a strong man one day. Enduring hardship is important, and I'm encouraging by helping." Andrew was silent, but he beamed from his heart outward.

In this way each gave voluntary help to one another. Love grew by expression in this way. What if I had not endured that first tough correction to teach them to work? Our own example speaks volumes. All my help to teach and to train them in the right skills and attitude toward labor came back to me at least tenfold. Was it worth the effort—the death of self's ways? Oh, yes! Love in our teaching and correcting is the glue that binds our children's hearts to ours.

This work of character development, under God, is our first work—even above community service and church work. Nothing should keep us from the work that lies nearest. Nothing is more important!

I had each of my sons learn to take full responsibility for the laundry at ages six or seven. By ages ten to twelve, they did the whole day's meal preparation and took over the management of the housekeeping and gardening. Through this they learned self-government under God; they learned order, efficiency, how to organize a task, thoroughness, and how to operate in a specific time frame to accomplish a set task. This was very valuable learning. Business training is taking full responsibility for a task start to finish and doing it well and faithfully. Thus at an early age they learned the skills necessary to be good businessmen. Where could they better learn these talents than in their own home?

Jim began teaching them to change the oil in the car, change the tires, clean the brakes, and grease all the necessary parts when they were ten and twelve years old. I asked Andrew to do a plumbing job when he was about ten years old. He did well. Have you been underestimating your child's talents and abilities? When they were about ten and twelve years old, each of the boys planned and prepared the meals in entirety for the day—twice a week. They ran chain saws alone, for they had proven themselves responsible. They loved helping to cut and collect firewood. They regularly chopped kindling and wood for the kitchen cookstove. At this age they were almost as quick and skillful in household duties as I was. We had become an effective and efficient team. From August to September we would can eight hundred quarts or more of fruits and vegetables, not to mention all the drying we did. We knew how to work hard, but we still found time to play hard as well. It was the training in those earlier years, under God's tutorship, that brought this blessing to us, and God can do the same for you!

About age twelve, the boys also applied this work ethic to jobs for our neighbors. Then, when they were about fourteen or so, they ran their own contracting business in addition to home-schooling. By eighteen, they each ran their own real estate businesses. The extremely valuable lessons that made all this possible were learned as young men in their homes under God and their parents.

Sad to say, I have known an eight-year-old boy who thought rinsing dishes while my son washed them was slave labor. I've known nine- and twelve-year-old girls that didn't know how to cook, how to do house-work, sew, or have a system for washing the dishes! I've known eight-year-old boys and girls that appeared not to know which end of the broom to use. They had no idea of a system to sweep the kitchen floor; they just dragged it around haphazardly. How very sad!

This is evidence of a mother's unfaithfulness to do her God-given work. She has mismanaged the use of her time and talent. I can tell you these mothers' lives are hard! It wasn't easier to let their children just "come up." The exhibition of passion is the result of the mother's course of indulgence. "The rod and reproof give wisdom: but a child left to [himself] bringeth his mother to shame" (Proverbs 29:15). If this is you, look to the God in heaven for direct guidance, and He will bring you out of your dilemma as surely as He brought Israel out of Egypt. He will teach you how to redeem your dropped stitches and begin right where you are.

If your children don't like being with you, ask yourself why. Be honest. Then correct your wrong course in Jesus and make your home different starting today. Your history need not continue.

Work approached as fun is beneficial. It can be done cheerfully, daily, in a matter-of-fact way that will become automatic. What a blessing! The children, rightly trained in neatness, order, routine, and regularity, will be a tremendous blessing in your home, in the work-place, in the church, and in society. A visitor to my home once said at lunchtime, "Everything seems to just happen automatically here; how is that?"

"It didn't happen by chance," I responded. "It's a daily routine for rising, worshiping, doing laundry, meal preparation, eating, clean-up work, play, family time, and bedtime."

My children carried responsibilities because that was our normal, daily routine. They needed little direction from the sidelines because it was our way of life—with or without me. I typically cooked ahead in preparation for more talk time with our guests. So it didn't just happen; it's the blessing of a planned daily routine. And so it can be with you.

Jesus, my General, wants to be your General as well. He may not lead you in the identical way He has led me, because we have different personalities and different family needs. But the fruit will have the stamp of Christ's character and power amidst your unique family unit. *My family is not the pattern.* The age at which we had our boys assuming certain tasks and responsibilities is not necessarily your pattern. Jesus is your sure pattern, and our homes are the school where we learn to express that pattern.

"Whatsoever thy hand findeth to do, do [it] with thy might" (Ecclesiastes 9:10). We must deny, restrain, and starve the expressions of the flesh—irritation, confusion, anxiety, despair, low self-esteem, fretfulness, faultfinding, sassiness, bad language, disorderliness, laziness, poor work habits, and even shyness. The thoughts, feelings, habits, and tastes must be redeemed to God's side of the equation. We must cooperate with Him to cultivate pleasant conversation, new habits of orderliness, skillfulness, good and diligent work habits. We need the power of God so that this transformation may take place at the level of our child's thoughts and feelings.

Getting the heart is getting "Disorderly Dora" to cooperate with God's right thoughts and disposition and come out of her wrong way. Our child often mirrors us. If we do not like what we see, we must let God change us, and while we are learning new ways, we can teach our child. You will understand the particular struggles of "Disorderly Dora," for they will often be the same as yours. You will want to show her a better way and not let her continue in disorderly habits, which are a curse. Pray for God to direct your steps and give you the right words to say to gain her heart in cooperation.

" 'Disorderly Dora,' you don't want to do it that way; you want to do it this way instead." Then show her how to hang up her dress nicely rather than leaving it in a heap on the floor. "Poor dress! We want to keep it looking very nice by hanging it up right away. And it will save me time later from having to iron it. This is good for me."

Now, let Dora re-enact the same thing you just demonstrated to her. If her heart is not with you, it will be obvious by her countenance and attitude. Pray for God to show you what to address and what to leave alone. If it is obvious that you do not have her cooperation, you may need to go to firmer measures. Then return in a sweet spirit to the matter of hanging up the dress. You want her to put forth the effort to do right in the right spirit. You don't want just outward conformity; you want heart-obedience.

Instruct and correct her in a Christlike spirit until she finally cooperates. Then give encouraging, approving words so that she will repeat this better way. The new way is awkward at first, so encourage it. If you need to have her do it three or more times to get it right, do it. You are after the heart. Tell her often that she can be neat and orderly in Jesus and show her practically how to do that. When she falls and fails, don't criticize or condemn her, but rather entreat her to return to God. Then be the ready hands to take her to Him. Gaining right thoughts on the throne of the heart is freedom from disorder. Use prayer at any time during the instruction and discipline to make real Christ's presence and power. Tell them they can change in Jesus' power.

Make the right desirable. Parenting has everything to do with expelling wrong thoughts and inculcating right thoughts. "Clearing the dishes is lots of fun. Let me show you the way." "Sweeping the floor right can make the job go more quickly. Let me show you how." Enlist the child's hope, joy, and courage to change.

Deuteronomy admonishes us to teach our children to know God personally. They need practical understanding of how He delivers us from our sin with a mighty hand and how He has commanded our homes to be neat, clean, and orderly. We are to utterly slay all the giants—the false gods and false ways in our life. Teach your children how Jesus is there to heal them of all their sins and to strengthen every weakness. We need never lose a battle against self. When we are on God's side, we are the majority. We are to teach and train our children as Moses taught Israel—under God. Our happiest, safest course of life is to hear His voice, obey His ways, and go to battle under His generalship. We are to teach all these things to our children when we rise up, while we work, when we eat, and when we lie down. This is the most important work and purpose for our life on this planet.

If we, as parents, neglect to teach our children the art of useful labor, we hurt and damage them for the present and future life. The home will be unkempt, untidy, or even unclean. The kitchen will have stacks of dirty dishes. Grumbling and arguing will be commonplace; tools and other things will chronically be lost, jumbled, or difficult to find. Meals will not be regular or planned, and the yard, garden, and car will be in perpetual disorder or uncleanness. This is going after other gods, and your children will perpetuate this family dysfunction.

The physical disorder of the home graphically describes *our spiritual condition* as well. The same slackness, the same lack of neatness, order, and thoroughness seen in the home management will also be lacking in the management of the mind and heart. Wrong thoughts, feelings, emotions, and habits will prevail. The clutter and disorder of the home describe the clutter and disorder that are in the mind and heart. Both the home and the character are terribly damaged and in need of a Savior. Will you be the leader, under God, to correct these imbalances in the power of heaven?

A great and important field of labor is before the mother at home. If true Christian mothers will present to society children who have integrity of character, firm principles, good work habits, and sound morals, they will have performed the most important of all missionary labors. Children thoroughly educated to take their place in society, trained in useful labor as unto the Lord, are the greatest evidence of Christianity that can be given to the world. The faithful parent will not be occupied in other pursuits that keep them from this greater work. Mothers will teach their children to share with them the domestic duties so that they may have a knowledge of practical life. These children will regard useful employment as essential to happiness, ennobling rather than degrading. It will prepare them for life as a mother or a father one day, having Jesus as a constant Companion and a familiar Friend and Problem Solver.

These are the children entrusted to your care. The hand that rocks the cradle rules the world. The influence of the parents—to a large degree—determines whether the child will be like Ahab, a bad king who was self-serving, self-directed, and led with cruelty and oppression, or like David, a good king who was God-directed and led in a balance of justice and mercy.

How you use your time is your choice. Useful labor is God's tool to develop good attributes and to help us experience redemption from sin and selfishness. In doing this work, the mother is doing the work God has given her to do. Educating and training her children to serve God is the highest service that parents can render to God.

What will you do?

The Lone Embrace
A Special Word of Encouragement for Single Parents

Providing a set routine, useful labor, and the skills to do that labor under God are your keys to a successful single-parent family. You can cut off Satan's use of idle time as his workshop by making practical household duties a pleasant occupation and by exercising your children in the expression of proper appreciation. Also, direct them in how to use their time in well-directed, useful lines in your absence, while you are at your job.

When the laundry, cooking, and cleaning are done, inspire them to other habits of industry, such as needlework or sewing for girls, and carpentry or mechanics for boys. Direct their industry according to their age, ability, and interests. Once they are in their teens, you can direct that industry into experiencing different occupations so that their time and energy are positively occupied. This will be your fortress, under God, against the devil's wiles to lure your children into evil, destructive lines. Be not overcome of evil, but crowd out evil with sufficient wholesome, useful labor.

Chapter 17
BALANCE

"A just weight and balance [are] the LORD's" (Proverbs 16:11).

$\mathcal{I}$ was in an antique store playing with an old scale that operated on a balance spring. It took skill and precision to balance those scales when I used anything other than identical weights. Lack of experience and of familiarity with the various weights was my difficulty. The solution would be gaining familiarity and experience in their use. With practice, I'm sure I could learn the art of balancing the scale. How about you?

The parallel to balancing my life at home was simply profound. The first area in need of adjustment was that of balancing work and play. This scale helped me to see the big picture. I needed to experiment with consulting God on how to become better balanced in work and play.

Jim has lovingly called me "Martha" because of my strong work ethic and my drive to complete one task before starting another. My inclination is never to play unless the work is all done—and there is always another task or home improvement I could be doing. My grandmother instilled this concept into my being. Yes, I was imbalanced toward the work side. I know otter-type friends who are imbalanced toward the play side. They neglect properly caring for their home, training their children in efficient work habits, and developing a proper schedule because play is an impulsive priority that crowds out work. The point is that imbalance on either side has its problems and needs correction.

Jesus is our solution. He wants to pull us out of whichever ditch we find ourselves in and to place us in the middle of the road. He will remove weights from the heavy side and place a weight on the other side to achieve balance. That means we must experiment with making changes and then evaluate if that adjustment was the right balance—too much or too little? God wants the otter to work more and the worker to play more. And we must cooperate as need be by shifting our use of time.

At ages four and six, my boys were too heavy on the play side. I was the slave to the home duties, and God wanted to bring me out of that comfortable ditch. So He had me call them in to fold the clothes, and I met resistance. We worked through the necessary attitude changes, and with Jesus' leading, consequences were successful in prompting these changes in my children. In hindsight, that was good. The next step was to add the list of personal-care chores and a second list—the chore list—to divide up the daily household duties. God was shifting my weights of time and energy to the work side of the balance scale for my boys. This was a positive change.

Now God shifted me personally to play more with my boys in the free time I had gained. Going for a walk with the boys, talking or picking flowers, was fine with me. But these boys were growing up in Montana, which prompted adventure. They wanted me to climb trees with them, go for bike rides, and play hide and seek outside after dark, and these were not as desirable to me as other activities. God prompted me to see a need to change my attitude toward these activities. As I cooperated, so did He!

Next, the game of Mother, may I? came to mind, and we played it. This was a fun way to teach the boys to listen carefully, to think, and to follow directions appropriately. The skill required in this game went beyond the game to everyday life. God showed me that He was using this game to build a new foundation in the boys' minds that I was a good authority figure. It's fun; you play, laugh, and enjoy each other. It was a good balancer for me. God is so good at shifting weights of various sizes into and out of our lives. I recommend playing Mother, may I? It's great fun!

Once we began school, God prompted me to play store with the boys. Even if we had only twenty minutes, we'd play with what time we had before we had to return to our schedule. We would price books and other items and put them on the living room bookshelf, and it was our store. I'd ring up their purchases on our play cash register. They'd count out their money, and I'd count out their change. They learned honesty, integrity, and courtesy in this play. We had such fun! Soon the boys wanted to be the merchant, and salesmanship began. Counting money and making change was excellent learning and an excellent use of our time.

Matthew would say, "Your purchase was five dollars and fifty cents out of ten dollars." Then he would count out the change coin by coin and dollar by dollar—"that's six dollars, . . . seven, . . . eight, . . . nine, . . . and ten dollars. Thank you!"

Teaching the boys the art and procedure of making change was important learning. This play also taught them how to socialize and be interested in their customers' needs. It's good to help your customer find what he is looking for. I found all this play fun; it was like playing house as a little girl.

But God again put His finger on the scale, adjusting my balance of work and play. He challenged me to enjoy "boy play" and to put my heart into it more. By His grace, I did. Attitudes had to be surrendered and better ones put in their place. This shifting of weights was not natural, but it was possible through connection with Christ. We played duck, duck, goose, and soon I enjoyed it. Then the tag I had learned to enjoy turned into hide-and-seek in the woods after dark. Another attitude adjustment was necessary, and again God performed that miracle in my heart and mind. Soon I enjoyed this, too, with relish. God is good. Then came mountain climbing, swimming in iceberg-cold lakes, and bike rides that got longer and longer! All these turned into success stories. It's a challenge to remain balanced, for it is an ever-changing balancing act with age and family interests. Once balanced is not always balanced. Balance requires perpetual evaluation.

Jim, too, was prompted by God to enter into play with the boys. One day Jim saw the boys arguing in the large sandbox we had made for them.

"This is my side!" Matthew said.

"No, this is *my* side!" Andrew argued.

"Jim, they don't know how to play with their trucks. I think that's why they argue. I've shown them how to play somewhat, but they need their father's expanded ideas. Can you teach them some fun things to do?" I asked.

"Me? Oh, I don't want to do that," Jim responded. But his time with God was paying off, and he inquired what God would have him to do. Very soon Jim was out in the sandbox with the boys.

"Vroom, vroom," went the trucks. They built lakes, dams, and waterways together. Such awesome fun they had! Squeaks and squeals of delight were heard. When Jim came in, he told me he didn't know how to play. I thought he did marvelously!

"Beep, beep, beep!" I'd hear when they'd back up their trucks. Jim taught them how to make towns and roads. An ambulance came to rescue injured people on the roads and in their homes. Tow trucks rescued people who slipped over the hill. A prayer was heard, and then "Putt, putt, putt!" The rescue was successful, and a "Hurrah, hurrah!" came from all three "boys." A father's influence in play is very far reaching and can be a strong influence for good. Whatever Father did, they imitated and expanded when they were alone.

This was valuable training in how to play. It taught them how to think and how to respond while cultivating integrity, honesty, helpfulness, and the ability to see what is truly important in life.

God had to balance Jim and me by adding play to our daily routine. Every evening at 6:30 P.M., it was family fun time. The adjustments were good once the shifting of the balance scale rested and settled in place. While going through these changes, I determined alone with God that I would be involved in my husband's and sons' interests and not miss out on their changing joys, be that in work or play.

It is amazing to me how many parents don't know how to play or work with their children. They have been taught that children are in one place and parents are in another. Jim and I found that our boys loved being with us more than anything else. Our children want us! Don't miss out on this bonding of their hearts to yours. If you need to change, you can if you allow God's divine power to attend your human effort.

When our boys were seven and nine years old, academic subjects began with school at home. If I had it to do over again, I would start schooling sooner than I did. I was living out a misconception I believed at the time. Again, I am not the pattern; Jesus is. Don't follow me; rather, follow Jesus' leading. Jesus will help you sort through what's best for you and when. But with this addition of school to our lives came the need for more balancing and more changing.

The first few months of school were very frustrating because the "best" curriculum for phonics and reading didn't work for us. The boys were excited about school, but that enthusiasm quickly waned. After three months, they still could not read. Something had to change. Jim knew it needed to be the curriculum. However, to abandon it felt like failure to me. Yet, I came to see that this particular curriculum was the wrong weight in the "scales" of *our* life. It may work for others, but not for us. I changed to Rod and Staff textbooks and phonics programs, which proved to be a blessing. It was an excellent curriculum for us. It grounded my boys in mastering the basics. By the second week, they were reading well and enjoying learning. What a thrill! This was a good change that brought success and balance into our home.

As home-schooling progressed, increasing problems of the will now arose in our daily routine. Again, I took time to evaluate the difficulty with God, Jim, and reason. Both Jim and God suggested there was too much mental work for the boys and not enough physical occupation to balance it out. It is good for all children to have a balance of both the mental and physical exercise daily.

So I evaluated our present routine. The boys had personal worship and family worship—that was mental. Then they had house chores and breakfast, which were physical activities, but not very strenuous. By 10:00 A.M. the house was in order and school began, which was mental work. School lasted until 3:00 P.M. I had observed that problems regarding the will typically were most common after three or four hours of school.

"Lord, would more physical activity help my boys? If so, what will bring about balance for us?"

Time with God gave me a plan. I'd do one school subject, then do fifteen minutes or so of activity that was physical—work or play—to break up all the mental taxation. In the beginning I struggled internally, thinking, "My friend schools her girls, and they are done with school by 1:00 P.M. They appear to have no problems with the will as we do. What's the matter with me, anyway? Or what is wrong with my boys? Her girls can do subject after subject without any difficulty. It would be so nice for it to be that way for us!

"Sally, you must do what is best for you and your boys, led by Me, not by a person. Families, dispositions, and constitutions vary. This does not make one better than another. I want you free to be you. I want your boys to be the best each of them can be in Me. Remember David could not wear Saul's armor; neither can you necessarily do things the way others can."

I altered the schedule to meet this need, and it was perfect for us. Providing for my boys' needs of balance between mental and physical activity offset many of our problems with the will. The mental weariness had been contributing to greater proneness to irritability. Boys are different from girls, I understand. Maybe so!

Another weight-shifting idea came to mind once this attitude was in place. I made each subject a one-hour slot in my schedule. Not all subjects took a whole hour. This would be a positive motivation for the boys to govern themselves, and it would give us another spot for physical exercise. We agreed that if the boys worked diligently and finished their subject early, they could go for a bike ride or work on an outside project of their choice. This would be a positive motivation for the boys to govern themselves. This delighted them and added another balance to our lives.

A ten-minute bike ride gave vim and vigor to Andrew to face understanding his math lesson. Fifteen minutes of shoveling snow around the cabin not only helped Father and provided good fellowship but brought oxygen to a weary mind, making it sharp for English class. Digging an igloo or cross-country skiing down the driveway for those few moments whisked away the cobwebs in their minds. A fun and lively game of Mother, may I? lifted their spirits. Working in the greenhouse, raking the lawn, de-barking fence rails with a drawknife, or whatever we had available to do worked wonders to free up their minds for more school. Along with school, the house, yard, gardens, and even the garage and car were kept neat, clean, and orderly. What a blessing was ours in choosing to make God-led decisions that would bring balance to our lives.

I liked the boys' recreation or occupation to be pleasant, yet still accomplish something practical. It proved to be a good balance while eliminating idle time as the devil's workshop.

What do I mean by recreation and occupation, you may ask?

I consider recreation to be going for a bike ride, swimming, hiking, playing "Mother, may I?" knitting, crocheting, recreational reading of a character-building story, ball games such as catch and throw the ball, kickball, bat and ball, croquet, a relaxing stroll, time to think, or just relaxing in the warm sunshine.

Occupation, on the other hand, would be more like a work project or a task one looks upon as fun. At ages ten and twelve the boys built a bicycle obstacle course through the woods using the moments and larger portions of free time. Once, they hand dug, into the steep hillside behind the garage, a pathway down to the road. This was a big project for the boys and brought them much joy. They built it to bike, sled, and walk on. This was a pleasant occupation that accomplished practical things and challenged them.

Useful occupation begins with little projects and grows to bigger ones as the child's abilities and confidence grow. Bike riding, digging igloos in the snow, shoveling snow, pounding nails in a board to learn how to hammer—all these are useful occupations. Our second summer in Montana, we prepared for and built a greenhouse. The boys helped haul rock for the foundation and helped stir the cement in the wheelbarrow. They helped pound nails in the roof and do whatever else they could. Garden posts and rails needed to be de-barked for our garden fences. The boys found this grand work, and their muscles grew as they dug postholes for the fencing. At ages six and eight, they began building birdhouses. It was on-the-job training because neither Jim nor I had any experience in such things. So they began with a picture, some tools, and trial and error. Matthew built a jungle-gym set out of logs at age ten, beginning by chopping down trees with an axe for the lumber and using a drawknife to make the logs smooth. It was tall enough for a six-foot man to hang from the cross bars without touching the ground. Andrew, aged eight, built a baby swing out of small limbs he cut and gathered; later he built a very nice adult swing upon which Jim and I established swing time. Next, the boys built a set of parallel bars and learned how to hang and jump on them. Helping the contractor build our guest cabin was great training for our boys and an excellent practical occupation. Useful labor developed skillful work habits while training them in perseverance and endurance, and giving them many experiences in problem solving. These activities helped keep our school time balanced with physical exercise and made summertime fun.

We made opportunities for useful occupation in order to have something at hand to interest our boys. If it wasn't there, we made something practical happen—a home improvement, for example, that they could learn to do. What is at hand where you live? Nothing, you say? Go to God and let Him help inspire you with some practical occupation for your children beginning right now in your home. Make something happen. Our boys are so grateful for all the skills they have today because of the direction we gave in their young years. The older they got, the larger and more useful the activities became. You will be able to read more on this topic in my next book on raising teenagers.

God wants balance in our homes, and only time with Him will keep us balanced. Can we become overbalanced in the area of occupation and recreation? Can we become underbalanced? We need His wisdom in shifting around those weights!

As our home-schooling progressed, Jim started up a real-estate practice, so a phone graced our home after more than three years without one. The addition of that phone created another imbalance that needed to be addressed.

Friends and relatives began to call, so glad to be able to reach us. But this made it more difficult to remain on our schedule. I made all my food from scratch, home-schooled the boys, kept a tidy home, and wanted daily time for God, Jim, and family play. These things got so easily crowded out.

"Lord, where is the balance by adding phone calls to my day? Experience has shown me that something will be rushed or eliminated."

God led me to learn to say "no" and not always "yes," as was my nature.

Sometimes I'd say "yes" when I should have said "no." For example, during school I sometimes neglected my own children in order to help another mother with her child on the phone. Saying, "yes" without seeking to know and do God's will only made it easier to say "yes" automatically. It cost me dearly in math class and in the character of my sons. Thankfully, I saw my error and cooperated with God to say "no" and "yes" under His direction. I had to cooperate with Jesus in how to pick up this dropped stitch of character—correcting this imbalance.

Where is the balance? Because of my trials and errors, I became familiar with these *weights of time* in phone calls—the pluses and minuses. I needed to learn to filter each call through Christ to know what I should do. I took some calls and made them brief. Others I deferred until later. And some required a "no" so that school would not be impeded.

I learned to say "no" gracefully. It got easier, and God led me to find balance by seeing that the education of my children was to be my "business." During these set hours, I could not be distracted from my purpose. I was convinced it was not God's will to delay my boys' education in order to talk on the phone during school time. If my "business" hours were 10:00 A.M. to 5:00 P.M., I needed to be there during those times with all my energy to do my business. Educating my boys academically is a most important work. I need not feel guilty to say "no" to other's business in order to make a daily success of this one. God would not lay a second business on me to crowd out the first, but Satan would. God wants us to be thorough in our work—diligent but not overworked. So who would push me to overwork or to substitute another work? Not God! He wants us to do a few things well, to be skilled at what we put our hand to. So I had to pick my priorities and let the world go by hurriedly without me. I determined to do the work God had laid at my door and do it to the best of my ability. God loves to lead us to balance.

Soon my new priority was keenly tested. My church wanted help with this program or that social event, a Bible study or cooking for a needy person, baby-sitting or mowing an elderly person's lawn, building this or that, or a fundraiser. Now each of these things may be a truly worthy project, but if I do all or even some of them, what happens to my boys' education? It gets crowded out—delayed—and Satan is very happy! As a family, we had to consult God regarding His will for us in each call upon our time and resources. Is this a call from God or a call from man? So I learned that in doing God's will for my life, I will not always please man. Pleasing God is more important, I decided.

"Lord," I concluded, "it doesn't matter if sister So-and-So appears to be able to do more than I can. All that matters is, Am I doing Your will and not neglecting my post of duty nor leaving undone the work you gave me to do? Help me see that balance taking place in my life day by day!"

God spoke to my heart, *"You see, Satan wants to crowd out your time with Me, your communication time with your spouse, your children's social and academic development, and their character formation. One needs time to connect, to bond with one another. So Satan will always oppose and try to crowd out the important things in life. He is most successful using 'good' to crowd out the best use of your time. It's a closer test!"*

"The scales on the balance have some very fine adjustments," I mused. "So through familiarity, experimentation, and evaluation under God I will find the balance for how to use my time."

As you determine what your business is, under God, you may

have to restructure your priorities. You will need heavenly wisdom to do that rightly. And when you do, even though others may not understand or agree, you will find the peace in God that you desire in following Him.

Another area in need of balance is our parenting approach. We all tend to err on one side or the other.

Some approach parenting from the too-soft side and are indulgent toward their children by avoiding correction, letting them come up like weeds; they are more sentimental than practical. They typically excuse or avoid bad behavior. They see firmness and consistency in Christ as unloving. They misrepresent Christ as One with whom anything goes—that God loves evil, and there is no need for change. These poor parenting practices instill detrimental lies and imbalances into your children's concepts and life.

On the other hand, some approach parenting from the too-firm side and are harsh, angry, dominant, dictatorial, forceful, or compelling, expecting their "little soldiers" to march cheerfully under their oppressive, demeaning banner—wrongly calling this love. They lack the balance of compassion and love. They do not give the child proper room for growth or a parent's hearing ear. These wrongly represent Christ as cold, dogmatic, unloving, and heartless.

Too much management is as bad as too little management. To avoid the ditch on either side, we need God personally directing our lives, and we must cooperate with the Holy Spirit in shifting the weights from our too-strong side to our weak side to achieve the balance we need.

God wants to bring us all, step by step, to the middle of the road, where it's safe to travel. It's dangerous to travel in either ditch. God wants mercy and justice to balance each other. Recognize that God will have you exercise your weak trait to strengthen those muscles, not to goad you to a greater imbalance in your strength. This will require a close work, a close evaluation. So commune with God and learn from Him how to respond before you commune with your children in a corrective situation. Balance is worth it, for it will bring about symmetry of character in all family members and a happier home. Isn't that what you want?

Balance is truly an endless subject. Thoughts have been shared here, and you and God can practically apply what is valuable for you and then expand its application. To achieve balanced parenting, we all need

God as our Head, directing our steps to come out of our familiar ditch that is so strangely comfortable, and stand in the middle of the road. The towing strap that gets us out of either ditch is faith in Christ. The power is grace from God, empowering our choices and enabling us to cooperate with Him to do His will, not ours.

The Lone Embrace
A Special Word of Encouragement for Single Parents

God calls you to be the patriarch of your single-parent family. Even under your circumstances you can lead your children aright in God. Your gender does not matter—God wants you to "marry" Him. God makes up for any imbalance in your life, for He'll bring you out of it if you follow Him. Follow Him as He leads you to be the cheerful, pleasant companion, teacher, and co-worker with your children that God intends you to be. Make your home atmosphere heavenly. Balance your children's occupation, recreation, academics, and play, and all aspects of your family life.

As you "marry" Christ and follow Him, your drawbacks don't matter, for you can be complete in Him. Man's difficulty is God's opportunity. If you gain that balance in Him, your children will long for your company and compassion, wanting to be by your side and to develop a character after God their Father. You will have accomplished the best in life.

Chapter 18
IMPORTANCE OF A SCHEDULE

"And thou shalt teach them diligently unto thy children, and shalt talk of them when thou sittest in thine house, and when thou walkest by the way, and when thou liest down, and when thou risest up" (Deuteronomy 6:7).

Hophni and Phinehas were the sons of Eli, the high priest of Israel. They grew up listening to instructions in righteous living and had advanced knowledge of right and wrong. As young men, they were consecrated to the priesthood. They wore the sacred garments, performed the ritual services, and instructed the people. And yet, their service was a mockery to God because they spurned godly living. They used the forms of religion for personal selfish gain. While they professed to represent God, they knew Him not.

How could that be—*they knew not God?*

Faulty, imbalanced training produced this fruit. Eli was neglectful of exercising the firmer virtues with them while they were young. He was still unwilling to correct their imbalances as youth and young men. The effort and discipline needed was distasteful to him. God had asked father Eli to remove his sons from office because they were causing Israel to sin. They had used their positions of authority to perpetuate stealing, lying, intimidation, and fornication. This brought much pain and heartache to Eli. God impressed upon his heart what to do, but again he was too indulgent and sentimental. It was too hard to bring proper consequences upon them. Eli wanted God to do Eli's work of disciplining and parenting, for it was uncomfortable to him.

Aren't we guilty of this, too, when we hope that the church, our pastor, or anyone else will teach and train our children in upright living? We want others to pick up our dropped stitches. Then we wrongly blame others for our child's misbehavior. But this is not God's way. The work of parents cannot be transferred to God; He will not do for us what we can do for ourselves! He requires us to nurture (love) and admonish (give consequences to) our children in the way of God from their beginning and to train them up, to see to it that they do the right.

Hophni and Phinehas were accustomed to following their own will above that of God. They knew about God—but did not know God in their hearts and minds because their parents were unwise in the use of their time and neglected to deal with the true character development. "Because sentence against an evil work is not executed speedily, therefore the heart of the sons of men is fully set in them to do evil" (Ecclesiastes 8:11). As boys and men, Hophni and Phinehas knew another voice, another god, working in their hearts and minds. That voice was Satan, who took up the slack and trained them effectively with *his* thoughts and habits for *his* service of evil and selfishness, and they followed him. God finally removed them from the priesthood by allowing the Philistines to slay them in battle, and Eli's outcome is questionable. Eli was responsible for the character defects he could have changed in his sons!

Is indulgence love? Is life really easier this way? Do you want this to happen to your children? What is the best safeguard for training your children in the service of God so that they will come to know God personally in order to serve Him and not self?

A proper schedule is a vital tool in this process. Yes! Indeed, the schedule is the basket that carries in it the tools of training. It provides the structure that makes you the master of circumstances rather than the victim of happenstance. Under God, it makes possible the matching of your priorities with how you actually spend your time. It takes time to be holy.

An essential tool for knowing God is scheduling talk time with Him daily so that both parent and child can come to know His voice speaking to their hearts, minds, and souls in their personal worship time. Can you come to know someone without talking or spending time with them? A proper schedule will give time for this.

Our life needs to be so regular in personal time with God at the beginning of our day that Satan can have no access to us. God cannot be in charge of our lives unless we have given Him permission day by day. Satan wants us to see worship time as unimportant or just to be negligent or inconsistent so that he can have more access to the mind and heart to do his dastardly deeds, and we become comfortable with his thoughts in place of God's thoughts—for our tendency is downward, not upward! So we need to connect and commune with God in heaven so that He can change us into His image.

I was a night person and preferred staying up late at night; I would get out of bed just in time to launch into the duties of my day. God challenged my thinking: *"If you seek after Me in the middle or the end of the day and not the early morning, who has been leading you before you sought Me?"*

"Another god?" I answered. "Oh, I don't want Satan directing me!"

"And how do you successfully battle against Satan and self without a vital connection to Christ?" He added.

"Well, I can't do that either! I need to change my concept and my schedule. Truly, Jesus rose up early, and He is a safe example to follow," I decided. And God empowered me to be an early riser. It was difficult at first, but it comes naturally to me now and is far more rewarding.

Deuteronomy 6:7 tells us "teach them diligently." So what are we to teach diligently to our children? We are to teach them His "statutes"—which are His thoughts and purposes for our lives. Teach diligently His judgments—which are His loving, yet firm, consequences for going in the way of evil. Teach diligently His rules of conduct—how we should think, feel, respond, and love one another through His power and might. And teach diligently His Ten Commandments, which have to do with all these things. What we instill early in life goes with them for eternity. They will learn either to follow the God in heaven or Satan, the god of this world. A schedule gives our children the time and opportunity to know God's voice speaking to their hearts through experience.

Children aged five to seven can be taught a good pattern of prayer. Start with a short amount of time and lengthen it as they build these skills and God leads you. Teach them not only to ask God for this and that but also to take some time to sit quietly before God so that He can talk to them. Teach them how to discern thoughts from God as opposed to thoughts from self or Satan, using Scripture as the unerring standard. Also schedule time in their daily routine to read God's Word. Teach them to read a verse—or a portion of a verse—and to sit back to think what that verse means to them, in their home, today. If they don't read yet, have them listen to the Bible on a cassette tape, turning it on and off to think about it. Or a good illustrative Bible storybook can bring home the lesson in a quiet fashion as well. Teach them to turn the pages slowly and to think about the story. Teach them to ask God for understanding through His Holy Spirit to direct their reasoning. Teach them to evaluate their thoughts. Is it according to God's word, His principles, and His character? Surrender to God's leading and Word is all-important, and is what Hophni and Phinehas and Lucifer lacked training in.

By ages eight to twelve this experience of seeking and surrendering to God's leading will deepen and broaden. Teach them how to do word studies, topical studies, and cross-referencing using a concordance. Expose them to a wide selection of safe religious history books. They need to be taught the distinction between true and false study. Varying their study approaches keeps interest high. When a difficulty arises in their lives, have them study out God's will on that topic. All these avenues help them to come to know God intellectually. Now take what they have learned that day and apply their knowledge to how to treat their sibling or respond to their parents or restrain a negative trait in their character led by God. Now that knowledge about God becomes an experience. They discover that God can change them, and they are happier.

"Mommy, I want to be like Jesus. He is so kind and good. I don't ever want to be ugly again."

"That is Jesus knocking at your heart's door, dear. He is asking you if you want Him to come in."

"But I asked Him to do that in my prayer time this morning. Isn't that enough?"

"No, dear. Every moment of the day you again have a choice either to follow God and right or Satan and wrong. One moment you have a good thought, and another moment, you have an ugly thought. God will not force you to do His will. He asks you over and over throughout your day if you still want to follow Him. God wants permission to redeem your character every moment. So what is He after?"

"He is after my thoughts and feelings."

"That's right, son! For God to redeem or change your character, which is your thoughts and feelings, He needs your permission in the moment to change them. Jesus doesn't want to share the throne of your heart with Satan. So He asks you if you want Him to come in. He wants to clean out the room in your heart that needs cleaning, but He won't do it without your consent and cooperation. One moment you need your disposition cleaned, another your attitude, another your temper. This is how He puts His character—His thoughts and feelings—into you when you cooperate. It's letting Jesus come in. It's opening the door wide for Him to enter. This is yielding up your will, like you read about in your Bible. Now God's new thoughts flow into your habits, dispositions, and passions—freeing you to serve God and right. So you will become like Him."

"I see," he replied.

"Satan doesn't like you to have your personal worship and learn to let God's mind work in you. For when you come to know Jesus and how to let His divine power re-create you into His image, Satan's power over you is broken. You are set free to be good and to do right. By reading, seeing, or hearing God's Word, not only are you learning about Him, but if you apply that knowledge through the day, you will experience God changing you inside. Then you will want to follow God more."

"I do, Mother. I do. I want only Jesus in my heart. I will give Him my heart as often as He calls for it today."

What a loss to everyone when we do not schedule in personal worship time that kindles such conversations and learning experiences as this! Without this time set aside to become acquainted with our Maker, we will naturally hear only the voice of Hophni's and Phinehas's god. And we follow whatever we become familiar with. It takes effort and planning, executed regularly, to help our children come to know the voice of the God of heaven.

Satan well knows that his power is broken over parents and children alike when Christ is in charge of their life—especially their thoughts and feelings. The Holy Spirit will teach the willing mind to discern good thoughts versus evil thoughts, feelings, and dispositions. When evil is exposed for what it truly is and the child is trained to cry out to God and let go of those wrong ways, Satan trembles, well knowing that he is a defeated foe. That is why Satan does not want our children and youth to come to know Jesus personally and practically in this way. So he attempts to crowd out all the time he can from personal and family worships. He quite likes being unhindered in leading our children under his cloud of selfishness without God being a part of that equation.

Knowing this, God recorded in Deuteronomy 6:7, regarding his commandments, that we should "teach them diligently . . . when thou sittest . . . when thou walkest . . . when thou liest down . . . and when thou risest up." Begin seeking Him at the beginning of your day and all day long. End your day still seeking, communing, and remaining connected to Him. This is the parent's work given by God to do!

Closely related to personal worship time is the tool of regular morning and evening family worship time. Properly conducted, it provides a safe and happy place to discuss the Christian walk, to answer questions that arose in the child's personal time, and to instruct about God's character.

Hopefully, the father has found the freedom and power to be in Christ and to be the priest of his household under God morning and evening, fulfilling his God-given responsibilities. My Jim felt inadequate, awkward, and incapable at first, but as he cooperated with God, he has become very skilled at making family worship a highlight in the day for the entire family. We all have to learn of that personal God who can empower us to fulfill our part in His program.

Family worship is truly our first work for eternity. Our regularity to seek God in this way demonstrates loudly to our children that, yes, this is important for life. We don't allow any little thing to crowd it out.

A well-planned schedule has other benefits as well.

"Mom, I'm hungry. When is lunch?" Amber asked.

"Don't bother me now; I'm doing something important. I'll make lunch when I get to it!" Mother responded irritably.

Later: "Mom, I'm really hungry. Can we eat now?"

"Just go and find something in the kitchen to eat. I need to sleep now."

So Amber rummaged through a dirty kitchen, with dishes here and there. She got out some bread. It was rather crusty and hard from sitting out unwrapped, but it was all she could find. She spread some peanut butter on the bread and sat down at a sticky table where the breakfast dishes were still sitting.

What will Amber's home likely look like when she grows up? There is no set or regular time for even a meal. She doesn't know what to expect or when to expect it. Isn't it sad what we do to our children? Is this God's will? God is very dependable and timely. Shouldn't we be also? We can change in Him.

Our schedule, as a *training tool* for regularity, is a great blessing. It can alleviate many conflicts in the home by simply bringing in the element of predictability. It helps to define our purpose and direction in life and makes family teamwork possible. Today, irregularity and disorder are rampant and are extremely destructive to our families. Almost everything is happening; circumstances rule. This is not God's way. God is a God of order and dispatch. He has a time for everything and everything in its time. Under Christ's management, we are to run our homes like a well-oiled machine. Our children need to be trained in the art of neatness, order, and thoroughness in all they put their hand to. Keeping our home tidy can be done quickly and well and then maintained with little attentions often. God does not want housekeeping to be a tedious, never-ending job. This happens because of a lack of proper training in the skill of efficient, diligent workmanship.

A schedule is not to be an Egyptian taskmaster, whipping you moment-by-moment, but rather a familiar friend, keeping proper parameters in your life so that the essentials get done in our God-given time instead of the nonessentials taking precedence. As you let God truly lead you out of your bondage of negative, defeating thoughts, feelings, attitudes, habits, and dispositions about housekeeping, you will be freed to discover a schedule as your friend. Now you are equipped to teach this to your children. Now you know a Savior who can change your thoughts and attitudes and direct your steps in a better line. Now you can be free to have a happy, neat, clean, and orderly home. It's a little taste of heaven.

In order for your schedule to be your helper and not your enemy, you need to build some flex into your day. Instead of preparing a schedule incremented into fifteen- or thirty-minute slots, which pushes you, make it an hourly scheduling so that you have more time than is needed, which will give you flex for a brief phone call or a will problem. Stay focused on the task that is scheduled for a particular time. If it's cleaning, clean. If it's doing school, do it with all your heart and mind. If it's cooking, cook. If it's shopping, shop. Don't dawdle out of your time frame. It's so easy to shop an hour longer than you need to—and so hard to pick up the slack later. If it's worship time, lend your mind entirely, not divided. When your home is neat and in order, your mind rests, your emotions become calm, and your mind is more sensitive to God. To remain focused and remain within your allotted time frame is a discipline that becomes a good friend because you find that under God you can accomplish the desires of your heart.

If you bring this into your home, you will give your children a wonderful heritage of a proper schedule. Regularity allows consistency in time with God so that He doesn't get crowded out. Organization is cultivated, and great things can be accomplished in less time. A well-structured home is well appreciated; it is something one can count on. A well-structured schedule and the disciplines in lines of practical duties done quickly and well allows time for other productive things, bringing a happy, balanced life. Truly this is a talent. We have the privilege of passing this talent on to our children. It starts their journey with God, already out of Egypt and on the way to Canaan, the Land of Promise.

In my book *Parenting by the Spirit* are two chapters that go into aspects of beginning a schedule. If you'd like further ideas on this topic, see "Putting on the Brakes" and "Does Your Schedule Match Your Priorities?"

Our physical homes picture graphically the state of our spiritual house management. Our hearts and minds look in the same condition of clutter and mess to God as our physical homes. That is why God directed Moses to go down from the mountain and begin the spiritual reformation with Israel by putting their tents, their clothes, and their things in order. It was a lesson in sanctifying their hearts and homes for Him.

Training tools to know Jesus include scheduling time to prepare the meal, time to eat the meal, and time to clean it up after. Hasty meals and cleanup engender irritation, which wounds and alienates family members. We need to establish regular meal times, work time, school time, personal time, and family time. What you do not schedule in regularly will, in all likelihood, get crowded out. There will always be too many things one can do in a day, and the unimportant will crowd out the important. Or an easy-going personality will be inclined to do what is pleasant instead of what is needful. So using your God-led reason, establish your skeleton schedule first, getting comfortable in a routine, and then add in the other details you consider important. In this way the important can crowd out the unimportant.

God wants us to schedule our life, doesn't He? Of course! But what if we *say* we should be on a schedule, *express a desire* for a scheduled life, but never get around to implementing a regular bedtime, rising time, eating time, worship time, or working time? What will our children do? They will do as we do, not as we say. We will perpetuate bad habits—hindering their walk with God. Without regular scheduled time with God, can we *really* know Him? No; that's absurd! Our life says loudly that it doesn't matter what time we go to bed or get up. It says God isn't important; it is just something we say but do not do. We will be without power to live the Christian life in our self-directed existence. We will pass on that powerless experience to our children, provoking them to discouragement. What we do speaks louder than what we say.

This lack of schedule will make you like Eli—letting your children come up like weeds, cultivated in doing their own will not God's, without direction, without proper training or consequences, teaching them that there are no consequences for going against God. Are you willing to let Satan work his evil work in the thoughts, feelings, dispositions, and responses of your children so that they are destructive soldiers in his army? No, no, a thousand times no! They must come to know God.

But what is the cost of not repeating Eli's story with its sad ending? It is facing my weaknesses and learning how to overcome self in Jesus—and then teaching this to my children, in the balance of love and firmness.

My past experience doesn't matter; nor does my lack of training, my spouse's lack of cooperation, my leader's failure to lead the family, or my children's lack of desire or cooperation. All that really matters is what God is asking me to do. If God is asking me to step out in faith—that which is not seen, yet believed—I must choose to step out and do what I see and know is right. In Him, I can get on a schedule and keep it. If I have to swim upstream, so be it; God's strength is sufficient! If I have to go against my child's will, God's wisdom is great enough to show me how to gain his heart. I'll tune my ear to heaven for counsel. If I have to face my history and my habits that are opposed to Him, I can know that God is stronger than my history or any habit. In Him we are omnipotent against the pull of our history.

"Because they have no changes, therefore they fear not God" (Psalm 55:19). This means we do not know God as it is our privilege to know Him. This, too, can change.

We can deny the wrong thoughts, habits, or history in the power of Jesus. With my hand in His, following His leading, victory is guaranteed. We have a heaven to win and a hell to shun. We have a warfare before us. We are to fight giants, evicting them from our land, and our General, Jesus, is willing to lead us successfully in this battle.

Then why aren't we successful more often? Eli found the task of disciplining his sons too hard for his personality. Many mothers find scheduling their lives a failure. Why? Trying to do it in our own strength doesn't work. You need to learn to do it in Jesus. Hanging onto our old ways, while trying to follow God's way, is self-defeating because God doesn't possess your whole heart. You must give up entirely on the old way, wrap both arms around Jesus, and go forward, knowing you are a spiritual paralytic whom God will heal.

Believe that you can change. Believe that you can mature in Christ and come out of those slothful habits of your childhood. This is vitally important for success. God is your General. Become proficient in knowing and doing what He directs you to do each moment. Put your hand to the plow. Be willing to change, to discipline yourself, and to say "no" to many things so that you have time to say "yes" to the right things. Be courageous in Him. As you begin to do what you know you should do, He comes into your life and changes your thoughts and feelings. If, like Lot's wife, you long for the old way, God cannot change you. You will stay where you are just like a pillar of salt—unmoved and miserable. You must come out of your comfort zone by faith in Jesus and follow Him.

Mothers, come to Jesus with your perplexities. You will find grace sufficient to help you manage your children's character and train them in skillful work habits, timeliness, and staying on a schedule. Jesus wants to help us redeem negative, ugly attitudes, thoughts, and feelings. If your children's thoughts are wrong, their feelings will be wrong. Help them acquire habits of self-control in Jesus. Tell them that they do not want to invite evil angels into their lives to control their thoughts and feelings. That's misery! Teach your children to bring their sins and shortcomings to Jesus, asking for forgiveness and believing that He pardons, receives, and cleanses them. It's the way to true happiness.

Train the will and impulses of your children so that the young tendrils entwine about God for support. Teach them to ask the Lord to help them in the little things, to be helpful, to see the small duties that need to be done, and to do them in a good spirit. In this training program, time spent with God and our example are essential.

We need to be missionaries to our children and youth by teaching them to do those things needful to be done in the home. Instead of repining that you cannot do great things in some foreign missionary field, improve your opportunities in the home field, and your work will be acceptable to God. Securing the hearts of your children for eternity is a more important work for you than anything you might do for those far away from home. Be faithful in the performance of the little things that may seem unimportant to you. Your true missionary spirit will convert your children to follow Christ. It is the willingness to do the duties that lie in your path that will prove you worthy of being entrusted with larger responsibilities by God. Mother, sweep those floors, shake those rugs, wash those dishes, do the laundry, iron, clean, scrub, and put the house in order with the spirit of Christ, while teaching your children to do the same. Teaching our own children how to walk with God is the greatest missionary outreach we can do.

Family time is an important part of our schedule. It gives us time to talk, time to play, laugh, and enjoy each other. It's valuable time to bind the heart of the child to the parent under God. Following a schedule will result in many, many other benefits. We have talked about only the essential things that need to be in our everyday schedule. To have room for the essentials, we will have to simplify our present life and, under God, find the balance to add all the other necessities for our life.

We need to make our lives quieter. Less is more. Effort is valuable. Don't wait for a miracle to take place that will require no effort or struggle, for if you do, you will be sorely disappointed. A miraculous transformation without any effort or cooperation on our part is not God's plan of action. Pray to God about the changes you need to make, and then put forth all the effort you can to answer your own prayers and bring them to pass.

You need Jesus as your General in this majestic task of scheduling your life in a proper balance. Christ will be with you just as He was with the three Hebrews in the fiery furnace. He delivered them by loosing the ropes that bound them while they were *in the fire* of affliction. He will also loose your ropes of sin, selfishness, any habit, and all history that bind both you and your children *in your fires of affliction.* This is a God-honoring work! He is the great I AM. "I [am] the LORD, the God of all flesh: is there any thing too hard for Me?" (Jeremiah 32:27).

THE LONE EMBRACE
A SPECIAL WORD OF ENCOURAGEMENT FOR SINGLE PARENTS

What all single parents need is a true friend to help organize their life and get everything important done. That helper is your schedule, under God! Even your home can be improved; it can run like a well-oiled machine, bringing peace and order. I've known single parents who have tried embracing a schedule with God's leading who have reported success beyond their hopes and dreams. Schedules had failed them before, but not this time. They began by letting God have their thoughts and feelings and create in them right attitudes and dispositions. Wow, what a difference Jesus can make!

No longer are you at the mercy of your history or the whim of childish demands. Your life can be in control thanks to Jesus being willing to be your General and the Leader in your home. Taking time to talk and counsel with God regularly is your key to success. Yes, it requires decision, determination to change, forethought, planning, and teaching diligently our family team as Deuteronomy instructs us. But once this is in place and functioning, the importance of our schedule becomes evident, and is now seen as the friend and helper God intended it to be. May God's presence be with you!

Chapter 19

A CHILD'S BEST FRIEND

"I am a companion of all [them] that fear thee, and of them that keep thy precepts" (Psalm 119:63).

Our boys were ten and twelve years old. Six years had passed since we had moved to the mountains to learn how to let God be our Lord and to find out if Christianity had the power to change us. Jim and I had changed a great deal and fortified our marriage by opening communication to an unprecedented level. Our boys had come a long way in being good, faithful workers. Chores were second nature, charts were no longer necessary, and the work was done cheerfully and automatically. Life was great!

One day, church friends had just left our home after lunch. I put the boys to doing up all the dishes; they were a great team. I got the house back in order. Then it happened! I saw the boys standing at the sink grumbling at each other.

"Boys, what's the matter?" I asked.

No answer came. They just stared at each other. Their countenance made me think it was pretty serious. They appeared angry, which didn't make sense, for we didn't battle over doing dishes anymore.

Jim and I together asked, "Boys, what's going on?"

"We're just your slaves!" they responded with bitterness. "You had us just to do **your** dishes!"

"We what . . . ?" I responded.

"Come over here and let's talk." Jim intervened.

"You had us just so we'd do your dishes! We work too hard! We do home-school six days a week; that's against the law, you know! We do more than one lesson per class per day; that's wrong!" Matthew and Andrew shared all their feelings of injustice.

"Who told you these things?" Father asked wisely. "We had been functioning for a long time in harmony with joyful work habits."

"The pastor's boys told us so," Andrew admitted (see 1 Corinthians 15:33).

"Lord, what would Thou have us to do?" both Jim and I asked silently.

"Reasoning is the best place to start," the Holy Spirit impressed on our minds. *"Find out what the lying thoughts are and try to correct them by cultivating the opposite thoughts. Bring them to Me to be enabled to change."*

"Boys, you are not slaves. You are part of the family team. These are **our** dishes, as you well know. When you do the dishes, Father and I are doing other things. We don't sit in the chair just making you work and work! We all work together so that we have time to play together. No one is a slave here. Your thoughts are not reasonable," I said.

"What else did these boys tell you?" Father asked.

"They said it is against the law to do school six days a week. We should be going to school only five days a week, and we should have off all holidays and snow days. You are unfair to us!"

"Boys, these are all lies you have been told. Satan likes to insinuate lies to make you discontented. And this lie is making you doubt our love. This is terrible. Listen, boys, you have it good. We do school six days a week and we do double school almost every day for a purpose, don't we? When we have guests here and you are ahead of your school schedule, you have the opportunity to have a day off. You won't get that in regular school. When we are traveling, you do school in the car, but when we are at special places and you're ahead, you get the day off for sightseeing. Not too bad, is it? Would you rather just do a smaller daily work load and do it from September to June rather than from October to April and lose these privileges?" I appealed to their reason kindly.

Both boys resisted this sound logic and reason. They were still feeling the strong emotion of injustice, and the discussion did not engender surrender.

"Lord, what would Thou have us to do?" Jim and I entreated again.

"Table the discussion. It is time for a break," the Lord said gently.

Jim and I both struggled with this; we had to surrender our frustrations to Him in order to follow His counsel. We ended the discussion and gave the boys no consequences. We asked them to take their feelings to the Lord in their personal time in the morning to sort out what was right and to seek what the Lord would have them to do. They finished the dishes coolly.

That night Jim and I prayed to God about this terribly uncomfortable situation. We wondered if we had made a mistake by not getting them to surrender their negative attitudes. The only course by which we could have subdued this attitude at the moment would have been to dominate them by parental force or autocratic rule. We wondered, Why didn't God change them?

Years later it became clear to me. God never forces the conscience. They were both convinced they were right and had revealed a serious wrong to their parents. A man convinced against his will is of the same opinion still. Pressuring them at that time would not win their hearts in the long run. God's directions were to pray and give them some time for Him to work in their hearts and minds. We needed to remain sensitive to the Lord directing our steps. Our boys must freely give up their wrong thoughts to God.

That evening God reminded me that He had spoken to my heart earlier that day. I recalled that I had been talking with a lady when I saw the boys in a lively conversation with the pastor's sons and that the Lord was calling me, *"Go over there and see what they're talking about."*

"That would be so awkward," I had responded. "It's not comfortable to interrupt my conversation with this lady." My conscience troubled me, but I stayed where I was.

"You need to go over there to know what is being said amongst them. You can be discreet," the Lord called again.

Again, I chose not to go. So our present scenario was partially my fault: I hadn't been the parent I needed to be; I hadn't done what God asked me to do. It would have been easier to deal with the situation then. Now, it was harder.

For the next two days, this remained heavy upon our thoughts. I studied all I could find on the subject of lying thoughts, and I discovered that a lie, often told, is finally believed, but that the truth, often told, is also finally believed. I read my Bible and prayed to God for wisdom. There seemed so much silence from heaven. Jim and I felt we needed to be careful not to overly stress this issue, but also not to avoid the subject with our children. We wanted to find balance. We directed the boys to spend time with God to sort it out and gave space for God to work. We even gave them opportunity to take their Bibles and go sit out under a tree to talk this over with God during the day.

God spoke to my mind, *"Keep your heart warm, sweet, and sympathetic toward the pastor's boys as well as your sons. Give your wrong thoughts to Me and think on solutions to avoid these situations in the future. Forgive the pastor's sons. Suffer your boys to come unto Me. I am with you."*

Jim and I stayed sensitive to the promptings of the Holy Spirit so that our example would uplift and not tear down. We spoke when we sensed God prompting us. When there was silence from heaven, we preceded cautiously, saying little or nothing. At the end of the day, Jim talked openly with the boys and drew out their thoughts. We allowed them to express exactly what they thought. With each day, the burden and passion lessened, and the truth did win in the end. With time, simple reasoning, and God working in our behalf with their minds and thinking process, they cast out the lying thoughts as lies. The boys cooperated, and in a few days we were back to our former normal, happy workers, cheerfully doing their share of the home duties.

Discipline is discipleing my child to Christ. It was discipline for us to follow Exodus 14:14—"The LORD shall fight for you, and ye shall hold your peace." Time with God solved many problems. Our time with God kept our hearts loving, yet firm and consistently honest. Their time with God brought them out of the lying thoughts.

Time also allowed the boys to see our true love toward them as shown by our not harassing or compelling them to see things our way. Their critical spirit led them to watch closely their parents' work about the home during this time. They observed our faithful work efforts that we put forth all day for them in meals, school, home care, and play. And I think these acts of normal life were the voice of truth from God that spoke loudest of the love and fairness of our home. This was reality, and the lies fell away as unworthy of thought. Their hearts had to reclaim the truth in place of these lies. God had to regain the mind and heart they had yielded to Satan. Rehearsing those lies over and over had wounded both them and us.

Parents can cooperate with God to change their children's rough spots as well as reach out to protect and redirect them when there are poor influences from other children. We can overprotect them as well as underprotect. So we need to be under God to bring the balance we need into our families. On special occasions, we were able to help our children's associates to come up higher when their hearts were open for help, love, and instruction.

This experience made us more observant of our boys' conversations with other children and youth and gave us a desire to be more involved with all their associations. We wanted to know what they were hearing and be able to offset error at its origin and teach them how to be Bereans, checking whether what they hear is so before they take it all in. God had shown us over these past six years how to be their pleasant companions in work, play, and recreation. They loved to be with us whatever we were doing. We needed to become that *true friend* with our children as God wanted us to be. So we expanded our involvement with their friends, making ourselves pleasant associates with them. Talking openly with our boys, with each listening to the other, became second nature to us.

Parents must become the most desirable people to be around on this earth. Not by indulging our children's selfishness, not by giving in to their wrong concepts or unwise wants, but by being under the lordship of Jesus Christ. By being sweet, pleasant, and cheerful, with good problem-solving techniques when they err or get out of Christ. By instructing them and calling them to a decision to do the right. By bringing them to Jesus so that He can touch their mind and hearts to do what's right. By giving firm, consistent consequences in a loving fashion for wrong choices. By training them in right thoughts, and responses in a way that is practical and at the level of their understanding. By being there and not deserting them.

In prayer to God I said, "Jim and I want Jesus to be our constant Companion and to become our best Friend. I'm discovering a degree of that here, but I want more."

"I want the best for you. I'll never ask you to do something that is detrimental to you. Although I will ask you to do hard things with your hand in Mine, it is for your best interest. I can be your faithful Friend whenever you choose Me. But Sally, I'd like to be Matthew's and Andrew's best Friend now while they are young."

"Hmm . . . I've thought of that before, but I haven't made a practical daily effort to bring that experience into their life. Lord how do I make that tangible to them?"

"Remember the day Andrew drove his bike to the neighbors' house and you had to work to get that bad spirit surrendered before he left? My companionship directed him aright how to respond to the two grizzly bears he met down the road because now I, not Satan, had his heart. In order for Me

to work My will and spirit into his mind and heart, I needed his coopera-
tion as well. Without his cooperation, all the power of heaven is neutralized
because I will not go against his will.

"I want you to teach your boys of Me like Hannah did Samuel. There is
a part you must play as a parent, teaching them of My character and My
approach so that they recognize Me when I call upon them. Teach them to
turn to Me in every trial, need, and joy. Plan experiences to exercise thoughts
of Me throughout their day."

I opened my Bible to Samuel. Hannah made God real to Samuel
from a very young age. I asked God to help me. She must have used the
common things in Samuel's life to teach him about Christ. Perhaps
when Samuel built a fire, his mother inspired him with thoughts of
God as a cleansing fire, burning up things that are not worthy of keeping. Then, when God would come to Samuel's mind, with His still
small voice, asking him to let go of his anger or resentment, Samuel
knew God wanted to get rid of those hurtful thoughts and give him
good thoughts and feelings instead. And Samuel cooperated to let God
burn up the evil thoughts and feelings in his mind that were not
Christlike. He chose to think right thoughts instead.

Hannah must have presented Christ as the water of life, the foun-
tain of all blessings, and how He cares when a sparrow falls to the ground.
Therefore Samuel knew that God cared when he was hurting—physically, mentally, or spiritually—and that He could help him by bringing
life, and refreshing blessings. Hannah made object lessons from the
sun, the stars, the trees, and the animals about him. Samuel thought
about what his mother taught him and repeated them to himself. When
he saw these things, thoughts of God were brought to his mind. With
all these reminders of God, Samuel was more inclined to turn to Him
as his familiar Friend. Through daily experiences as these, turning to
God became his habit.

"Jesus, I want this experience for my boys," I prayed. "I want to
connect every common thing in our home and life with You in order to
give them good thoughts to ponder."

"Go forward. I will instruct you and teach you in the way which thou
shalt go. As you study, I will give you ideas, plans, right interpretations,
right approaches, and object lessons."

I thought more about Hannah. She must have talked with Samuel
about the reality of angels being there to help him when he chose to be

good and do right and that he could look to the unseen God as his God, his constant Companion, and his best Friend. She must have told him that God would be there to help him at any time. That he could call upon Him and discover His Presence always.

"Lord, this is what I want to do as well. Direct me."

"Not all association is good association. Choose, guide, and direct your sons' friendships according to what you want them to imitate. As they get older and become the leaders, your children can give a positive influence and lead their friends to Jesus as their problem solver, Companion, and Friend."

In God's Word I found guidelines such as Proverbs 13:20: "He that walketh with wise [men] shall be wise: but a companion of fools shall be destroyed." Proverbs 28:7: "Whoso keepeth the law [is] a wise son: but he that is a companion of riotous [men] shameth his father." God doesn't want us to have detrimental associations for our children. God wants us to be wise with what we allow and do not allow. Yet we need the balance of not being haughty or feeling that we are better than others. Although some of my sons' associates don't yet know God, they can be safe if God gives permission and I'm involved in their activities to steer them aright. I'm willing to learn and be slow to judge.

"Gregarious Gary" runs up to one of his friends, "Cliquey Cleo," who is with some other fellows.

"Gregarious Gary" says, "Hi, how are you doing? Want to play something?"

"Cliquey Cleo" gives him a look that seems to say, "Go away!" His body language gives the definite impression "I don't want to be with you." Then he says with his nose in the air, "I can't right now."

Gary is so sad. This had happened a few days before as well. Several families went to the petting zoo together. "Cliquey Cleo" was petting a baby goat. Gary came up to Cleo after a while and asked, "Can I hold him now?"

"No," "Cliquey Cleo" retorted, "I just got him."

Then "Rough Randy" came up, not knowing what had just taken place, and asked, " 'Cliquey Cleo,' can I hold the goat?"

"Okay," "Cliquey Cleo" replied very nicely.

"Gregarious Gary" has a talk with his parents on these types of issues that keep reoccurring. Gary and Cleo have lots of fun together at his house or whenever just the two of them are together. But when

"Rough Randy" or his friends come, Gary is undesirable company to Cleo.

Mother is sensitive to seek counsel of God. She knows that Gary wants a good friend badly. But she tells him, "These boys are not good associates for you. It's obvious Cleo wants to belong to this 'cliquey' group. God doesn't want exclusiveness like that. You will have to let go of this friendship. Jesus wants to be your best Friend. He will never leave you nor forsake you like this boy. Jesus wants you to walk and talk with Him like Enoch did. He will help you not to hate or be hurt by 'Cliquey Cleo' and his friends, and you can be there in heart when one of them needs a real friend."

Gary goes to a quiet place to talk with God about all of this. His thoughts confirm what mother is saying. He still isn't ready to give up, so outing after outing, Cleo continues treating him in the same fashion. When no one else is around, Gary is a great friend and they have fun together. But as soon as someone "Cliquey Cleo" prefers is present, he ignores Gary.

At a church outing for the youth, Cleo gives a toy car to each boy there—except Gary. Afterwards, they all go to Cleo's house for refreshments and some fun together. Cleo and his friends change into camouflage clothing and get their toy guns. This is not acceptable in Gregarious Gary's home. Gary says, "Let's play hide-and-seek instead."

"No, we're playing army. If you're a sissy, you don't have to play," "Cliquey Cleo" says harshly.

Gary comes crying to Mother because all his efforts, patience, tolerance, and prayers have done nothing to change their friendship. He doesn't look down on them for playing guns; he just wants to be able to do something they all could do. He is emotionally worn down with these repeated rejections.

"I don't want to go anywhere ever again. I don't want to play with any of those boys again." Gary says, exasperated.

"Gary, that's a hurt response. Let's go to Jesus to find a better solution," Mother says encouragingly.

Gary can't talk then, he needs time alone to sort things out. After some time at home, in prayer, and a study of association in God's Word, nine-year-old "Gregarious Gary" comes to his conclusion: "My mother and father are my best companions; we have fun together, and they are often here for me. Jesus will become my best Friend, for He will never reject me. He loves me, and I want to get to know Him better. And one day perhaps God will bring me an upright friend who shares high ideals and a love for Jesus, too. That would be wonderful, but I'm no longer going to pine for Cleo's friendship. He's free to choose the friends he chooses. I'll be thankful for what I have."

With the continued exercise of these thoughts in Christ, Gary is freed to be "Gregarious Gary" with all those he comes in contact with—without fear of another rejection.

We need to reason through with our children what are the characteristics of good and not-so-good friends. Often the child's ideals and decisions are a product of our discussions. Then we need to provide opportunities for them to meet good friends or we need to be that good friend that is there for them so that they aren't driven to debilitating friendships. And we must learn, under God, how to make Jesus a real, tangible friend to our children in a practical way day by day. Jesus can fulfill our children's need for wholesome friendship. Then we need to go to the school at Jesus' feet each day to learn how to incorporate this experience with Jesus into our daily life. The Holy Spirit will give us ideas as we ask for them. It's our work to experiment with these ideas and adapt them to our situation. Providence will lead, and we will learn with our children.

As both Gary and his parents gained this precious experience, he grew into a special friendship with Jesus. When he became a teen, he found younger boys flocking to him. His influence for good was far reaching. He fulfilled his desire for wholesome friendship by providing it to these younger members of God's family. He did not want them to experience rejection and the lack of a good friend. He pointed them to Jesus as their Friend, sharing tender stories of how Jesus healed his wounded heart and showed him a better way. And how happy he became talking and working with Jesus!

"Abraham believed God . . . he was called the Friend of God" (James 2:23). "Ask, and it shall be given you; seek, and ye shall find; knock, and it shall be opened unto you" (Luke 11:9). I concluded Jesus wants to be my sons' best Friend and began sharing these concepts and texts with my boys. We had some interesting conversations, which positively colored experiences that followed.

Matthew went out under a tree with his Bible, taking his frustrations to Jesus to talk them through. God reasoned with him and directed his thoughts and feelings in another direction. Matthew cooperated with that reasoning. God transformed his sadness into joy, his frustration into acceptance by looking at the situation from God's positive perspective. Matthew chose to change his ideas and views for God's.

To this day, Matthew, aged twenty-seven, uses the same problem-solving technique in times of current frustrations, hurts, or perplexities. He turns to God to counsel with his best Friend, Jesus. What we parents cultivate in our children during childhood will go with them for life.

Only by acquaintance and association with Christ will we become like Him. We become changed by what we behold. Do you want your child to be like other children or to be like Jesus? You can make an eternal difference in your child's life by making Christ real to him.

Andrew surrendered his ugly disposition at last, prayed for protection, and went on his bike to the neighbors' on an errand. Sometimes it takes firmness and discipline in order for our child to discover God as his constant Companion and best Friend in a tangible way. It's worth it! I wanted to establish the habit of prayer, communion, and the attitude of dependence upon God when Andrew went for any bike ride. It took tenacity under God to gain this surrender. I had a sense that this was very important for his life. Little did I know then that this was God guiding me at the moment.

Andrew had traveled about a quarter of a mile from the house when he came upon two good-sized grizzly bears at the top of a knoll in the road. They stood in the middle of the road and would not let Andrew pass. They didn't move; they just stared at him. Andrew and Jesus conversed over his options.

Andrew said, "I think I can scare them, and they will let me by."

"That would not be a good idea," the Holy Spirit impressed him.

Andrew was only eight years old and didn't realize you don't shout to scare a grizzly bear. That may work for black bears, but for a grizzly it is considered a challenge and will often kindle a charge.

Andrew said, "Well, I could ride my bike around them through the woods over downed trees and rugged terrain. I'm a good biker. They'll never catch me."

"Maybe you won't be fast enough," God intervened in his thoughts.

Andrew didn't understand that running from a grizzly bear is an invitation for a chase.

"Andrew, wouldn't it be great for Mother and Matthew to see these two grizzlies? Why don't you go home to tell them?" God suggested.

Andrew yielded to this thought and returned home to tell us the good news. The bears were gone when we arrived in the truck. But the lesson was well understood—that God is a good Companion and a faithful Friend to direct us aright! Prayer is not only important but essential. We want to teach these essential truths to our children not only intellectually but also experientially.

Andrew is twenty-five years old now, and because of this early training that took root he knows habitually how to consult God about handling difficult problems in his personal life and business. He prays before he travels in his car, on his bicycle, or goes for a long run. God keeps him safe and directs his steps. He is an elder in his church and is on the nominating committee. He recognizes his need of God in order to give good counsel and direction in these important positions of life. Giving him good problem-solving techniques and the tools of union and communion with God has prepared him to fill these positions as an ambassador of God giving sound counsel. Andrew and his wife, Sarah, recently had their first son, Landon James, and now he has the blessed privilege of teaching his own son of this mighty God that is his personal Savior and familiar Friend. Even infants can know Jesus personally, if the parents do. (See Luke 1:41, 44).

Teaching our young children of the reality of God as their personal Friend, Counselor, and Savior can be passed on from generation to generation for good. What a loss if we neglect this training or let it be crowded out because of other less-important pursuits. What a legacy is our privilege if we take up this all-important work of introducing our children to Jesus! What will you do?

Matthew, age twelve, was cross-country skiing alone up the back bench to a series of roads and trails in the forest behind our home. He loves high adventure, and he found it! He came across moose droppings and tracks. He decided to follow them to see if he could track down this moose, and sure enough he did! It was a good size bull moose that had recently lost its antlers. These animals are bigger than a large horse and can be very mean if angered.

Matthew wanted to see how close he could come. When he came within fifty feet, this moose would turn to face him, the hair raised on the back of its neck and shoulders. Then he'd scrape the ground and snort.

"Matthew, it isn't wise to come any closer. Back off right now," God said.

And he backed off, thinking, "Well, let's see if it is the same distance on all sides that he reacts to." His inquisitive mind had to know. The moose responded similarly each time he approached. Then Matthew ventured closer still.

"That's enough, Matthew. See the hair on his back rise? You can push it too far. His head is down ready to charge. Back off and give him his space," God instructed.

I'm so thankful for God being Matthew's constant Companion and Friend. Jesus held off that moose while He reasoned with Matthew to honor proper boundaries for that animal. Matthew did heed God's counsel and warning. He found the adventure he sought safely with Jesus. Don't you want God with your children?

Today, Matthew still has high adventure in his nature, but he also talks with God amidst his trials. Even though his curious nature is impetuous, God can alter and influence him to find a good balance. The training of those young years is very far reaching; it is worthy of the time, effort, and inconvenience involved in planning and executing learning experiences with God. We also need to follow God's lessons that present themselves in the moment in answer to our prayers.

Take these occasions to instruct your children to rely upon divine aid in their difficulties and dangers. They will not lack power to curb their fears, impulses, or bad judgment calls due to inexperience. We cooperate to connect them with Jesus, the source of wisdom, who will give them discernment between right and wrong. This will help them become not only safe but also morally strong.

Andrew was four years old, and we were up at Bowman Lake enjoying the pristine glacier-fed lake, the pure, clean, ultra cold water there, and all the beauty speaking of our Creator God. We soon discovered that the deer there were unusually friendly. Accustomed to being fed by campers, a deer came up boldly to the boys. Seeing others feeding the deer, we followed suit. We shared our wholesome whole grain bread with them. At this point we were not experienced with deer. Matthew broke off a piece of bread, and the deer took it gently from his open hand. Andrew followed his brother's example. The deer took his bread then placed her hoof firmly on his stomach and pushed him down.

"God spoke clearly to Andrew's reason, *"Stand up right away."*

With a sense of urgency, he stood up rather than staying down and came to us right away. We didn't understand, so we took Andrew back to the deer and fed her. As long as we were there, she was fine. But she did the same thing as soon as we had left his side.

"I don't think that deer likes me," Andrew said. "She doesn't do that to Matthew—only to me."

God directed Andrew aright. We have since learned that dominant does use their hooves to show dominance to any deer lower than themselves. Matthew was taller than this deer, but Andrew was shorter. That is why she did it only to him. Deer quickly learn to get out of the way of flailing hooves. Andrew's best move was to get up right away. I believe God influenced this deer to be relatively gentle. We have seen how viciously they can use their hooves on others. God is trying to be our best Friend and show us in situations like this that He is with us, always ready to give us directions.

This was a good experience for our boys at ages four and six. God is a good Friend. Only a few years later the boys befriended deer after deer in our yard. They learned wonderful lessons of patience and the time necessary to gain a wild deer's trust. These lessons of gentleness with patience were treasures in drawing the deer close. And later lessons of firmness were necessary to keep a pet deer off our front porch to protect him from getting his little hooves caught in the spaces between our decking and possibly breaking a leg. The boys not only fed deer from a bowl but petted them on their necks while they ate. Some were so friendly that the boys could brush them down with a brush like a pet dog.

Learning to walk and talk with God helped the boys break down the barrier of fear in the deer. This is their secret ingredient for these special friendships with the deer. It's like the unseen friendship with God developed into a tangible, touchable friendship with these deer. Few have ever experienced this special relationship. Their friendship with God paid off in wonderful unexpected dividends.

When human friendship is slim or far between, God supplies the lack somehow. He is a big God. Along with the deer friends He gave them chipmunks, golden mantel squirrels, ground squirrels, bunnies, and a very special friendship with a wild bear cub. It began as a lesson for me, to help me overcome my fear of bears. My fears were first faced with this cub's mother, and then this bear cub followed up those lessons for many years to come. The boys named the cub "Lonesome" because she was always alone. They enjoyed her friendship for many years. God uses nature to minister His tangibleness, His watch care, His protection, His guidance, and His love to us. Friendship with God will pay wonderful dividends for you as well. Try Him.

I may not feel God's physical hands about me to calm my soul. I may not audibly hear His voice to my reason or conscience. But I know He is there for me. I know His love, for it is made tangible through other means of His choosing. For our family, nature was one of those avenues. Teach your children about God in whatever way you can, and God will open the windows of heaven to pour you out a blessing too big for you to hold. He loves us and longs to reveal Himself to us.

THE LONE EMBRACE
A SPECIAL WORD OF ENCOURAGEMENT FOR SINGLE PARENTS

God has exceeding power that He wants to bestow upon us. His power is above all principalities and powers. God puts all things under Jesus' feet so that He may be head over all things. God wants to quicken us—give us life where there is none—so that we may serve Him aright. He will strengthen you in the inner man by His Spirit and transform you by the renewing of your mind (see Ephesians 1:19-22; 2:1; 3:16, 17; Romans 12:2). Every single parent needs this kind of power and inward strength. Making God your best Friend, walking with Him, and talking with Him like Enoch did will bring this empowerment into your life.

That means no more frustrations that have to be tackled alone. No more entanglements that bring discouragement and confusion without Him at your side. For now you have a Friend that will never leave you nor forsake you. He will always be with you in all your troubles. He will calm your emotions and take away all your fears.

God says to every one of you, *"I'm your forever Friend. My friendship is different from any friendship you have ever had. I'm always here for you. Call upon Me anytime, and I will answer you. I love you and want to redeem you to serve righteousness. Try Me and see for yourself."*

Chapter 20

DEVELOPING CHARACTER

"Whereof I am made a . . . [ministering parent], according to the gift of the grace of God given to me by the effectual working of his power"
(Ephesians 3:7).

"Boys, we need the power of God in us in order to be the kind, helpful person that we and Jesus want us to be. To change our wrong thoughts, feelings, lifestyle, or habits, we need a vital connection with Jesus so that the sap from His tree of righteous living can flow into us and re-create us into His image."

"But, Mother, I try and try not to be foolish, but it doesn't work," Matthew responded.

"Me, too. I've tried and tried to not be slothful, and I still am," Andrew said in frustration. "I want to be diligent, but it is so hard."

"To develop the right character—the right thoughts and feelings—we need to be ever communicating with Jesus to know His will, and always cooperating with what He is putting in our minds and hearts to do," I responded.

"Now this crosses the big self in us. It is not natural or easy, but it is beneficial when we follow God's way over self's way. We must come to see that doing right in self's power is not good enough—this is why we fail. Every effort, in self, must fail. Our failure needs to be our motivator to reach out to God and find a different way to change that is effective. We must learn to do the right in Jesus' power while we cooperate by doing all we can do. Learning to be the branch connected to the vine is what we need to learn the most," I added.

"We don't get it!" they responded.

I was tempted to be upset and angry at their childish response. Hadn't I told them this many times? But instead, I chose to turn to God for wisdom and strength to be the parent He wants me to be and to respond in a way worthy of imitation.

"First you need to have personal worship time with God to learn by experience how to talk with Him and how He talks with you in the Scriptures—to your conscience and your reason. Second, you need to be willing in mind, heart, and muscle to cooperate when Jesus asks you to do something differently than you are used to doing it. And third, do it depending upon Jesus' strength and wisdom to perform a change on the inside while you cooperate outwardly with all your heart. When we walk with God in this way, He will work in you to will and to do of His good pleasure [see Philippians 2:13]. You can change successfully in this way."

And so we continued to make headway in understanding.

Later that day Matthew was responding angrily towards Andrew, his brother.

"Matthew!" I responded, lovingly, entreating him with just a look.

Ashamed, he turned his head away. We don't always need to instruct, reprove, or correct our children verbally. He knew his own spirit.

Very soon Matthew responded to God asking, "What am I supposed to do?"

God spoke clearly to his heart, *"Put off your anger. Put on the new man* [Colossians 3:8-10]. *Pity your brother instead of demeaning him with angry retorts. Entreat him with velvet on your steel. How would you like to be treated if this were you?"*

Instead of turning away from these God-led thoughts or ignoring them as he typically had done before, Matthew chose to listen. Then he chose to cooperate with God instead of his fleshly thoughts and responses. The outcome was lovely. Everyone was pleased, but especially the holy angels that were there working with all our hearts.

As I reflected on this, I was delighted to see that I, too, had chosen to heed God's entreaty to my heart by not responding in belittling anger or pitiless hail to Matthew. I just called for his heart by speaking his name to interrupt the old pattern. Heeding the voice of God was the reason for this success. God performed His mighty work to will and to do His good pleasure, as we cooperated to a good end. I was God's little mouthpiece to gain Matthew's attention and to arrest the course he was taking. But God performed the miracle to change his thoughts, and feelings inside—and Matthew's response corresponded to the inward change.

Building character is interrupting the old fleshly ways so that there is an opportunity for our children to hear God and to choose to cooperate with His ways instead. But they don't always listen, do they? So building character can also be instructing them practically in what are good and evil thoughts and feelings, and how they should respond. It's teaching them the basics. But even knowing what is right isn't always sufficient to bring about change. So real growth in character building means going all the way to a deeper training of the will; that is, to see to it, with God directing your steps, that your child does what he knows is right. At times, consequences and motivations will need to be part of the program of learning. Keeping in touch with what your child is thinking and feeling, and why he responds the way he does is a work that takes much effort and prayer, day in and day out, year after year.

My boys, ages eight and ten, had made friends of many of the deer that frequented our yard. They named their deer Big Nose, Friendly, Baby Saved, Loco, Dainty Toes, and other names according to their outstanding traits. The boys would spend a fair amount of time morning and evening with these deer, gaining their trust, getting closer and closer to each of these animals, which was very rewarding.

They fed these deer with cracked corn this morning and came inside for family worship. It was late fall, and hunting season had been in progress for a few weeks. The boys earnestly prayed for protection of their many deer friends every morning and evening. We were in the middle of worship at daybreak when we heard a loud gun shot!

My stomach wrenched at the sound, as had Jim's and the boys'.

Matthew said, "That was one of our deer friends, I'm sure. That was so close! Father, we need to go and see!" Fear and apprehension were obvious.

Jim and the boys went down our back hill to the road below to investigate. I stayed back. Soon they returned. All three of them returned crying.

"It was Big Nose. They shot her! We saw her struggling to breathe— she is suffering awful. Father said we couldn't stay there to watch. Hunters are awful men!! They shoot innocent animals. The deer don't stand a chance. These road hunters are illegal. They shone a light in her eyes to blind her and shot her." And Matthew went on.

Andrew voiced his heartache as well with vehemence. "I hate hunters. They kill our pet deer. I'll never talk with another hunter ever again. They are all bad! They killed Big Nose, my favorite deer. She ate out of my bowl for the first time this morning." And tears flowed profusely.

We all cried, hugged, and prayed to God to soothe and comfort our sorrows and to let Big Nose die without suffering long. The reality of imagining her suffering was too much for all of us.

"Let's sit down for worship," Father said. "We need to talk about this further. God wants us not to hate the hunters but to forgive them. Let's consider what Jesus would do were He in our situation."

"I don't know if I want to talk about forgiveness. This hurts too much. It isn't fair! I think Jesus would hate hunters too," Matthew responded, giving voice to his pain. And Andrew agreed.

The countenances of both boys showed painful, emotional hurt at the loss of the deer. My heart was pained that they had to experience this. We talked about forgiveness. We talked about the fact that not all hunters hunt in this illegal, cruel way. Not all hunters are bad.

"We hurt over this, but we can't hate. Jesus looks upon hate as murder. So we must yield up our hate to God and take His forgiveness in its place or we are no better than the hunters as you see them. We must realize that some hunters hunt fairly. Not all are poachers and shine deer. Some hunt deer to eat better meat. We can't fault all hunters for what these men did here today. Your father hunted deer before the Lord asked him to quit; he wasn't bad. We need to give our hurt to God and let God bring justice to the bad hunters," I added.

"I will never like any hunter ever again. A hunter killed Big Nose," Andrew said.

Through the day I prayed for the boys in their struggles—that God could reach their hearts to comfort their sorrows and bring reason back to the throne of their hearts. I saw them struggle periodically and would pray or talk as needed.

During the day, I had to be firm when one son voiced hate vehemently toward the hunters. His feelings were ruling and hurting him terribly, and my son was cooperating.

"Lord, what shall I do?"

"This is harmful to Matthew. He needs to yield up these ill feelings to Me to subdue for him. If he doesn't, they will continue to wound and hurt him and all around him even further. Hateful thoughts hurt the hater. Restrain this expression now."

"Okay, Lord. Be with my words, gain his heart, and offer him freedom."

Reasoning didn't work this time, so I had to send him on a grizzly run and give him time with God, and then we talked, and he was subdued considerably by yielding up his wrong thoughts to God.

Andrew's response now doubted God. "We asked God to protect our deer. Why didn't He? We have prayed every day!"

"God's ways are best. We must trust God even when we do not understand. God lets evil run its course so that we can abhor sin and see it for what it truly is. Sin and selfishness hurt everyone. This can help you choose to follow God more closely, or you will do hurtful things to others if you don't let God have all of you."

This reasoning worked a heart change in Andrew, and he stopped thinking doubting thoughts about God.

That evening during family worship, we talked over some Bible texts that could bring a nice balance to the boys. Little by little, their hate subsided, and forgiveness took its place by our loving persistence to win their hearts and bring them in touch with God day by day and moment by moment.

Two weeks after this incident, a real estate client came by to talk with Jim about some property. Lonesome, our wild pet bear, came for a visit while this hunter and his wife were there. I offered the husband the opportunity to feed our pet bear, and he declined. But his wife fed Lonesome. The boys entered into conversation with the husband in his camouflage clothing. A friendship began; he was such a nice fellow—an honest and a fair hunter. This man became a good friend of my boys and was the final step for our boys to fully forgive the illegal hunter who shot their pet deer, Big Nose.

God had a plan to give opportunity for the boys to see that not all hunters are alike. Some poor people hunt wild game to feed their families, and do so fairly. God can provide for some in this way. The boys' attitude was strongly influenced in a Christlike direction.

This is character development. Taking wrong thoughts and feelings, bringing them to Christ, and cooperating to think new thoughts, and being willing to change. It's in Christ's power that this is possible for us and our children to forgive.

Do you listen to your child with a listening ear and heart? Do you know what he is thinking or struggling with? Are you willing to put forth the effort necessary to learn and do this? It is so very important. This work of studying your child's disposition and directing his steps to God to be changed can *never* be laid aside without undoing the work you have begun. Consistency is essential! Developing character must become our life's priority.

Reasoning with your children or telling them what they should do may be sufficient at times, but rarely is this the case before they have learned to connect themselves to God and find the joys of obedience for themselves. So the parent must be willing in heart and mind to do whatever it takes to get them connected, and keep them connected, to God. It will take effort—sometimes, much effort—and much self-control to do so in the right spirit and bring them to a truehearted surrender in Jesus. Having a happy, sweet home is worth it!

God wants parents to be there for their children, consistently, to instruct them, to be willing to give consequences as needed, and to gain a true connection with God to bring about change. If we are under God, as the underteacher we need to be, He will direct our steps to gain the heart and mind of our child into Jesus' hand. This is when true character transformation happens. Do you need a miracle? God can work with you to make it a reality in your heart, home, and family.

Talking with our children and youth is important! Get into what they think by probing to the depths of their heart with questions and by being interested in them. Don't do so in a critical, demeaning manner, but do so honestly caring for them. We must be interested in what they are thinking and feeling. Our disinterest often engenders those negatives responses. If we don't know what they think, how can we direct them aright? Once we know how they are thinking wrongly, we can go to God to make a plan for how we can correct, evict, and replace wrong thoughts with heaven-led right thoughts, intelligently, lovingly, and consistently. Dealing at the level of their thoughts, feelings, and responses correctively is true character development.

Character development is fostering a personal union and communion with God so that Jesus has access to our child's thoughts and feelings, offering them ideas for a better response. As often as the child cooperates with heaven's alternative direction, beautiful miracles of character transformation occur. It is the indwelling, re-creative power of Christ that makes this difference.

We can aid or hinder God's reaching out to our child or youth. We have a part in cooperating as God leads us so that His power can work effectually in and through us for our children.

"Whereof I am made a . . . [ministering parent], according to the gift of the grace of God given to me by the effectual working of his power" (Ephesians 3:7). We want effectual power!

Peter and Paula are the parents of Carol and Edsel. "What are your ideals for your children?" a visitor asked Peter and Paula.

"We are on fire for the Lord. We long to raise our children for Him and have them follow right principles. We have moved to the country at great expense to provide the best home environment we can. We love our children so much." And Peter ruffled Carol's hair and kissed her profusely. "We'd do anything for our children to give them the best," he stated with enthusiasm.

"We want our children to love and serve the Lord. We want all the strife and disobedience that is too common in our home to leave and our children to become happy, obedient, and helpful. We want to help other families do the same. There is nothing I wouldn't do to bring that to pass. Our desires are to see our children receive the crown of eternal life in heaven," Paula added with passion.

They had worship together and went to put the last breakfast items on the table.

Paula asked "Complaining Carol" to get the milk and juice from the refrigerator and put it on the table. An argument ensued.

"Why do I have to get them? Ask Edsel!" Carol complained vehemently.

Paula entreated her three times. The third time, "Complaining Carol" simply disappeared into the living room in a huff to play the piano without doing what she was asked to do. No consequences for this behavior were given.

Mother was getting irritated, so she asked her son, "Evasive Edsel" to put the items on the table.

"I'll do it as soon as I finish what I'm doing on the computer," responded Edsel, as he had done many times before.

Now Paula was ready to blow her stack because past experience says Edsel won't ever finish playing at the computer. He is accustomed to forgetting his promises because Mother will often let him get away with it and simply do it herself.

Now Peter came into the picture. "Go help your mother right now, 'Evasive Edsel!' Have you no respect for your parents? Why aren't you helpful? Can't you do anything right? Don't you appreciate all I have done for you? Get out there and at least try to be good." Father's remarks were like pitiless hail and were accompanied with irritation and a demeaning spirit.

Now Edsel plopped the milk and juice on the table and slumped in his chair for breakfast looking hurt and resentful.

The visitor opened up the conversation by offering suggestions for a different approach—if these parents were open to new ideas. Peter and Paula both justified their course, making many excuses for why they did what they did.

"You see, if I correct the children, my husband opposes me." And Paula gave examples. "When I correct the children, they disrespect me." And she gave several illustrations of this. "It's easier to do it myself," she said at last, feeling guilty and exasperated.

"Have you tried to talk these things over with your husband calmly at the proper time?"

"He won't listen. I don't cross him. I let him do what he thinks is right. He gets so demeaning to me when I tell him anything," Paula responded.

"But isn't it harder to remain as you are than to risk changing?"

"I suppose it is," Paula said, but her demeanor showed her fear of change.

As they talked further on this subject, new ideas were kindled about how to deal with her children.

Peter was also approached, in a helping attitude, regarding what he needed to do and what traits his present course would create in his children. "Peter, you need time with God so that He can impress your heart with what and how you need to change. Give God permission to change you and cooperate with Him to do the opposite of what is natural to you. These are essential disciplines to which you need to submit. Your inconvenience is not to be considered. You need to give your children discipline that will motivate a change in their responses or self will become stronger. You can't do this without having Christ within you. Talking things over with your wife is so important. The two of you need to be united in your goals and direction. You need to play and work with your children in a nurturing spirit instead of your demeaning, critical spirit. Without these changes, led of God, your children will become increasingly selfish and pull further away from you."

"I want our children to do what they know is right!" he retorted with fretfulness and faultfinding in his voice. "No one had to tell me what to do as a child. I did my work well without anyone overseeing me. I tell my children over and over what they should do. It's disgusting! I expect them to do what I tell them to do without a question. I don't want to be bothered by them." Frustration spewed forth from his mind and heart, increasing his present irritation and confirming him in his former way.

A year later, there was little notable change in either parent. The children helped in some small chores about the house, but it was done with a poor spirit and a complaining attitude. Paula continued in her indulgent ways, requesting obedience over and over until she became upset. Then her anger spewed out as before. The children responded in the same way. Paula still found it next to impossible to approach her husband to discuss issues of child rearing or marriage difficulties. As a result, her resentment toward her husband grew. She continued to respond to him in a negative, unloving, and destructive manner.

When a good friend was visiting, Peter commented, "These kids are useless. I get so angry around them. They want to ride their bikes across *my* lawn; they don't have any respect for the lawn looking nice. I told them not to use *my* soccer ball on the concrete, yet I find them playing ball on the driveway and scuffing up the soccer ball. I won't let them wash my cars because they might scratch them. They won't do it right! 'Evasive Edsel' only wants to be on the computer. When I work with him and show him how to work, he doesn't do it just as I would do it. He doesn't think. And my wife—she doesn't love and respect me like she should!" he concluded.

"Your children are a byproduct of your parenting approaches—or lack of parenting. Their character—their thoughts, feelings, and responses to you—are a direct result of your lack of respect to them. Your verbal and nonverbal dealings with them convince them you don't love them. They obey you out of fear. They are frustrated because they still can't please you even when they try their best. You are demeaning and too exacting. Why would they want to please someone who they think hates them?" his friend said lovingly.

"Change in your children must begin with you! If they know they are loved, they will receive instruction and correction. But your present course is creating resentment, hatred, and wrath in your dealings with them. It's up to you to pass down to them an example worthy of imitation. Your children will not gain the character and relationship with God they need in order to gain the crown of eternal life unless you first let God change you and then teach them in an attractive, practical, and real way how to come to Jesus."

The seriousness of the conversation lent itself to self-evaluation and introspection. Time was given to let Peter and Paula digest these thoughts.

Later that day, the children came up enthusiastically to remind Father of his promise to play kickball.

"Oh, not now. I'm too tired to play," Peter said.

"But you promised," both children complained. "You never play with us."

"Just sit down over there and be happy with TV and all the toys I've given you. We adults need to talk," Peter retorted with irritation.

The children's shoulders shrugged, and they went to play alone. Disappointment in play was common. Rarely did Father play with them.

Soon the children went out to play with the soccer ball; at times it went onto the concrete. They were having fun. Then Father came out to reprove them angrily for being on the concrete and not playing on the lawn with *his* soccer ball as he had told them to. Then he came back inside to vent his frustration with them to his wife and visitors.

Paula said, "Peter, things are more important to you than are your children and I. You always place a greater value on things than you do on us. That silly soccer ball was given to us to have fun with. You limit the children so severely that they can't have appropriate fun because it will cost you something. Do you want me to place that soccer ball in our curio cabinet to keep it from being scratched? When you are old and wonder why your children don't want to come home with their families to spend time with you, I'll give you your scratch-free, shiny soccer ball to hug, cuddle, and talk to. The money you have saved will be useless and unfulfilling. Is that what you really want? Don't you prefer your children's love and devotion instead?" Paula was pleading with honest feelings of pity in her heart.

Peter sat silently for a while without a response. Then his good friend lovingly called to his heart, saying, "You said you'd do anything to raise your children to follow after Christ and help others to do so. To do that you need to let God have you first and right now. Your present approach is alienating your children from you in heart, and ultimately it will alienate them from God. Will you let God have your heart, thoughts, feelings, responses, and inclinations and do what He'd have you to do?"

Peter was humbled and serious. "You're right. God has been calling for my heart for over a year now, and I have spurned him, not wanting to yield up my old ways. I have wanted to do God's will, but to do it *my way!* I've wanted the easy life of sitting on the beach, thinking I deserved not to be bothered. I never saw how selfish I was until I was scolding them over the soccer ball. I saw my son's tears and realized how often I had been hurting him. It was like I saw myself for the first time. I'm going to spend more time with God and let Him have me day by day. And as I gain this experience, I intend to show my children the way in a new and Christlike spirit. I'm determined to wrap both my arms around Christ and not cling to my wrong selfish desires."

This family had thought for many years they were raising their children for Christ when in reality they were cultivating Satan's character traits in them instead. They gave them religious formality, but they lacked training in Christ's character traits of helpfulness, kindness, and the joy of proper obedience with loving consequences. They failed to train them how to deal with wrong thoughts, feelings, and habits through communion and connection with Christ. They never taught their children how to deal with their response to unfairness, harshness, and anger in a Christlike spirit. The children were never taught how to approach the erring, fretful parent and voice redemptively how they were being hurt and wounded and becoming hopeless under their present treatment. Having no way to deal with difficulties or to resolve conflicts engenders either a despairing or a combative response.

Many parents think that they are raising their children for Christ as long as they provide them with food, clothes, and shelter; take them to church for social or educational reasons; and involve them in sports or other social activities with other children. This is a very superficial view. God wants our children—and us—to serve Him with all of our hearts and minds (see Matthew 22:37). In practical terms, God wants all of us—our thoughts, desires, emotions, feelings, and responses, and even our countenance. God wants all our habits to be upright. By His power, through faith and connection with Him, this is possible. "My sheep hear my voice, . . . and they follow me," Jesus said (John 10:27).

All children want to be loved and appreciated and to have a sense of belonging. They want to be trained in habits that will not need changing later. In the training process, they do not see the big picture, that it is desirable to give up this bad habit for a good habit. But we parents should see it. And we can lovingly help them over the hurdles of habits that need changing in order for them to have a happier better life with, and in, Jesus. It brings them great rejoicing to show them that their lying thoughts and bad habits need to be given up and that they need to cultivate right habits in their stead by following Jesus. Show them in practical terms how they can choose to be happy and helpful in following right. It is a pleasant experience if it's done in Jesus.

Your children will wrap their arms about you with gratitude and joy when they understand what you did for them by having them face their wrong ways. If we persevere in proper parental training, enduring hardness and resisting the desire of our fleshly nature for a life of ease and no responsibility, our children will grasp God and heaven. When they get their crown, they will give thanks to their parents for the part faithful parents have played in their salvation. And they will cast their crown at Jesus' feet. What a day of rejoicing that will be!

Unfortunately, few parents are willing to do what it takes to accomplish this. As a result, our world is daily becoming more and more like Sodom and Gomorrah. Satan is the prince of this world, and he exercises his power over our children, preparing his great army for battle against right, good, and God.

Parents can no longer look upon this matter of training their children properly as an inconvenience. Training your children to know and follow Jesus in all their thoughts and feelings must become the priority of your life and be seen as a work worthy of your efforts. It will also become the greatest joy of your life.

We cannot afford to be superficial in our desire to raise our children for Jesus. We cannot afford to repel, delay, and resist the work necessary to bring this to pass in their hearts, minds, and lives. We must possess the gift of the indwelling Christ, grace and power to live above the pull of our flesh, in order to bring this precious gift to our children. Doing battle against sin, self, and Satan is not an easy work, but it is a worthy, rewarding work. What a joy to see "Dishonest Henry" be transformed into "Honest Henry" through his cooperation with grace. What a miracle to see "Slothful Daniel" become "Diligent

Daniel" in Jesus. Seeing them struggle against the old ways and choosing to follow Christ's new ways instead touches the very cords of our hearts and rings the bell of victory. "Sassy Susie" becomes "Sweet Sue," but never without a struggle against the flesh according to her years. But, oh, how sweet the victory of being set free from our history of serving self to serve the living God in heaven!

Peter and Paula, whom we saw earlier in this chapter, took up the work of battling against their fleshly ways and matured in Jesus. They came out from under the rule of self by coming into Jesus' character-transforming arms. Was it difficult? It surely was! But, oh, how it transformed their hearts, lives, and home! To help others before you possess this genuine experience is only perpetuating in them your own weak, failing experience. It's not worth sharing until you possess it. Once Christ is working in your family, you are prepared to help others.

As Carol's parents exemplified the character development that was taking place in their own lives, they were able to demonstrate to "Critical Carol" how to become "Optimistic Carol" in her thoughts and attitudes toward work. Carol saw them struggling; she liked the change she saw in them. Discussing in family worship the battle that was being carried out for their thoughts kindled new thoughts for Carol. This discussion helped "Critical Carol" develop new thoughts in her mind and heart, which then flowed into her personal worship. She had a new and hopeful understanding of redemption. Mother gave her more and more work in order to correct the misconception that a little work was too much. Inch by inch, Carol changed. As they concentrated on cultivating a sweet attitude about serving and working to help others, a giant leap occurred. The more Carol was willing to say out loud that she enjoyed doing dishes and that this task was only a small one, the more it actually became so! "As he thinketh in his heart, so is he" (Proverbs 23:7). Carol began going to Jesus personally about her grumbling, critical attitude toward work; she cooperated with Him in avoiding such thoughts and feelings, fostering, instead, right thoughts under God. And He transformed her thoughts, feelings, and responses into those of heaven. Our "Critical Carol" can become "Optimistic Carol," helping cheerfully about the home.

When our children learn to think right thoughts, to cry out to Jesus for power and wisdom to change, and to cooperate so that Jesus can perform a miracle in their hearts and minds, thus changing their habits—this is character development. And the same is true of us parents.

Paula had to restrain her anger and go to God in the same way that her daughter was doing. When she wanted to do the task herself and avoid conflict, she responded to God's call to her heart that she must help Carol do the dishes, sweep the floor, or scrub the tub thoroughly— not allowing her bad habits to grow stronger. Instead, Mother took "Critical Carol" through the process of surrender—whatever it took to bring her to Jesus. At times, this battle to follow Jesus was severe. Mother implemented disciplines, consequences, and motivations; she found she could do so without harshness and anger. Life in the home was getting better. "Critical Carol" was becoming "Optimistic Carol," and home more sweet and pleasant.

Likewise, Father had to restrain his "don't bother me" attitude and get involved in the character development of his children. What a struggle it was to release his old ways to Jesus and do His will—to play with his children or to teach them in the right spirit, giving them room to be different from him. But soon the blessing was evident. Now his children wanted to be by his side instead of avoiding him. Peter had a particularly strong distaste for discipline, schedule, and consistency because of his history. He faced his issues with Christ and discovered by experience that discipline was love. It wasn't love for his children to let them pursue a wrong course and then rail on them for how bad they were. He discovered that he got miles further with encouraging words, appreciation, and letting them learn with some individuality mixed in. All the fretful, faultfinding, demeaning approach of former years had gained him nothing by comparison. His greatest joy was the unbelievable amount of love, respect, and truehearted service he gained from his entire family.

Now the home was working. The children's inability to work, resentment, and ugly responses were melting away. "How did we ever live the way we did before?" Peter asked. "Now I see that it wasn't Paula and the kids who were creating the evil atmosphere in the home—it was I!"

You may not struggle in the same way Peter and Paula did. Instead, you may stumble with overinvolvement in your occupation, earning more money than you need. Or you may be in bondage to slothful work habits that have not been overcome, keeping you from earning a livelihood without spending excessive hours to accomplish a little work. For others, the problem may be sports, needless shopping, socializing, appetite, distractions, even crafts taking your precious hours. Whatever you have to deal with, face it as Peter and Paula did by first allowing Jesus to change you. Then learn how to win the hearts of your children into Jesus' hand so that He can re-create their characters and fit them for heaven. This is of greater value than anything the world may offer as a substitute.

God speaks to each of us in Ephesians 6:4. "And, ye fathers [all parents], provoke not your children to wrath: but bring them up in the nurture and admonition of the Lord." God will personally give us all the wisdom we need if we come to Him for the power to develop His character in our homes and evict the spirit and character of Satan by God's power. "And they shall be all taught of God" (John 6:45).

Building character begins with resisting my wrong thoughts, feelings, habits, inclinations, desires, and responses. As Jesus frees you from serving other masters, you are free to bring your children out of their bondage in thought, word, and deed. This is true character building.

Will you stand up as Peter and Paula did, facing your shortcomings with Christ, being redeemed to serve God, not considering the inconvenience to yourself? Will you do whatever it takes, under God, to bring your children out of self and to nurture and admonish them in God's way?

The Lone Embrace
A Special Word of Encouragement for Single Parents

The foundation of our character building is Jesus Christ, the Chief Cornerstone. It is upon Him that we can build aright. There is no other foundation that will stand the test. What is the test, you ask? Our true character is revealed in a crisis. Character is tested when the pressure is on, when the heat is high, when unfairness reigns. Whom do we serve then—God or Satan? When we are under provocation, our *true character* is revealed. What are your thoughts, feelings, and responses then? That is your true character!

I think the word *crisis* is the proper word to describe a single parent's life. Be it an ugly divorce; the traumatic death of a spouse, leaving you alone and helpless; a financial collapse due to divorce; or a spouse that left you to carry the burdens—these are all major crises. You need God as your Foundation, your Spouse, your Comforter, your Wisdom in how to raise your children. He will be your Guide through life's muddied pathways. You are not alone, as Satan, the doubter, would have you think. Christ is ever with you. God's love and care for you is as big as your need. He can make a way of escape if you give Him your whole heart, mind, and soul. Building character in your children during your times of crises will begin with you. They will respond as you lead them. In proportion to your surrender and cooperation will be your success in directing your flock.

Let your great need and your children's need be the motivating force to go forward with God to discover that He is the one sure Foundation upon which you can depend. He will always be there for you. He will direct your thoughts and feelings out of self and despair into Christ and hope. As you choose to be Christ's child, He will re-create you into His likeness. As you choose to deny the undesirable traits of character, He will be there to slay their influence and strengthen you for the battle. Then you and your children can become like Enoch, as you long to be. Character development in Christ is your secret to success.

Chapter 21

THE PARENTS' FAITH

"Who against hope believed in hope, . . . So shall thy seed be" (Romans 4:18).

Recently, I came across a story in our local paper of a young boy who was missing and presumed dead from drowning. My heart went out to that poor mother. I knew how I would feel if *my* child were sucked under the icy water!

As I have traveled the globe, I have observed more human suffering, worry, and heartbreak than I ever knew existed. And much of this suffering centers upon parents' concern for the welfare of their children. Their children are disobedient, disgruntled, reactionary, or despairing. Many have left the faith and are disinterested in spiritual things. They have bad habits and terrible associates, are unwilling workers in the home, or have gotten into drugs and are often out getting a street education. Sometimes we worry about their physical danger, but most often we fear that they will make poor choices that will forever mar their happiness or, worse, eliminate their walk with God.

When one's children are in danger of loss, the grief is terrible. Yet in the very homes where life has become such a burden to bear I have seen the Life Giver's message of the role of the parent's faith come like a healing balm. These same homes become scenes of great rejoicing when the seemingly impossible happens, and faith on the part of the parents saves those precious children who seemed forever lost. Miracles still happen in answer to a parent's faith.

In the days of Christ, the city of Capernaum, located near the northwest corner of the Lake of Galilee, was a busy, active town. Jesus called His first disciples along the Capernaum waterfront. Not long after these men left their nets, Christ and His little group found themselves receiving an eager, expectant greeting in Cana, a town in the Galilean hill country some twenty miles from Capernaum. Why all the fuss? This was the man who had recently turned water into wine at the wedding feast there!

In the midst of the excitement, a distraught man arrives seeking Christ. He is an important nobleman in Capernaum, but now his rich robes are travel stained, and his face bears the strain of the uphill journey undertaken in great haste since daybreak. It has taken him hours to get to Cana, and each minute may be his son's last. A father's love has urged him tirelessly up the rocky roads from Capernaum. He is desperate.

He comes to Christ and beseeches Him to "come down, and heal his son: for he was at the point of death" (John 4:47). Here is the hand of faith raised to seek divine assistance. As Paul says, "By faith, we have peace with God through our Lord Jesus Christ: . . . access . . . into this grace . . . and rejoice in hope" (Romans 5:1, 2). Even this early in Christ's ministry, this man had heard enough about Him to see Him as his only help. Remember, Jesus had not yet healed a single person according to the Bible record, yet this man had traveled twenty miles while his son was dying to seek help. He could see in Christ access to the Almighty.

This man has a real trial, yet when he sees a way to access God, he acts upon it. Even then, his faith is sorely tested; Christ's words stun him, "Except ye see signs and wonders, ye will not believe" (John 4:48). In speaking to this nobleman, Jesus is really addressing the crowd that has gathered hoping to see another miracle. He will not disappoint them, for He is planning a great miracle. But how Jesus' words must have tried the spirit and emotions of this father. Jesus doesn't seek to crush his spirit—only to teach him to persevere. "Suffering produces perseverance; perseverance, character; and character, hope" (Romans 5:3, 4, NIV). The nobleman has learned this lesson well; again he pleads, "Sir, come down ere my child die" (John 4:49). Can't you just hear the agony in his voice as he cries, "Come down before my little baby dies"?

"Go thy way; thy son liveth," Christ declares (verse 50), delighting in the man's faith and perseverance.

Now that the promise of healing has been given, the father has a harder choice. He must *act* upon his faith. Does he really believe God has healed his son? Will he leave the Master behind and set out with nothing more than his faith in the promise? Herein lies the problem for every one of us who desires the salvation of our children. God assures us that He has the power to solve our problems, but they seem so overwhelming. We find ourselves in the same position as this nobleman.

Will we exercise faith? Will we believe God has done what He says when there is no immediate evidence of transformation? The nobleman has no cell phone to call and check the condition of his son. He has to rely fully on faith, and so must we!

As he heads down the hill the next day, he is met by servants sent with the glorious words that his son is well. "When did the change begin?" he inquires.

"At 1:00 P.M.," his servant answers.

The very moment that Jesus gave His promise! So too with us! Unlike the nobleman, we may be in for a long journey before we see healing and recovery. Yet when we look back upon the situation, we will find that it began to get better the minute we sought help from our heavenly Father.

None of us knows in advance all the twists and turns our lives will take, and yet, no event takes God by surprise, no problem leaves Him uncertain of the solution. Consider for a minute the Old Testament story of the great woman of faith who lived in Shunem. She decided that God's prophet Elisha should have a dwelling place in her home and prevailed upon her husband to build an addition for his use. Elisha was pleased by her gift and wanted to repay her kindness, offering to help even to the point of using his contacts with the royal family. But she turned him down. At last he told her that he would pray and that she would have a son a year later. The prophet's words were fulfilled, but the story doesn't end with that joyous birth. After a few years, her son died.

Why did God allow such a happy story to turn so tragic, so traumatic? We must be careful in assigning motives to God's actions because so much is still hidden from our understanding. Yet we can understand a little, and I like to think that perhaps He allowed it because He knew that there was going to be a tired mother or a discouraged father who needed the encouraging message found in this story of His power and a mother's faith. He knew that little Sally Hohnberger would be prone to depression when my situations looked so very bleak, and that I would cling to the stories of God's mercy as the only hope for my children's salvation because I knew that I had no strength or ability. Yet the key for unlocking God's salvation for our children is found in this very story. That's why I share it with you now.

The tiny baby promised by the prophet had grown into boyhood—

old enough to work in the field. The day had been hot from the time the sun rose over the horizon. Now, during this most routine of activities, the child fell to the ground clutching at his head. They brought him to his mother, and she cared for him as best she could. But despite her best efforts, her son died.

Death was the final closing of the door of hope, leaving her nothing except to bury her child—and all her hopes and dreams for his future along with him. There was nothing anyone could do, and yet she didn't respond as we might expect. She rode off to find the prophet of God. We don't know whether she held out some hope of recovery even at this stage or whether she felt uncertain that her son's death was God's plan, or whether she simply wanted to share her burden with the one who had promised a son to her, but we can be sure that others would have considered her behavior odd and irrational—riding off as she did and spending the better part of the day in travel when the ceremonial law demanded a quick burial.

Yet, this woman was not irrational. God had given her this child through the promise of His prophet, and she placed her dead child in the prophet's bed before she went to summon him. Her action was more than coincidence; it was symbolic. Placing her child in the prophet's bed was symbolic of laying her helpless, hopeless burden in God's hand, trusting Him with the outcome, whatever that might be.

We, too, should place in God's hands our hopeless burdens for the character defects of our children and ourselves. We, too, must go forth right now to find Christ at all costs, putting aside all other occupations so that we may bring Christ back into our hearts and the heart of our child. We need to be willing to unite Christ to our apparently dead child so that He can breathe into him a new life. Once we make that vital connection with Christ, our child can be healed of his deadly disease. We must exercise our faith and cooperate with Christ so that He can heal them. This may not seem to be rational behavior, but God is able to quicken a new life.

Jesus says to us today, "If thou canst believe, all things [are] possible to him that believeth"(Mark 9:23).

And we can say in response with tears and action, "Lord, I believe; help thou mine unbelief" (verse 24).

The prophet Elisha hurried to the room, and the Bible says he lay

3 3 3 3 3 3 3

upon the child and breathed into his nostrils. He did this repeatedly, and the child came back to life! Some scholars have suggested that this was simply a case of mouth-to-mouth resuscitation, but I believe God honored this mother's faith and gave her back her son's life. This child was dead! She had placed him in God's hands, and Elisha, as His representative, did just what God did when He created Adam. He breathed in his nostrils, and man became a living soul. The son was restored thanks to *a mother's faith*.

Often we take action, thinking that we are carrying out our own ideas, only to find out later that we were following the express purposes of God. When, in desperation, Moses' mother decided to preserve her child's life in the basket, she had no idea that she was preserving her nation's savior. Yet, in the face of overwhelming odds, her faith that she could still do something to save her son's life freed God's hands to work a mighty miracle and prepare the way for His people's salvation.

Our children can be dead to good works. "I can't do those dishes." "I won't sweep that floor." "You can't make me do my schoolwork!" Taking them to Christ can quicken in them a new life if we have faith, cry out to God, and do our work.

Our children can be dead to spiritual things. They sleep during prayer, are inattentive or distractive during family worship; they may cry, fuss, or scream when called to prayer, or look ugly and defiant at our efforts to help them do good. "I won't pray." We need to ride on our horse to find Jesus. We need to ask Him to breathe His own life-giving breath into us as well as into our children. We need to have courage to ask "Lord, what wilt thou have me to do?" (Acts 9:6). And then we need to have the courage to do whatever He suggests in order to help our child place his heart into the hands of Jesus. This takes faith on our part to trust God's Word against our feelings and emotions.

The lengths to which a parent will go to help a child are limitless. I can't help but think of another desperate mother whose daughter was possessed by an evil spirit (see Mark 7:24-30). More than anything, this woman wanted her daughter freed from this spirit, but would this Jewish rabbi help her?

She had reason to doubt. After all, she was a Greek, not a Jew. I'm sure that many times she thought about going to Jesus, only to shrink back uncertainly. She had heard of Jesus and His compassion for others, and it kindled a small flame of hope in her heart, but how small was that flame and how easily it could be doused by the attitudes and actions of Jesus' countrymen. Had it been any other rabbi, she knew she would be rejected. At last she decided that rejection would be bearable, for at least she would have tried. She must have been cut out of the same fabric as Theodore Roosevelt, who said, "Far better to have tried and failed than to be among that poor, sad number who live in the twilight knowing neither victory or defeat." She would put forth the effort and do battle on her daughter's behalf. This is what Matthew 11:12 means when it refers to the violent taking the kingdom of God by force. So she came to Christ, seeking His help. She fell at His feet and pled, "Won't you please cast this evil spirit out of my daughter?"

Jesus said, "Let the children first be filled: for it is not meet to take the children's bread, and cast [it] unto the dogs" (Mark 7:27).

She understood the import of what He said—the insult to her national pride and the personal offense that demeaned her worth as a person—yet now that she had entered the field of conflict, she was not willing to leave without a victory; her weapons of warfare were as effective as any ever wielded by the mightiest soldier. She showed great humility, never worrying about how she appeared if only she could obtain that for which she came. She replied in reasoned and truthful terms, "Yes, Lord: yet even the dogs under the table eat the children's crumbs" (verse 28). Her faith was still hoping. God's crumbs would be enough for her need.

In the next moment the victory was won. "And he said unto her, For this saying go thy way; the devil is gone out of thy daughter" (verse 29).

She had determined that she would not take "no" for an answer, and because of her faith and perseverance, she gained that which she desired. She is a living example of Romans 4:18, "who against hope believed in hope." In other words, "As your faith is—so shall it be granted you." What a promise to us as parents!

As parents, we often encounter lying thoughts from the devil in our children's thinking. We need to pray to God with perseverance, like the woman of Shunem, for the blessings and wisdom we need to direct our children so that they can be healed of the evil spirits with which they are cooperating right now. When we have done all we can do to correct our children, then we are to bring them to Jesus so that His Holy Spirit can make their dispositions mild and gentle. Jesus can tell the evil spirits to leave with authority and heal our hearts and homes in the process. He will never turn us away.

I think back over my own life—my own journey into faith and my tottering first steps to exercise that faith—and I realize it has been a long, long pathway. Jumping into new ways can be scary sometimes. I often felt like I was jumping off a steep cliff of uncertainty and wondered if I'd survive the landing. Until I learned by experience that God's faithful character and His ways were best in calling me to jump in faith.

Along the way, God has healed my wounds, and the winds of change have altered my life many times. I have found that the way to Christ comes only by submitting my will to His and cooperating with Him. I know that slavery to sin is bondage to self. I know that only through death to self-will can I truly find life in Christ. My old areas of struggle with such issues as diet, anger, despair, fear, and resentment now seem only small steppingstones, where once they appeared as unmovable mountains. Now I dance easily through those battles as a seasoned soldier. Now I realize that these early battles were but the opening round of conflict with the devil and with self. Like a soldier who has fought his way off the beachhead, I now see spread before me the whole country of my character that I must conquer. I know that it is impossible for me alone to accomplish the task before me. Thankfully, I have also learned that nothing is too difficult for my God. As God has led me and released me from so many forms of bondage, I have tasted true freedom in His law and in His love, and I am able to give Him more and more control.

Freedom comes with a price, dear friends, and the price I've paid has been extremely high. But because I've paid so dearly, the lessons are of incredible value. Some of those lessons include the following: Faith must be exercised in order to become a great blessing. Faith is not dependant upon my feelings. Faith is more than belief and is inseparably linked with actions. And, finally, faith is simple in operation and powerful in its results. Faith connects us to the power of Christ that changes us, healing both our children and us in the inner man. God is there for you.

I think of Paul's majestic words in Hebrews 11: "Now faith is the substance of things hoped for, the evidence of things not seen" (verse 1). Here faith is linked over and over with actions: By faith, the elders obtained; by faith, Abel offered; by faith, Enoch was translated. The chapter goes on to describe those who through faith subdued king-doms, wrought righteousness, obtained promises, stopped the mouth of lions, quenched the violence of fire, escaped the edge of the sword, and were made strong out of weakness. In verse 32, Paul laments a lack of time to tell all he'd like to say, and I agree, for time would fail me to tell of Jairus' daughter, of baby Joash, of the widow of Nain's son, of demoniacs saved, of the blind restored to sight, and of many other won-ders and miracles—all of which demonstrate that our God is able to save to the uttermost those who trust Him (see Hebrews 7:25). God is in the business of providing unexpected salvation in the midst of hope-less situations.

This has been the experience of my life, and my heart is filled with thankfulness for God's great mercy to me and my family. So I add my voice to the crowd of witnesses encouraging you to trust Him with your future. In looking back over my life, I see God's hand working long before I ever knew him. In a sense, God our Father illustrated the ulti-mate faith of a parent. Even when our earthly parents despair of a solu-tion, our heavenly Father has faith in our future. At a time when every-one else might give up on us, He still believes in what we may become. Our children are really His. They are precious blessings just loaned to us for a little while. This tale of divine love reaching out after me is the story of my life. I contemplate the words and the message contained in Hebrews 11 as I walk along the North Fork of the Flathead River, en-joying the wilderness, enjoying the God who made it, thinking about His watch care over me before I even knew Him. At last my thoughts turn once more to the little boy who drowned in the icy water.

The area where I live draws people from all over the country to enjoy the wilderness and the river. But swift, cold water, wonderful though it is, has a dark side. It can destroy mercilessly. This tragedy happened south of where we live, toward the Bob Marshall Wilderness Area. The family decided that the father and the boys would take a short river trip in their canoe while the mother drove downstream to pick them up.

Anyone river-wise in this area might have questioned the wisdom of their choice, given the extremely cold water so early in the season, but they were experienced canoeists. The boys had taken other trips with their father with no problems. They had researched this area of the river and were told there were no rapids, so they donned life jackets, and the father and his two sons, three and five years old, set out for a delightful outing.

No great, unforeseen event altered their plans—just a little choppy water, and soon they capsized. Shocked by the cold, the father surfaced near the older boy, but three-year-old Jacob was gone. Struggling through the numbingly cold water, the father and his five-year-old son reached the shore, where their cries for help had alerted the residents of a nearby cabin. The people quickly called 911 and worked to warm the boy.

Sheriff's officers, crews from the fire department, search-and-rescue units, and ambulances were dispatched. A number of rangers had just returned from a wilderness trip and were eating lunch when they heard the news and rushed to the site with rescue gear and a kayak. While the first responders searched the banks for the youngster, Ranger Kevin Hammonds launched his kayak.

"I was really hoping to see him resting on the side of the river, scared and maybe crying," Hammonds reported later. But as he paddled and time slipped by, his hopes dimmed. All he could think about was how cold the river was, how fast the current was, and all the time that had passed since the child had disappeared. His conclusion was depressingly clear. "I knew," he commented, "it was going to be a bad kind of scene."

After covering more than a mile of the river, the ranger turned a corner and spotted a life jacket in the distance. As he drew closer, he could see the child was hung up on a submerged rock. Running his craft ashore, he radioed the location of his find and waded into waist-deep freezing water to reach the child.

It was a sight to make anyone's heart stand still in horror—a little three-year-old, whose life was just beginning, lying limp in the water. When Hammonds checked him, his lips were blue, the eyes open, and the pupils fixed. The boy had no respirations and no pulse. As the ranger put it later, "He looked as dead as dead can be." Knowing he could hardly begin CPR in the water, Hammonds threw the cold limp form over his shoulder and rushed up the bank to the first level spot he could find and began performing CPR on the lifeless child.

CPR is hard work—ask anyone who has ever performed it—and Hammonds had the stress of the river rescue, his own exposure to the freezing water, and the added nightmare of working on a dead child. So it was with no little relief that he greeted the sight of the helicopter that came screaming upstream and landed on a gravel bed some three hundred feet away. Gratefully he turned Jacob's care over to the experts.

"My first impression was that he was dead. He was white, pulseless, breathless—zero signs of life," reported the flight nurse. The medics worked to warm him, administered drugs, and placed a breathing tube down his throat, but things looked very grim. Next was the difficult trip back to the helicopter. The ground was so difficult to traverse. By the time his rescuers reached the helicopter with Jacob, more than an hour had passed since he had been dumped in the river, and they knew that the already overwhelming odds against this little fellow's life being saved had only worsened.

Although warned of what to expect, the trauma team at the Kalispell Medical Center was still taken aback at Jacob's condition. As one member exclaimed, "He was clinically dead. He was! His temperature was sixty-nine degrees. People have survived colder temperatures, but it's rare."

Jacob's parents reached the emergency room, and the doctors were honest with them about their son's condition. One emergency room physician later described Jacob as "a little ice cube." And the local newspaper would report later, "The hospital was about to give everything it had to that little ice cube."

Hopeless situations! Have you ever been in one as a parent? Do you perhaps feel that you are in one right now? Does it seem that the hearts of your loved ones have become as cold as ice, refusing to respond to your most intense efforts to revitalize them? There is hope in the One who is the Life Giver, hope even when the one in peril can't—or won't—ask for help. God has always been the God of the impossible, and He can perform His mighty works in your home and life just as easily as He has for others in ages past. While we must be careful when we assess the reasons for God's intervention in the course of human events, it is certain that the prayer of faith has saved many a soul. The prayer of faith has altered human history and continues to do so.

After more than an hour at the Kalispell Medical Center, Jacob's heart began to beat and a pulse was once more present. His eyes opened. Everyone was delighted, but he was still in critical condition. The nagging question looming in every mind was: How much brain damage had he suffered after more than two hours without a heartbeat?" The hospital decided to fly him to the Pediatric Intensive Care unit in Spokane, Washington, but before he left, the doctors wanted his parents to have a chance to see him and at least know he was alive. When his parents entered the room, no one could believe what happened. Jacob turned his head and fluttered his eyes! Many of those looking on found tears distorting their own vision. Little Jacob was loaded onto the air ambulance; his plane was the *last* plane to take off before the airport closed for runway maintenance!

At Spokane, his recovery was breathtaking. In forty-eight hours he was fully recovered and ready for discharge! Everyone said he was a miracle boy. In retrospect, so many things went right. A cabin on the otherwise uninhabited section of river, someone with a cell phone and service that actually worked, three rangers who just happened to be in the right place with a kayak, a helicopter medical team able to land within a hundred yards of where Jacob was found, an emergency room team that wouldn't give up, and a flight to intensive care that was able to leave just before the airport closed. Was all this just luck? Mere coincidence? You and I know better than that. God is forever caring for us even when we don't know Him. Angels were there guiding all who would cooperate. I don't want you to miss the point of this story—Jacob was saved because many people wouldn't give up, even when it was absolutely hopeless.

Are you willing to be the next testimonial of God's power to save a child from the icy waters of worldliness, retrieving them from the heavy currents of selfish habits and weak character traits, and being redeemed from the lifeless forms of Christianity common today? God can save your child through your true faith as a parent in His ability to rescue the perishing. Come to Him. Set aside all other occupations, recreations, or pursuits—make your child's character development the foremost thing in your life. Cooperate with God in giving instructions to your children in how to come to Jesus and experience knowing Him as their personal Savior. They will find that God is real and able to rescue them from self. They will find that character transformation is both real and possible. This type of healing begins with our faith in God, in heeding His guidance in nurturing our children in His ways consistently day after day. The cost may appear high to us, but the dividends are outstanding.

I don't know what problems you will face, and no one knows what

the future may bring. God will be there with you in the good times and
the bad to direct your course. We may be certain that there will come
times of crisis and sorrow that will sorely tempt us to let go and give up.
Remember these children are not ours to do with as we wish; rather,
they belong to God, and He has entrusted them to us to raise to serve
Him and righteousness. I believe that many a parent will enter heaven
and hear Jesus express His gratitude for their efforts on behalf of His
children. Exactly what He will say I don't know.

How will we respond to God for His part, His effort, and His guidance to rescue both our children and us from the slough of this earthli-
ness in us? I can find no words to improve upon those spoken by Jacob's
mother after her son's recovery: "Thank You, Lord, for saving my son's
life through these people. Thank You for not giving up on us. You just
kept going and kept going, and it worked. I want to thank you from the
bottom of my heart."

This book is not about other's lives; it is about you and your home
and your children. Unleash your faith in God; be that instrument under His guidance to rescue your perishing children, to heal your sick,
and to set the captives free in your home today. You can be the next
miracle!

Appendix
14 DISCIPLINE IDEAS

A Spanking

1. Use spanking to establish authority.
2. Spank what has disobeyed:
    • hand for taking what mother says not to take
    • mouth for speaking sassily
    • bottom for miscellaneous infractions
3. Never spank with harshness, anger, or irritation.

Spanking must be done before God with the parent in a surrendered position to God and an attitude of wanting to bring the child to a truly surrendered and changed heart attitude so that he has the power to do right through Christ. We bring our child to Christ in prayer to choose to do right.

This method works well while the child is young; use it while it works. Spanking can be used on occasion when the child is considerably older; do it as God leads you.

A Grizzly Run

A grizzly run is used to subdue the unwilling, unreasoning attitude in a given situation through a physical output of energy. Set up a running course, of your discretion as to the distance necessary. We have a quarter-mile run for minor needs and a one-half- to one-mile run for more severe negative, unreasonable attitudes when they present themselves. Rules need to be set up before this discipline is used.

1. When told to go on a grizzly run, there will be no arguing or reasoning under any circumstances; the child will go immediately when he is told. If he doesn't follow these rules, severe punishment will be given without discussion. If tested on this, you must follow through to establish this rule.

2. The child must run as fast as he can; if he doesn't, he will rerun the course. (This will require you to set standards, knowing your child.) If the

child is argumentative, you will need to run with him and establish your word as law. Remember, make no compromise with evil (a selfish heart/will). The success or failure of this method rests with the parents, whether their word is law or not. It's up to you to establish this.

3. Benefits:

- A grizzly run helps get out the resistive spirit. It is a physical way of softening the spirit, making the child more open to correction and willing to call out to God to change.
- It prepares the child to talk with reason and be more willing to listen.

4. If the run does not soften the child, send him for a second run—or whatever is necessary.

5. Make the distance sufficient to work a desire to reform. (Lessens fighting energy).

6. When passion is high, reasoning is ineffective; consult with God what to do next.

Housework

1. Housework teaches helpfulness, perseverance, love, and how to work. Self needs to be laid aside.

2. When correction is necessary, almost always self (I want my way) arises. This type of discipline cultivates the opposite characteristic—self-surrender!

3. Training in surrender, yielding, and submitting deals with the will, not the mind only. Submitting to manual labor requires that self yield to the parent.

4. The child learns useful work in the learning process of the surrender of the will through Christ.

5. Work ideas:

- Do all the meal dishes today. See to it the attitude and countenance are surrendered.
- Work for mother one hour, chores of her choice.
- Do chores for the one you have wronged.
- Clean out and organize the garage or attic—cheerfully, well, timely.
- For a bad attitude when asked to scrub the tub, give the child the job for six months or a year until he learns to do it cheerfully and well.

We want to motivate the will being placed on the Lord's side of right doing; a change in habits, demeanor, and cheerfulness; and giving of oneself to help others. This can only be done properly when the child is taken to Christ before, during, and after the process of discipline.

Unaided by Christ, they cannot change on the inside. We can have outward conformity in humanity and discipline alone, but an inward transformation of the heart and disposition is possible only when they are united and submitted through Christ.

Yardwork

1. Yardwork is good hard physical work.

2. It must be done cheerfully; you want a surrendered experience.

3. The child should pray while working.

4. Deal with stubbornness and resentment if they arise. How? "Lord, what would you have me to do?" May require a second or third task.

5. The love of self must be surrendered to God. This requires a decision on the child's part.

6. Yardwork gives time outside with God. God woos the child to Him to yield up self and selfishness.

7. God can change their hearts and feelings, but not until they submit and cry out for help.

8. The mind must be convinced; there is no other way before it chooses to yield. Be firm, parents, but be also "in Christ."

9. Time alone with God and physical work often work wonderful reform and subduing of the heart. The heart can be thoughts, feelings, dispositions, and attitudes.

10. Realize this is perceived as a big trial to the child.

11. Teach them and train them to call out to God in all their trials of life, self.

12. Spare not for their crying, parents. Do what is right. Be directed of God.

13. This discipline takes time; it is a process of unlearning and relearning in many cases.

14. This discipline will require the *firmer virtues*—decisiveness, positive requirements, courage, force, perseverance. It is a battle for their soul. Who will rule?

15. Double dig garden soil. Point them to Christ to change their will/feelings.

16. Pull weeds in the garden, cultivate the soil, plant in plants or seeds.

17. Set a time period for the work or an amount to be done. See to it that it is done.

18. When done, talk about what they have learned through all this.

19. See to it that surrender has taken place during and after the discipline.

Read a Spiritual Book or the Bible

1. Reading spiritual material can work conviction while the child is reading, if you are praying.

2. Send them to the Bible or to the Spirit of Prophecy to study for themselves when you don't agree on what is right. Let God's standard rule, not the child's or yours!

3. Share example of Matthew not feeling he needed supervision any longer at twelve years of age.

4. Make the reading material practical and applicable to the area of confusion.

5. For younger children, read them a story that depicts right over wrong doing.

6. I've sent my teenagers out under a tree, with their Bibles, to work through an attitude difficulty. I prayed while they were there. God blessed. Confession and surrender were the sweet fruit of this discipline—discipline being discipleing my child to Christ.

7. Time in their bedroom just to think about the wrong—while you pray—is helpful.

8. Finally, talk about the situation, as God leads you—when and how much.

Write a Love Letter to the One You Have Treated Unkindly

1. Writing a loving letter cultivates the opposite trait for the offense.

2. Often brother treats brother unkindly in word or deed.

3. The letter makes right the wrong, practices right in its place, and develops new habits.

4. A surrendered heart to God makes all the difference in the outcome.

Write Half or One Page of "Why I Did What I Did; What Is Wrong With It; and What I Need To Do Instead Next Time."

1. Writing about the offense teaches a good thinking process of restitution—making right a wrong.

2. This work helps them become prepared in heart and mind for what to do next time.

3. Here too, connections with Christ make all the difference for next time.

4. This activity gives reflection time for evaluation, confession, and repentance.

5. Pray during the discipline. Disciple your child to Christ.

Double School Today

1. Double school helps get ahead of schedule or catch up if we are behind.

2. This discipline teaches perseverance also, because it is much more than the child is used to.

Lose Free Time

1. In this discipline the child must work for the one offended during her free time. If mother was offended, do cooking, cleaning, organizing, etc. If brother, do his house chores, serve him in his work like Elisha did Elijah.

2. This discipline cultivates an opportunity to learn the joy of serving— once we surrender and God can change our hearts and dispositions, that is.

3. They need to submit to it cheerfully. Call for prayer, choice, surrender.

4. God needs to lead whether during this time they work alone or with parent.

Cause-and-Effect Disciplines

1. Cause and effect can be matter of fact: They spill the juice; they clean it up.

2. If they break a dish, they must glue it (fix it) or replace it at their expense (even if an accident).

3. When a child destructively destroys something, the child must replace it, do something helpful, and confess the wrong. We want to cultivate the opposite attitude, not just gain outward compliance.

4. The child must be taken to Christ to be changed in heart and mind and actions.

5. When the child commits an unloving act—hitting brother, speaking angrily to him—he should write a love letter or do a kindness. Again, cultivate the opposite trait. Let God lead you in what to do.

Cultivate the Opposite Trait for Weak Character Traits

1. If a child is *shy,* we often wrongly excuse disobedience by making an excuse—"She's shy." Instead, cultivate courage:
- Love and discipline require her to answer when spoken to.
- Love prays with her and has her talk to others—she must choose to surrender.
- Love shows her that with Jesus she can find power to do hard things—and do right.
- Communion with God will reveal to you the right time and wrong timing.

2. When a child is *too outgoing,* we often wrongly excuse disobedience by making an excuse—"He's not shy." Instead, cultivate reserve:
- Love and discipline require him to be quiet when parent requests him to be.
- Love prays with him and teaches him to surrender to parent, through Christ.
- Love shows him that with Jesus he can be quiet and happy too—and do right.

3. If the child is *slothful* in work habits:
- Love requires whole-hearted work—good thorough work,
- at dishes, sweeping floor, mowing lawn, doing laundry, ironing.
- Teach: "Whatsoever thy hand findeth to do, do [it] with thy might."
- Take him to Jesus so that he knows he can do right if he chooses.
- If he doesn't do a job well, he must redo that job plus one more.
- Do not allow wrong habits to develop. If you allow jobs done poorly, you teach the child that poor work is all right. Every act repeated becomes habit, and habits become their character!
- Give them hard physical work—the garden, mowing lawn, weeding, collecting wood, chopping wood, hauling stones, etc.
- Give them more detail work that requires exactness, such as organizing room/garage.
- Missing a meal is a really strong motivator. Use this wisely with God's direction.

A Consequence List for the Repeating Offenses

1. Make and display a list of the repeating offenses with their automatic consequences.

2. Make family aware of this new rule and way of government so that all know the way.

3. Example: Hitting—pay 50 cents on first offense and double thereafter. Not brushing your teeth before family worship in the morning—miss family fun.

4. Example: Getting into arguments while playing together—give time out on separate porches, and they need to settle it amongst themselves . . . then tell you how they worked it out.

5. Mother keeps a list of unpleasant jobs around the house to be used if needed.

Discipline Jars for Mothers Who Go Blank Coming Up With Disciplines

A discipline jar helps those of us who lack ideas at the time of conflict, yet we know a consequence is necessary. God helped our family come up with these ideas together, in a family counsel session. I shared that I had a problem going blank at the time when I needed ideas most. Then as a family, we decided on this method of discipline, and all participated in consequence ideas. The boys prepared the slips and placed them in jars to draw from. If you find any of these disciplines offensive, just do not use them. Replace them with other ideas as God leads you.

We had our children pray to God before pulling out a discipline from the jars, so God was involved in the discipline. They knew God would help them surrender and do what is right next time—if they learned to choose right. But for now, they chose a consequence for their wrong choices to disobey, to be unkind, or disrespectful. The way of transgressors is hard.

Remember in dealing with discipline, you are dealing with two selves—your self and your child's self. This is a battle for us to keep our self subdued under Christ, to do what we must in a Christlike manner. Second, we must then bring our child to that same surrendered position before God so that he, too, can be changed and do right. It is a good and worthy work, parents.

Major Infraction Jar

These are ideas we used. Change or create your own. These are intended only to kindle ideas to help your family become a well-ordered, well-disciplined, Christ-centered family, which says more in behalf of Christianity than all the sermons that can be preached.

- One chore for the one you've wronged
- Write a love letter to the one you've wronged
- Write a thankful list
- One full page of "What I did and the evils of it"
- One dollar to the one you've wronged
- Double schoolwork—A+ work
- Half a day of schoolwork
- One hour of work extra, mother's choice
- Grizzly run to the mailbox (two-thirds of a mile, nonstop)

Minor Infraction Jar
- Read a spiritual book for half an hour
- Fifty cents to the one you have wronged
- One reasonable favor for the one wronged
- Chore for the one wronged; I pick it
- Lose a half hour of my free time
- Write half a page: "What I've done wrong and how to correct it"
- No dessert
- Grizzly run to the gate (quarter-mile run, nonstop)

Privilege Jar
- Feet or back massage for fifteen minutes
- One-half hour walk with mother or father
- Pick dessert
- Get five dollars
- Pick family fun for the night
- Get one dollar
- Evening chores done for you
- Pick own meal
- Choose hike, swim, skiing, or canoeing outing
- Parents do a reasonable favor for you
- Morning chores done for you

These are intended to be creative inducements for choosing obedience and Christ over self and wrong ways, habits, or inclinations. We found the privilege jar a real blessing. God first works by blessings bestowed. If that program doesn't work, God works on blessings removed to motivate saying "no" to self and "yes" to God. Our boys were well motivated with the privilege jar. The privilege jar was made from a peanut butter jar with these ideas written out—each on a slip of construction paper. If the child willingly strove to do battle against self, through surrender to Christ, and kept his heart on the side of right, even if he struggled to decide, then he could draw from the privilege jar in the evening and receive the blessing.

Consequences were drawn from the consequence jars at the time of the offense, with prayer first. It is up to the parent to see to it that the will is properly surrendered. Parents, please be well versed with what is a true-surrendered heart and study to show yourself approved. God bless you.

Reward System

A reward system is built around a chart with thirty or more boardwalk-type blocks on it. Have your child draw a picture around it. Put this chart up on door in a place easily seen during the day. Choose an area of weakness in the child's character—like slothfulness, shyness, anger, complaining at math class, etc. Challenge him or her to say "no" to self and "yes" to God and right. Each day your child does that for the whole day, he can move his little marker on the chart. At the end of the course, he will gain his incentive. You can keep the incentive a secret or make it a known gift the child can earn by practicing self-denial. Choose for a reward something your child would like that contributes to family fun—like a fanny pack for hiking the mountains, a knife to take backpacking, etc. Small items can be as much an incentive as bigger items. It's a positive motivation.

In all these areas we are rewarding choices for good that go against a natural bent to do otherwise, and this is done on a positive approach instead of a negative one. Be honest with your evaluations. Did the child really earn a reward today? Talk with God through these situations. Are you praying for your child each day in the area you're working on? Are you nurturing your child to keep close, and cling, to Jesus, a power outside of himself, so that he can overcome in these areas? Pray with your child when it is a point on which he may waver. When he begins to fall into old habits, are you there encouraging him, pointing him to Jesus, making prayer a desirable way to overcome problems? Use prayer often to gain the advantage in this battle with self.

There is a place and need for consequences in our home management; don't neglect one way for the other exclusively. We can err and become unbalanced on either side!

If one form of discipline—positive or negative—does not motivate your child to correct his ways, or if you have to correct the same area often, re-evaluate and change the consequences. Find one that is effective. If mild measures do not bring reform, use the severest measures necessary to obtain obedience to right. Jesus will help you, if you ask Him! We do not want our child to remain in sin and evil habits of disobedience; we want them to connect to Christ so that He can lift them up higher and to experience the joy of obedience to mother and Jesus. God be with you as you disciple your child to Christ.

Rightfully done, parents, we will gain wonderful experience in how God is able to subdue and change both your and your child's thoughts, feelings, inclinations, and "I don't want tos." God says, "Work out your own salvation, with fear and trembling." In this way of governing our children, we can rightly direct them in the way of right doing and aid them to work out their own salvation also. They will know how to trust and surrender to a power outside of themselves. They, too, will gain a valuable experience in the Lord and learn how grace can save them. As they cooperate with Him, they will gain an experience of how God changes them.

Jim and Sally, 1986,
with Matthew, nine, and
Andrew, seven.

Andrew, 1985, at age
six—doing dishes
cheerfully.

Family backpacking
trip, 1989.

Sibling adoration,
Matthew and Andrew,
ages nine and eleven.

"Lonesome," a God-
given family pet, with
Matthew, ten, and
Andrew, eight. 1987.

"Lonesome" and
Andrew, age nine. 1988.

Deer friends are
common in our yard.

Matthew feeding
"Big Buck." 1989.

Matthew, age ten, helps
peel the fence rails.

Matthew, age ten, built
it all himself. 1987.

Matthew, age nine,
peeling logs. 1986.

Andrew, age eight,
builds his first
swing. 1987.

Andrew, age ten,
working big equipment.
1989.

Matthew, age
seven, builds his
first birdhouse.

Matthew, thirteen, and Andrew, eleven, learning carpentry skills at our guest cabin.

Matthew, age twelve, and his first chainsaw. 1989.

Other books from Jim and Sally Hohnberger!

Parenting by the Spirit
This is not your typical book on child-rearing. You won't find the latest be-havioral science techniques or talk-show psychology here. What you will find is an entirely new and surprising way to parent—by the Spirit. This is the first volume in Sally Hohnberger's projected series on raising your children—from infants to young adults—by the Spirit.
0-8163-2031-4. Paperback. US$12.99, Can$17.99

Come to the Quiet
Leaving a life of material comforts and dead spirituality in Wisconsin, Jim and Sally Hohnberger took up their search for an intimate life with God on a remote property in the Montana wilderness. In this book, Jim provides new details and lessons not included in *Escape to God*. If your life is too full of the cares of this world and you need to come to the quiet of resting in Jesus—this book shows you how.
0-8163-2032-2. Paperback. US$13.99, Can$20.99.

It's About People
In what may be his most important book yet, Jim Hohnberger attempts to reconcile the faith we preach with the gospel we live—when we disagree. Jim shows how Jesus' attitude and approach toward those who didn't receive Him was just as important as the truth He taught.
0-8163-1964-2. Paperback. US$10.99, Can$16.49.

Empowered Living
A thoughtful collection of principles and testimonies of how God can revolu-tionize your marriage, family, and your walk with God.
0-8163-1917-0. Paperback. US$14.99, Can$22.49.

Escape to God
How the Hohnberger family left the rat race behind in a search for genuine spirituality and the simple life.
0-8163-1805-0. Paperback. US$13.99, Can$20.99.

Order from your ABC by calling 1-800-765-6955, or get online and shop our virtual store at www.adventistbookcenter.com—as well as check out all the other brand new books from Pacific Press!

For more information on the Hohnbergers' ministry or other materials call 1-877-755-8300 or visit www.empoweredlivingministries.org.